The New
HOYLE

❖IIIIIIIIIIIIIIIIIIIII❖

Standard Games
INCLUDING

All Modern Card Games
New Laws of Contract Bridge and New Scoring Rules
Chess, Checkers, Backgammon, Camelot, Ping Pong
Bowling, Billiards, Pool, etc.

Edited by

PAUL H. SEYMOUR, M.S.

Formerly Bridge Editor of the Chicago Daily News, Broad-
caster over WMAQ, Author of "High Lights on Auction
Bridge," "Auction Bridge Simplified," "Simplified
Bridge—Auction and Contract," etc.

A LAIRD & LEE PUBLICATION

ALBERT WHITMAN & CO.
CHICAGO

PUBLISHER'S NOTE

This Famous Book has been greatly enlarged and carefully revised by Mr. Seymour to meet the needs of up-to-date card playing.

Contract Bridge in all its phases is fully covered.

We hope that this book, as a silent partner, will contribute much to the efficiency and to the peace of mind of the reader.

TABLE OF CONTENTS

7

TABLE OF CONTENTS—Continued

LIST OF ILLUSTRATIONS

WHIST

There are two forms of Whist, single table, in which four players alone are engaged, and duplicate, in which a number of tables play the same hands. As the single-table game is the foundation of duplicate, it will be described first.

The Pack.—Fifty-two cards, which rank from the Ace, King, Queen down to the deuce in play. Two packs are sometimes used, the still pack being shuffled by the dealer's partner. The backs should be of different colors.

Cutting.—The pack is spread face downward on the table and each player draws a card. The lowest two pairing against the highest two, and the highest choosing his seat and dealing the first hand. Ties cut again, but the second cut decides nothing but the tie.

Shuffling.—Any player may shuffle the cards, the dealer last. When two packs are in play it is not usual to shuffle the still pack, after it has been shuffled by the partner of the previous dealer. The pack is presented to the player on the right to be cut, and at least four cards must be left in each packet, the upper portion of the cut being always placed nearer the dealer, who reunites the parts himself.

Dealing.—The cards are dealt one at a time to each player in turn to the left until the entire pack has been distributed. The last card is turned up for the trump, but is part of the dealer's hand. The deal passes to the left.

The Trump Card.—This must be left face upward on the table until it is the dealer's turn to play to the first trick. Then he must take it into his hand, and it may not thereafter be named, although any player may be informed as to the suit.

THE PLAY

The player to the left of the dealer leads for the first trick, any card he pleases, and each player in turn to the left must follow suit if he can. Having none of the suit, he may discard or trump at pleasure. The highest card played wins the trick, trumps winning all other suits, and the winner of one trick leads for the next.

OBJECTS OF THE GAME

To win the greater number of tricks. The first six taken by either side count nothing. They are called the "book." All over six count one point each toward game, and the partners who first reach seven points are the winners.

Scoring.—The points made upon each hand are usually scored on a Whist marker, made for the purpose, or they may be kept count of by chips, or entered on a score pad; but it is essential that every player should be able to see the state of the score, and also how many tricks each side has taken in during the play.

Revokes.—The penalty for a revoke is to surrender two tricks to the side not in error, for each revoke made. The revoking players cannot win the game on that deal, but must stop at 6 up, no matter what they actually make.

Rubbers and Honors.—In the English form of the game, honors are counted, and rubbers are played. Partners holding all four honors, Ace, King, Queen, Jack, score 4 points toward game. Holding three of the four, 2 points. Game is 5, but if the score is 4 at the beginning of the deal, the odd trick must be made to win the game, as honors alone will not give a side game. Games vary in value. If the losers have no score, the game is worth 3. If they have 1 or 2, it is worth 2. If they have 3 or 4, it is worth 1. The side that first wins two games adds 2 points for the rubber, so that the smallest rubber possible is worth 1, the largest 8, called a "bumper."

In America the game is either 7 or 10 points, honors are not counted and a fixed amount is added for a rubber.

The Play.—Skill in Whist is a matter of close observation and a good memory for small cards. The opening lead is usually from the longest suit if there are trumps enough to support it; otherwise modern players lead from the short suits and try to get in their trumps separately from their partner's.

The Leads.—There are five conventional leads. The King shows that Ace, or Queen, or both, are in the leader's hand. The Ace denies the King, and is led from suits of 5 or more, and also from Ace-Queen-Jack-10, or Ace-Queen-Jack and others. The Jack is led from Jack-10, with or without others, or from King-Jack-10. Any smaller card is either the fourth-best or the "top of nothing." Trumps are led only when there is some object in leading them, such as great length, or a good plain suit to defend. The trump signal is to play a higher card and then a lower, when making no attempt to win the trick. The six and deuce played on the lead of King and Ace would be a call for the partner to lead trumps at the first opportunity.

Second and Third Hand.—The second hand plays high cards on small card led through him only when he holds a combination from which he would have led a high card. Holding Ace-King for instance, he would have led a high card, so he plays one of his high cards second hand. The third hand wins tricks as cheaply as possible. Holding both King and Queen, for instance, he plays the Queen on a small card led by his partner. He should finesse the Queen when holding Ace-Queen and others; finesse the

Jack holding Ace-Jack and others. Always return the higher of only two cards remaining of the partner's suit, and the lowest of four or more. Discard from the weakest suit unless the trump strength is declared against you. Then discard the best protected suit.

THE LAWS OF WHIST

1. *The Game.*—A game consists of 7 points, each trick above six counting 1. The value of the game is determined by deducting the loser's score from seven.

2. *Forming the Table.*—Partners are determined by cutting—the two highest play against the two lowest; the highest deals, and has the choice of seats and cards.

3. If two players cut intermediate cards of equal value, they cut again; the lower of the new cut plays with the original lowest.

4. If three players cut cards of equal value, they cut again. If the fourth has cut the highest card, he deals and the lowest two of the new cut are partners.

5. *Cutting.*—In cutting, the Ace is the highest card. All must cut from the same pack. If a player exposes more than one card, he must cut again. Drawing from the out-spread pack may be resorted to in place of cutting.

6. *Shuffling.*—Before every deal, the cards must be shuffled. When two packs are used, the dealer's partner must collect and shuffle the cards for the ensuing deal, and place them at his right hand. In all cases the dealer may shuffle last.

7. The pack must not be shuffled during the play of a hand, nor so as to expose the face of any card.

8. *Cutting to the Dealer.*—The dealer must present the pack to his right-hand adversary to be cut; the adversary must take a portion from the top of the pack and place it

toward the dealer. At least four cards must be left in each packet; the dealer must reunite the packets by placing the one not removed in cutting upon the other.

9. If in cutting or reuniting the separate packets a card is exposed, the pack must be re-shuffled by the dealer and cut again. If there is any confusion of the cards, or doubt as to the place where the pack was separated, there must be a new cut.

10. If the dealer re-shuffles the pack after it has been properly cut, he loses his deal.

11. *Dealing.*—When the pack has been properly cut and reunited, the dealer must distribute the cards, one at a time, to each player in regular rotation at his left. The last, which is the trump card, must be turned up before the dealer. At the end of the hand, or when the deal is lost, the deal passes to the player next to the dealer on his left, and so on to each in turn.

12. There must be a new deal by the same dealer:

I. If any card except the last is faced in the pack.

II. If, during the deal or during the play of the hand, the pack is proved incorrect or imperfect, but any prior score made with that pack shall stand.

13. If, during the deal, a card is exposed, the side not in fault may demand a new deal, provided neither of that side has touched a card. If a new deal does not take place, the exposed card is not liable to be called.

14. Any one dealing out of turn, or with his adversaries' pack, may be stopped before the trump card is turned, after which the deal is valid, and the pack, if changed, so remains.

15. *Misdealing.*—It is a misdeal:

I.   If the dealer omits to have the pack cut, and his adversaries discover the error before the trump card is turned and before looking at any of their cards.

II. If he deals a card incorrectly and fails to correct the error before dealing another.

III. If he counts the cards on the table or in the remainder of the pack.

IV. If, having a perfect pack, he does not deal to each player the proper number of cards and the error is discovered before all have played to the first trick.

V.   If he looks at the trump card before the deal is completed.

VI. If he places the trump card face downward upon his own or any other player's cards.

A misdeal loses the deal unless during the deal either of the adversaries touches a card, or in any other manner interrupts the dealer.

16. *The Trump Card.*—The dealer must leave the trump card face upward on the table until it is his turn to play to the first trick; if it is left on the table until after the second trick has been turned and quitted, it is liable to be called. After it has been lawfully taken up it must not be named, and any player naming it is liable to have his highest or his lowest trump called by either adversary. A player may, however, ask what the trump suit is.

17. *Irregularities in the Hands.*—If, at any time after all have played to the first trick (the pack being perfect), a player is found to have either more or less than his correct number of cards, and his adversaries have their right

number, the latter, upon the discovery of such surplus or deficiency, may consult and shall have the choice:

> To have a new deal; or,
>
> To have the hand played out; in which case the surplus or missing cards are not taken into account.

If either of the adversaries also has more or less than his correct number, there must be a new deal.

If any player has a surplus card by reason of an omission to play to a trick, his adversaries can exercise the foregoing privilege only after he has played to the trick following the one in which the omission occurred.

18. *Cards Liable to be Called.*—The following cards are liable to be called by either adversary:

> Every card faced upon the table otherwise than in the regular course of play, but not including a card led out of turn.
>
> Every card thrown with the one led or played to the current trick. The player must indicate the one led or played.
>
> Every card so held by a player that his partner sees any portion of its face.
>
> All the cards in a hand lowered or shown by a player so that his partner sees more than one card of it.
>
> Every card named by the player holding it.

19. All cards liable to be called must be placed and left face upward on the table. A player must lead or play them when they are called, providing he can do so without revoking. The call may be repeated at each trick until the card is played. A player cannot be prevented from leading or playing a card liable to be called; if he can get rid of it in the course of play no penalty remains.

20. If a player leads a card better than any of his ad-

versaries hold of the suit, and then leads one or more other cards without waiting for his partner to play, the latter may be called upon by either adversary to take the first trick, and the other cards thus improperly played are liable to be called; it makes no difference whether he plays them one after the other or throws them all on the table together. After the first card is played the others are liable to be called.

21.   A player having a card liable to be called must not play another until the adversaries have stated whether or not they wish to call the card liable to the penalty. If he plays another card without awaiting the decision of the adversaries, such other card also is liable to be called.

22.   *Leading Out of Turn.*—If any player leads out of turn, a suit may be called from him or his partner the first time it is the turn of either of them to lead. The penalty can be enforced only by the adversary on the right of the player from whom a suit can rightfully be called.

If a player called on to lead a suit has none of it, or if all have played to the false lead, no penalty can be enforced. If all have not played to the trick, the cards erroneously played to such false lead are not liable to be called, and must be taken back.

23.   *Playing Out of Turn.*—If the third hand plays before the second, the fourth hand may also play before the second.

24.   If the third hand has not played, and the fourth hand plays before the second, the latter may be called upon by the third hand to play his highest or lowest card of the suit led; or, if he has none, to trump or not to trump the trick.

25.   *Abandoned Hands.*—If all four players throw their

cards on the table, face upward, no further play of that hand is permitted. The result of the hand, as then claimed or admitted, is established; provided, that if a revoke is discovered, the revoke penalty attaches.

26. *Revoking.*—A revoke is a renounce in error not corrected in time. A player renounces in error when, holding one or more cards of the suit led, he plays a card of a different suit.

A renounce in error may be corrected by the player making it, before the trick in which it occurs has been turned and quitted, unless either he or his partner, whether in his right turn or otherwise, has led or played to the following trick, or unless his partner has asked whether or not he has any of the suit renounced.

27. If a player corrects his mistake in time to save a revoke, the card improperly played by him is liable to be called. Any player or players who have played after him may withdraw their cards and substitute others; the cards so withdrawn are not liable to be called.

28. The penalty for revoking is the transfer of two tricks from the revoking side to their adversaries. It can be enforced for as many revokes as occur during the hand. The revoking side cannot win the game in that hand. If both sides revoke, neither can win the game in that hand.

29. The revoking player and his partner may require the hand in which the revoke has been made to be played out, and score all points made by them up to the score of six.

30. At the end of a hand, the claimants of a revoke may search all the tricks. If the tricks have been mixed, the claim may be urged and proved, if possible; but no proof is necessary and the revoke is established if, after it has

been claimed, the accused player or his partner mixes the cards before they have been examined to the satisfaction of the adversaries.

31. The revoke can be claimed at any time before the cards have been presented and cut for the following deal, but not thereafter.

32. *Miscellaneous.*—Any one, during the play of a trick, and before the cards have been touched for the purpose of gathering them together, may demand that the players draw their cards.

33. If any one, prior to his partner playing, calls attention in any manner to the trick or to the score, the adversary last to play to the trick may require the offender's partner to play his highest or lowest of the suit led; or, if he has none, to trump or not to trump the trick.

34. If any player says, "I can win the rest," "The rest are ours," "We have the game," or words to that effect, his partner's cards must be laid upon the table, and are liable to be called.

35. When a trick has been turned and quitted, it must not again be seen until after the hand has been played. A violation of this law subjects the offender's side to the same penalty as in case of a lead out of turn.

36. If a player is lawfully called upon to play the highest or lowest of a suit, or to trump or not to trump a trick, or to lead a suit, and unnecessarily fails to comply, he is liable to the same penalty as if he had revoked.

37. In all cases where a penalty has been incurred, the offender must await the decision of the adversaries. If either of them, with or without his partner's consent, demands a penalty to which they are entitled, such decision is final. If the wrong adversary demands a penalty, or a wrong penalty is demanded, none can be enforced.

AUCTION BRIDGE

Auction Bridge is a game for four players, two being partners against the other two.

The Cards.—A full deck of fifty-two cards is used, which is composed of thirteen cards of each of the four suits, spades, hearts, diamonds, and clubs. Two packs are commonly used, and should be of distinctive backs. The partner of the dealer shuffles the still deck while the deal is in progress and places it at his right, which is at the left of the player who is to deal next.

Rank of the Cards.—In each suit the Ace is high, then King, Queen, Jack, ten and down to the two spot or deuce, which is low.

Drawing for Partners, Positions at the Table and Dealer.—The cards are spread on the table, face down, and each player draws one. The highest two become partners to play against the other two; the highest becomes the first dealer and has the choice of seats and cards.

Cutting.—The shuffled deck is presented to the player at the right of the dealer for cutting, which is done by dividing the deck into two packets (each of which must contain at least four cards) and placing the upper portion on the table towards the dealer. The dealer then completes the cut by placing the lower packet upon the portion just removed.

Dealing.—All of the cards are dealt out one at a time beginning with the player upon dealer's left.

Immediately after the deal the auction begins, which is bidding for the privilege of making the trump. Any suit may be declared trump or the game may be played without

a trump, called *No Trump*. Each suit and No Trump has
a different value as shown in the following table:—

Declaration.—

	Club	Diamond	Heart	Spade	No Trump
Each trick above book of 6 counts....	6	7	8	9	10
3 honors	30	30	30	30	30
4 honors (divided between partners)....	40	40	40	40	40
4 honors (in one hand)	80	80	80	80	100
5 honors (divided between partners)....	50	50	50	50	
5 honors (four in one hand)	90	90	90	90	
5 honors (in one hand)	100	100	100	100	

Game is 30 points; rubber (two games for one side)
250; grand slam (13 tricks) 100; small slam (12 tricks) 50.
Nothing can be scored towards game except by declarer,
and by him only when he fulfills his contract. Honors (Ace,
King, Queen, Jack and ten of trump, or the four Aces in
No Trump) are scored as held.

The first six tricks taken by declarer constitute the book
and do not count towards game, but each trick taken in
excess of the book counts according to the above table, 10
if the declaration is No Trump, 9 if Spades are the trump,
8 for Hearts, 7 for Diamonds and 6 for Clubs.

In the auction the dealer has the first right to make a
declaration and may bid from one to seven of any suit or
No Trump. The number that he bids indicates the number
of tricks (called odd tricks) above his book of six which
his side contracts to take. If he bids one No Trump or
one of a suit it means that his side must take one trick in
excess of their book or seven tricks altogether.

The dealer may pass if he does not care to make a bid
and after his declaration the auction continues around the
table to the left. Each declaration must be higher than
the preceding one—that is—it must be for a greater num-

ber of odd tricks or for the same number in a higher suit or No Trump. Thus three No Trump would overbid any other three bid, but four Clubs would outrank any three bid, although the numerical value of three No Trump (30) is greater than four Clubs (24).

The auction continues until three players in succession pass, then the last bid made becomes the declaration at which that hand is to be played. If all four players pass without a bid having been made the hand is thrown down and the next dealer deals.

Whichever player (of the side which wins the declaration) started that particular bid becomes the declarer and must play the hand. After the declarer has been determined the adversary on his left is called senior, the one on his right junior and his partner becomes the dummy.

The play of the hand is now begun by senior who leads any card from his hand. Immediately after this lead dummy's hand is placed on the table face up arranged in suits with the trump suit (if there is one) upon his right and the red and black suits alternating. Declarer must now play the two hands (the dummy and his own) and the play goes around towards the left.

In playing to a trick each player must follow suit if possible but if void of that suit may play any card desired; that is, he may trump or discard. The highest card on each trick wins unless one of them is a trump in which case the trump wins, and if more than one trump has been played to a trick the highest trump wins.

The winner of the first trick gathers the four cards and places them face down in front of him and leads to the second trick. This is continued until the thirteen tricks have been played and gathered in, when the scoring is done.

If the declarer has won as many tricks as his declaration guaranteed, he counts all tricks over his book at their proper value and enters it on the score pad below the line, and he places above the line the value of the honors held by either side. For example, suppose the declaration was four Spades and the declarer took six odd tricks (six above his book or twelve in all). His score below the line would be six times nine, or fifty-four, and if the opponents held three of the honors they would score thirty above the line. Declarer would also score fifty above the line for a small slam (because he took all the tricks but one). Since thirty or more makes a game, a line is drawn across the score sheet under the fifty-four and the next hand starts a new game.

If however, in the above example where the declaration is four Spades, the declarer takes only nine tricks (three odd) he is defeated and there is no score towards game (below the line). In this case the opponents score fifty above the line because they defeated the declarer by one trick. Thus when a declaration is defeated the opponents score fifty for each trick which the declarer failed to take (called under-tricks).

Doubling.—If, after the bidding has gone rather high, an opponent feels sure that he can defeat the declaration he has a right to double it, and if the other players then pass the last declaration is played doubled. If the declarer is defeated the opponents score double, or one hundred for each under-trick, but if the declarer wins a doubled declaration he scores double below the line for the number of odd tricks that he takes, fifty above the line for fulfilling his contract and fifty for each trick made above his contract.

Doubling does not affect the score for honors or for slams nor does it alter the size of the declaration during the auction. For instance, if a bid of four Spades is doubled a player may bid five of any other suit and such a subsequent bid nullifies a double.

Valuing a Hand for Bidding.—Card valuation is based upon *Honor Tricks* and *Playing Tricks.* An honor trick is a card or combination of cards which may reasonably be expected to take a trick, no matter what is trump or who the declarer may be. This is called valuing the honor tricks "defensively."

TABLE OF DEFENSIVE HONOR TRICKS

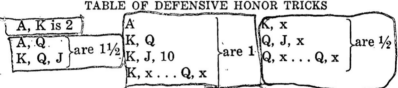

A, K is 2

A, Q
K, Q, J are 1½

A
K, Q
K, J, 10
K, x ... Q, x are 1

K, x
Q, J, x
Q, x ... Q, x are ½

x stands for any small card.

K, x... Q, x signifies a King and one in one suit and a Queen and one in another suit.

Experience teaches that in any deal, the four hands will contain eight or eight and a half honor tricks and that two partners will be able to take just about that proportion of the thirteen playing tricks that they hold of these eight honor tricks. If, therefore, a player holds two and a half honor tricks he may reasonably expect to take four playing tricks because two and a half is the same proportion of eight that four is of thirteen. If a player can take four tricks he may assume that his partner will be able to take his share of the remaining nine tricks, which is three and as this makes seven, he has a right to bid one.

Biddable Suits.—To be biddable a suit must contain at least four cards, and if it is of that length, it must contain one and-a half honor tricks. A five-card suit is biddable if it is headed by half-an honor trick and a suit that is longer a Jack and a higher honor. A five-card suit is biddable if it is headed by a Jack and a suit that is longer than five cards needs no honor trick strength to be biddable.

Examples of biddable suits:

Q, J, x, x   J, x, x, x, x   x, x, x, x, x, x

Rebiddable Suits.—To be rebiddable a suit must contain five cards headed by A, K, or any three honors, like Q, J, 10, x, x, or any six cards.

REQUIREMENTS FOR AN ORIGINAL BID

To bid one of a suit a hand should contain a biddable suit and three honor tricks or a rebiddable suit and two and a half honor tricks.

Counting Playing Tricks in the Bidding Hand.—Playing tricks in the bidding hand consist of honor tricks and "long suit" tricks. A "long" card is any card in a suit beyond three, that is, a four-card suit has one long card, a six-card suit has three long cards, etc. Each long card in the trump suit is counted one playing trick and each long card in a plain suit is counted a half a playing trick. Long cards should not be counted in any suits which have been bid by an opponent.

Example—Counting playing tricks in the bidding hand for a Spade bid:

S—A, K, x, x, x Two honor tricks and two long cards..4
H—A, x, x, x   One honor trick and one long card....1½
D—x, x, x   No playing trick value...............0
C—x   No playing trick value...............0

                                                      ———
                                                       5½

To make an original bid of one of a suit it is not necessary to count the playing tricks; a biddable suit and three honor tricks is sufficient, but if this player is to rebid on the second round he must count his playing tricks and unless his partner has denied assistance, he may rebid once for each playing trick in excess of four. If partner has passed when he should have shown assistance if he had it, the original bidder should have two extra tricks for each rebid.

An original suit bid should be made in preference to a No Trump unless holding a 3-3-3-4 distribution. With this distribution open with a No Trump if holding four Honor Tricks or three with eight honor cards, even in preference to a four-card biddable suit.

SECOND HAND BIDDING

Second hand should very seldom bid over dealer's one No Trump,—never unless there seems to be a good prospect of making game.

Over dealer's one of a suit, second hand may make a defensive bid with one and a half honor tricks and a five-card biddable suit or may bid No Trump if holding a strong hand with opponent's suit stopped twice.

The Informatory or Take-Out Double.—If, after dealer bids one No Trump, second hand finds that he also has a No Trump hand, he may use the take-out double to find out his partner's best suit. If he doubles a one No Trump, it says to his partner: "I have a No Trump hand also, partner, please bid your best suit." In responding to such a take-out double, the partner should bid a major suit if holding one of four cards and some reasonable help, in preference to a longer and stronger minor suit. If he has a poor hand he still must bid, in fact the poorer his hand is, the more imperative it is for him to bid. The only case where he may pass is where he has such a strong hand that he is certain that by allowing the opponent to play the hand at one No Trump doubled, a large penalty may be won. This is called a business or penalty pass because it changes the partner's take-out double to a penalty double. If dealer bids one of a suit and second hand has a good No Trump hand in all except that suit, he may again use the take-out double to get a bid from his partner. The rule to distinguish a take-out double from a penalty double is as follows: "Any double is a take-out double if it is of one No Trump or of one, two or three of a suit, made at the doubler's first opportunity and before the partner has bid or doubled. All other doubles are penalty doubles."

THIRD HAND BIDDING

When dealer bids a suit and second hand overbids, third hand would like to assist his partner by a raise and the first consideration here is the size and number of cards held in his partner's suit. A raise should never be given unless holding *"Adequate Trump Support,"* which is four small ones, or three if one is as high as the Queen. With that much of your partner's suit, there must be four playing tricks, and one additional raise may be given, if occasion requires it, for each playing trick over four.

Counting Playing Tricks in the Responding Hand.—In valuing a hand in support of partner's bid, the playing tricks consist of (1) trump tricks; (2) honor tricks in plain suits; (3) long plain suit tricks and (4) short suit or ruffing tricks. These are counted as follows:

In the trump suit (bid by partner) Four cards count ½
Five cards count 1
More than five.. 2

and in addition to these the Ace counts one, the King one and the Queen one-half.

Long suit tricks in plain suits are counted as in the bidding hand, i.e., each long card is counted ½ playing trick.

Honor tricks in the plain suits are counted as in the table given on page 25.

Short suit or ruffing tricks depend upon the length of the trump suit and are counted as follows:

	With three trumps	With more than three trumps
A doubleton counts.............	½	1
A singleton counts.......... .	1	2
A void suit counts.............	2	3

When holding two short suits, only one (the shorter) should be counted.

Another method of counting playing tricks in the responding hand is by a mechanical rule, as follows:

Add the number of cards in suit bid by partner to the number in the longest side suit, divide by two, subtract the number in the shortest side suit and add the number of honor tricks. Example—Partner bid a Heart.

S—A, x, x, x   4 plus 5 is 9, divided by 2 is 4½, minus
H—x, x, x, x   0 is 4½, plus 1 is 5½.
D—x, x, x, x, x
C—0

Still another shorter but less accurate method is to give one raise when holding trump support and (1), a void suit and a half an honor trick, or (2), a singleton and one honor trick or (3), even distribution and two honor tricks. If less than adequate trump support is held, third hand should make a denial bid in another suit if holding a biddable one with one and a half honor tricks. This he should do even if second hand has passed.

Third hand should also overbid his partner's one of a suit after an intervening pass, if he can *improve the bid*, that is, if he can bid a major suit or a No Trump over his partner's minor. A good major suit is considered better than a No

Trump, therefore third hand should not bid No Trump over partner's major unless holding less than adequate trump support in that major suit.

If dealer bids one No Trump and second hand passes, third hand should bid if he holds any of the following combinations:

(1) A major suit of original bidding strength.

(2) A very strong minor suit (eight tricks in the hand) bid three of it.

(3) A singleton and a major suit of defensive strength.

(4) A singleton and any six-card suit.

(5) Any two five-card suits, either one of original bidding strength.

(6) Any seven-card suit.

To raise partner's No Trump after an opposing suit bid, third hand should have opponent's suit twice stopped and one and a half honor tricks.

SUGGESTIONS FOR PLAY

Senior's opening lead to a No Trump should be the fourth best card of his longest suit unless that suit contains three honors, two of which are touching, in which case he should lead the top of the touching honors.

In a declared trump such a simple rule cannot be given but the following list of leads in the order of their preference should be used as a guide:—

(1) Ace from Ace, King and no others.

(2) King from Ace, King and others.

(3) Ace, lone or with one small one.

(4) Top of a three-card sequence.

(5) Top of a two-card sequence.

(6) Top of worthless two-card suit.

(7) Singleton, if holding four or less small trumps.

(8) Fourth best from long suit avoiding if possible four to the King or King-Jack.

(9) Ace from Ace and several others avoiding if possible Ace-Queen or Ace-Jack combinations.

If senior opens his partner's suit in a No Trump, he should lead his highest if holding only two or three without an honor as high as a Queen, but should lead low if holding three with such an honor or more than three. At a declared trump he should lead low if holding four or more, but his highest from all other combinations.

The Rule of Eleven.—Subtract the number of spots on the fourth best lead from eleven and the result shows the number of cards of that suit, *above* the one led, held by the other three players (not counting the leader). When senior leads his fourth best, declarer and junior can each tell, by applying this rule, how many the other one has above the one led.

Junior's Play.—If senior opens his own suit low, junior should win the trick if possible and return his next highest.

If senior opens his own suit high, junior should unblock, that is, play in such a manner that he will *not* win a trick with his last card of that suit. The proper way to unblock is to hold the smallest card to the last.

If senior opens junior's suit low, it means great length or an honor and if junior wins the trick he should return the suit low.

If senior opens junior's suit high and junior can tell that declarer holds one above it which cannot be captured, he should play low to force out declarer's high card while senior still has one of the suit to lead back later.

Declarer's Play.—After dummy's cards are exposed, declarer should take time to look over both hands and lay out a plan of play, deciding whether or not to extract trumps at once, which suits to lead first, what finesses to take, whether or not he needs to develop a hidden re-entry card in dummy and approximately how many tricks he can take.

Finessing.—Finessing is trying to take a trick with a card when there is a higher card unplayed, the location of which is unknown. If declarer has Ace-Queen and others in dummy and only small ones in his own hand, he should lead towards the Ace-Queen and if senior plays low he should play the Queen, which is called finessing against the King. If senior holds the King, the Queen will take the trick and the finesse wins but if junior has the King it will capture the Queen and the finesse loses. Such a finesse has just a 50-50 chance of winning and should always be taken unless some further consideration makes it unwise.

When holding Ace-Queen-Jack in the two hands, the Queen or Jack should be led towards the Ace and if not covered by second hand it should be finessed through.

When holding Ace-Queen-ten, the double finesse (against King and Jack) may be taken by playing the ten or the single finesse (against the King) by playing the Queen. The double finesse should be taken when holding less than nine cards in the suit in both hands, but the single finesse is better if holding nine or more.

Holding up an Ace.—When declarer holds just Ace and a few small cards of the suit opened by senior in a No Trump, he should hold the Ace up if he thinks he can exhaust junior of that suit *and* if he wants to finesse towards junior. If he cannot hold it up long enough to exhaust junior, or does not think junior can get the lead, there is no object in holding it up.

The Elimination Play.—This is a play which may sometimes be employed to avoid the risk of taking a finesse. When declarer has a major tenace, and can eliminate two suits from his two hands, he then throws the lead to senior who is compelled to lead up to the major tenace or to lead one of the eliminated suits allowing declarer to trump in dummy and discard the Queen of his tenace from his own hand. When this play can be brought in it always nets one trick for the declarer.

The Grand Coup.—This is where the remaining trumps are held by junior and declarer, and the latter has one more than the former—for instance, if junior has the King-Jack and declarer has the Ace-Queen and one small one. Played in the ordinary way declarer will be forced to take the eleventh trick and lead up to junior's tenace, assuring a trick to the King, but if declarer can get rid of his small trump and place the lead in dummy for the twelfth trick he can lead through junior's tenace and capture both. Declarer must therefore get rid of a trump, which is done by trumping a good card of dummy's. The play must be planned several tricks in advance.

The Squeeze Play.—This is an end play which frequently wins an extra trick. It consists of compelling the opponents, by discarding, to unguard one suit or give up the command of another. It requires rather careful reading of the opponents' hands towards the end of the play and is, therefore, common only to experts.

THREE-HAND AUCTION

Auction Bridge for three persons may be played in a number of ways. One is to deal four hands as in the regular game, one to each of the players and the fourth for dummy, and have the three players bid against each other. The successful bidder becomes the declarer and the fourth hand which is his dummy is placed opposite him between the other two players. This compels each player to bid upon his own hand without any inkling of what his dummy will contain and is so hazardous that it is sometimes called Cut-Throat Auction.

Another method is the same as this except that in dealing, every other one of dummy's cards is turned face up. This gives all players an equal chance of knowing *something* about the help they will receive and makes a better game. Individual scores must be kept and rubbers may be played or 125 added for each game.

TWO-HAND OR HONEYMOON BRIDGE

Two-hand or Honeymoon Bridge may be played in a great number of different ways, some of the most interesting of which are here given. They may be played as Auction or Contract as desired.

TWO-HAND BRIDGE, No. 1

This may be played by having racks to hold the cards of the two dummies. Each rack is placed in such a position that the cards may be seen by only one of the players. If one player sits in the south position at a table the other one would take the east position, south's dummy rack would be near the northeast corner of the table and east's near the southwest corner. The cards are dealt into four hands and each player sorts his dummy's cards and places them in the rack. In bidding each player sees his twenty-six cards and in the play, also, he always sees his own dummy but never that of his opponent.

TWO-HAND BRIDGE, No. 2

Another, and more interesting game for two players, is as follows:—The players sit as just described at the two sides of the table which are not opposite each other. The dealer in the south position deals the usual four hands but, in laying out the two dummy hands, the first card is turned face up, the next six cards are turned face down in a row with the first one and the last six turned face up, each one partly covering the six which are face down. This reveals seven cards of each dummy, which helps the players in their bidding and the subsequent play. The play is conducted as nearly like four-hand Auction as possible, each player playing two hands, and whenever one of dummy's cards is played under which another one lies, this under one is turned face up.

Considerable skill may be employed in this game, as a King or Queen will frequently be good before the Ace has been played, because it is covered up in a dummy and, frequently, small trumps may be used in dummy ruffing a suit, cards of which may be turned up there later.

TWO-HAND BRIDGE, No. 3

Thirteen cards are dealt to each player and the remaining twenty-six cards are laid aside face down.

The thirteen cards dealt to each player are then played at No Trump—the opponent of dealer leading. There are, of course, only two cards to a trick. The result is scored and the remaining cards are now dealt, thirteen to each player. Bidding for the privilege of making the declaration is now done, the dealer bidding first and his opponent over-bidding, doubling or passing. The declaration having been determined, these cards are played and the result scored as before.

The skill in playing this form of the game consists largely in remembering, during the bidding and play of the second twenty-six cards, which cards were played in the first round.

TWO-HAND BRIDGE, No. 4

Thirteen cards are dealt to each player and the twenty-seventh card is turned up and placed face up upon the other twenty-five cards which are placed face down.

For the first thirteen tricks there is no bidding but the hand is played at No Trump, the opponent of the dealer leading. The player winning the first trick takes up the exposed card from the top of the stock and his opponent takes the next card into his hand without showing it. The top card of the stock is now turned face up to be drawn by the winner of the next trick.

After thirteen tricks have been played and the stock is exhausted, the dealer starts bidding and after the declaration is determined the remaining thirteen tricks are played.

Sometimes the first thirteen tricks are not scored while some prefer to score them, but the chief interest of the game is in playing the second thirteen tricks.

While there is a stock, the leader tries to win or lose a trick according as to whether or not he desires the exposed card.

In bidding, a player must, of course, remember as well as possible what cards have been played in the first round and the more accurately he can do this, the more exactly can he know what cards remain in his opponent's hand, so that the game is a very great help in training one's memory and assisting him to learn to concentrate his thoughts. Since these faculties of concentration and memory are most essential to ordinary Bridge, these games serve a very useful purpose for self improvement.

PROGRESSIVE AUCTION

Progressive Auction is played where there are several tables and it is desirable to change partners. Four hands are played at each table and then a change is made. The winners at each table progress to the next higher table and there change partners. Winners remain at the head table and the losers go to the foot table. In scoring 125 points are added for a game made in one hand and at the end of the four hands the scores are added up, the smaller one subtracted from the larger, the winners recording upon their individual score cards this difference plus 100 points for winning and the losers recording the same difference as a MINUS score. If a hand is passed out without a bid, the same dealer deals again, but if this happens twice at the same round the dealer loses his deal and only three hands are played at that table.

CONTRACT BRIDGE

The main point of difference between Contract and Auction is that in the former only the number of odd tricks *contracted for* are scored in the trick column towards game while any won in excess of the contract are scored in the honor column. This materially alters the bidding and in general makes it desirable for the two partners to bid their hands to the limit.

The scoring is also very different and will be given first so as to aid in describing the game.

Each odd trick *contracted for* and won counts:

In No Trump, 1st trick 40; each succeeding trick 30.

In Spades or Hearts, 30.

In Diamonds or Clubs, 20.

The rank of the declarations is the same as in Auction, namely, No Trump, Spades, Hearts, Diamonds, Clubs.

Game:—A game consists of 100 points.

Vulnerability.—Either side is vulnerable when it has won one game; when the games are one all, both sides are vulnerable. Only the vulnerability of the declarer's side affects the bonuses and penalties.

PREMIUMS, BONUSES AND HONORS

(Scored in honor column)

For winning rubber of two games............ 700
For winning rubber of three games.......... 500
Four Aces in one hand at No Trump......... 150
Five suit honors in one hand.............. 150
Four suit honors in one hand............. 100
All other honors........................Nothing

	Not vulnerable		Vulnerable	
	Undoubled	Doubled	Undoubled	Doubled
For each extra trick...........	Trick Value	100	Trick Value	200
For small slam (when bid)......	500	500	750	750
For grand slam (when bid)......	1000	1000	1500	1500

Unbid slams made count nothing.

PENALTIES

(Scored in adversaries' honor column)

	Not vulnerable		Vulnerable	
	Undoubled	Doubled	Undoubled	Doubled
First Undertrick	50	100	100	200
Second Undertrick	50	200	100	300
Third Undertrick	50	200	100	300
Fourth Undertrick	50	200	100	300
Fifth Undertrick	50	200	100	300
Sixth Undertrick	50	200	100	300
Seventh Undertrick	50	200	100	300

If redoubled, twice the doubled value.

AGGREGATE PENALTIES

	Not vulnerable		Vulnerable	
	Undoubled	Doubled	Undoubled	Doubled
One Undertrick	50	100	100	200
Two Undertricks	100	300	200	500
Three Undertricks	150	500	300	800
Four Undertricks	200	700	400	1100
Five Undertricks	250	900	500	1400
Six Undertricks	300	1100	600	1700
Seven Undertricks	350	1300	700	2000

If redoubled, twice the doubled value.

REVOKE PENALTY

For first revoke...........................Two tricks

For each subsequent revoke by same side,
   same deal ....One trick

For additional laws see page 328.

Although the trick values are different, their relative values regarding the game remain the same as at Auction, namely, it still requires three odd tricks at No Trump, four at a major and five at a minor suit to make game, because the game at Contract is 100 points.

It has been said that in general it was desirable to bid the hands to their limit, but this statement must be somewhat qualified. It is best to start the bidding low so as to give your partner a better chance to tell you something about his hand and if his response does not give promise of game, to stop bidding at once. If a game seems possible, however, the bidding should be continued until that is reached and then stopped, unless such a wealth of high cards is shown in the two hands that a slam appears possible, in which case it is desirable to keep up the bidding until the slam is reached.

Valuation of Hands.—The best method of valuing a hand is that which has already been given for Auction, and therefore the reader is referred to pages 26-29 for the Honor Tricks, Biddable Suits and the manner of counting playing tricks in the bidding hand and in the responding hand.

Rules of 8 and of 4-5-6.—There are always about eight or eight and a half honor tricks in the four hands of any deal and it has been found that one side will take just about that proportion of the thirteen playing tricks that they hold of the eight honor tricks. This, as we saw in Auction, is why a player may bid one upon two and a half to 3 honor tricks, as this corresponds to about four playing tricks. In higher bidding we aim to determine the number of honor tricks the two hands hold and figure from that how high it is advisable to bid. Working out these proportions we find that four honor tricks will produce about one odd trick, five about two odd and six about three odd or game. These rules are wonderfully helpful in telling how high to bid.

Original Bids.—A bid of one of a suit shows a rebiddable suit and two and a half honor tricks or three honor tricks and a biddable suit.

A bid of two of a suit is peculiar to Contract and is made when the holding is so strong that a game seems assured, but this strength is distributed in three suits in such a manner that it becomes desirable to learn something about partner's hand. An original bid of two of a suit is therefore, "forcing" and partner *must* keep the bidding open even with a blank hand. The two bid signifies four and a half to five and a half honor tricks in three suits with about eight playing tricks, and after such a bid both partners must keep bidding until a game is reached.

Examples of Original Two Bids:

(1)	(2)	(3)
S—A, K, J, x, x, x	S—A, K	S—0
H—A, K, x	H—x, x, x, x	H—A, K, Q, x, x, x
D—K, Q, x	D—A, K, x, x	D—A, x
C—x	C—A, K, Q	C—K, Q, J, x, x

No. 1 has five honor tricks and eight playing tricks, bid two Spades.

No. 2 has six honor tricks and eight and a half playing tricks, bid two Diamonds (Here the A, K, Q of Clubs are counted three playing tricks).

No. 3 has four and a half honor tricks and eight and a half playing tricks, bid two Hearts.

An original No Trump bid is now only made with the 3-3-3-4 distribution and with this distribution should be made in preference to a biddable four card suit. A one No Trump shows four Honor Tricks or three and a half with eight honor cards (10 spot or higher). An original two No Trump shows five and a half or six Honor Tricks or five with nine honor cards and all suits well stopped. It is not forcing but strongly invitational.

An original bid of three of a major or four of a minor shows eight or nine playing tricks largely in one suit— it is not forcing and says to partner, this suit or nothing for me. The total number of honor tricks may not exceed two.

Original bids of four of a major or five of a minor (game bids) are pre-emptive bids and usually overbids, made upon hands which are strong in that one suit, but practically worthless for any other bid. They show about seven or eight playing tricks and may have as little as one and a half honor tricks.

Since original bids now require somewhat greater strength than formerly, it is no longer necessary to make any distinction as to the position at the table or as regards vulnerability.

SECOND HAND BIDDING

After an original bid has been made, the next player may make a so-called defensive bid of one of a suit if holding a biddable five-card suit and one and a half honor tricks in the hand or with a four-card biddable suit and two honor tricks.

If second hand has a strong holding, he may show three honor tricks by a take-out double or, if holding a singleton Ace or a void of the opponent's suit, he may show four tricks by overbidding in that suit.

Examples of Second Hand Bidding after Dealer's One Heart:

(1)	(2)
S—A, K, x, x, x	S—A, K, x, x
H—x, x	H—0
D—K, x, x	D—K, Q, x, x
C—A, x, x	C—A, x, x, x, x

With No. 1, opponent's one Heart should be doubled.
With No. 2, two Hearts should be bid.

Jump Over-call.—A second hand bid of one more than necessary to over-call dealer is called a Jump Over-call and is now used to show a strong two-suiter or a strong re-biddable suit with three Honor Tricks and seven or eight playing tricks. It is called semi-forcing.

THIRD HAND BIDDING

The first requirement for raising partner's suit bid of one or two is "Adequate Trump Support," which is four small ones or three if one is as high as the Queen. When partner opens with a bid higher than two, adequate trump support is not necessary when considering a raise as such a bid announces a trump suit of unusual strength. With adequate trump support, four playing tricks are required for one raise, five are enough for two raises and so on, and if a raise is to be given it should be for the full value of the hand at once.

If the hand does not contain adequate trump support, some other bid should be made if possible. If having any biddable suit and four playing tricks that suit should be bid and lacking a biddable suit one No Trump should be bid if holding one and a half honor tricks in two suits other than the one bid by partner.

If third hand is strong, a jump bid in another suit should be made, like two Spades over partner's one of any other suit or three Diamonds over partner's one Spade. This is a forcing bid and is called the "forcing jump take-out."

It shows three and a half honor tricks and affirms adequate trump support for partner's suit. After it, each partner must continue to bid until a game is reached and a raise in partner's suit may thus be given on the next round.

Third Hand's Response to Partner's Original Forcing Bid of Two of a Suit.—The first response should be to show the presence or absence of one honor trick. If holding less than one honor trick, the response MUST be two No Trump no matter how many playing tricks for the partner's suit may be held. The bidding must continue and on the next round the partner's suit may be raised if holding adequate trump support and any ruffing tricks. If lacking adequate trump support, the second response should be any biddable suit of if holding none, No Trump must be bid again. If holding adequate trump support and at least one honor trick, these values are worth one raise and any other honor tricks or ruffing tricks are additional raises. With any biddable suit and one honor trick, it is better to make a simple take-out in that suit first, so as to give partner this additional information and then give a raise on the second round. If holding some honor trick strength but no biddable suit and less than adequate trump support, a jump bid in No Trump should be made; three No Trump with one and a half to two honor tricks and four No Trump with more than two honor tricks. This last bid would show that a slam seems possible. If after partner makes a forcing bid of two of a suit, second hand over-calls, third hand may pass if holding a blank hand, but if the bidding comes around to him again and is still less than a game, he must keep the bidding open.

Third hand should raise his partner's three of a major or four of a minor suit with about two and a half playing tricks as these will be sufficient to bring the total to a game bid, but after partner's original game bid do not raise unless holding strength enough to go for a slam, that is, about four or five playing tricks.

After partner's one No Trump and a pass, third hand should raise to two No Trump with one plus to two Honor Tricks even if holding a biddable five or six card suit.

With two plus or more Honor Tricks he should bid three No Trump if holding good No Trump distribution but with a good five card suit and a singleton, he should make the forcing jump suit take-out.

He should make a simple suit take-out with any biddable five or six card suit if holding from one-half to one Honor Trick.

If holding less than one Honor Trick, he should pass unless holding a seven or eight card suit in which case he should bid two of it and if his partner says two No Trump he should bid three of it, which would be a sign-off bid.

After partner's original two No Trump, third hand should bid any biddable suit if holding one honor trick and a poor No Trump distribution or raise to three No Trump with one honor trick and good No Trump distribution.

Three Minimum Third Hand Bids.—If partner bids one of a suit and second hand passes, it is very desirable to keep the bidding open as partner may have a big hand. Therefore, in this situation, third hand should bid where a pass would be proper if second hand had made a bid.

Raise once with adequate trump support and two and a half playing tricks or if lacking trump support, make a simple take-out with any biddable suit and one honor trick, or if lacking both a biddable suit and trump support, bid one No Trump, if holding one plus honor trick.

Slam Bidding.—After a strength-showing response from either partner which shows a fit in some suit (like a double raise of an original bid of one of a suit or a forcing jump shift take-out) the following bids show Aces and Kings.

Four No Trump (forcing) shows three Aces or two Aces and a King of one of the bid suits.

Response to four No Trump. With two Aces or one Ace and the Kings of all bid suits, five No Trump MUST be bid. With one Ace and not holding the Kings of all bid suits, bid five of THAT suit and with no Ace, bid five in the lowest ranking bid suit. If player who bid four No Trump follows by a bid of five No Trump, it shows all four Aces.

Five No Trump (without previously bidding four No Trump) means that bidder lacks very little further assistance for a grand slam. If partner holds Ace of chosen trump suit or an outside Ace, and King or Queen of the trump suit he is requested to bid seven of the chosen suit. If holding an outside Ace but no high trump he should bid six of THAT suit and if holding King or Queen of trumps without an outside Ace, he should bid six of the trump suit.

Asking Bids.—After a strength-showing response to an original bid, like one Heart, pass, three Hearts (showing better than normal trump support and about two Honor Tricks) a bid of a different suit by the original bidder asks for the second round control of the newly bid suit and an additional Ace. Second round control would be a singleton or a guarded King. If holding such second round control and an outside Ace, the suit of that Ace should be bid. If holding the second round control but no Ace or an Ace without the second round control, a simple take-out in the trump suit should be made.

The asking bid must be a bid of four unless it is in Spades when it may be a bid of three. If the responding hand holds the Ace of the asked-for suit, he should raise once in that suit; if he has the second round control and two Aces, he should bid four No Trump. If the responding hand bids a new suit to show the Ace and the original bidder raises that suit, he is asking for the second round control of that suit, namely, Ace and King or singleton Ace, and if an affirmative answer can be made, it should be No Trump at the same level.

Since the play of the hand is exactly the same at Contract as it is at Auction, the reader is referred to Page 31 where suggestions for the play are given.

BACKGAMMON

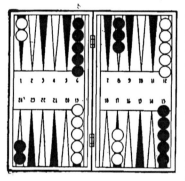

Old-fashioned Backgammon was a game for two persons, played with a set of checkers, fifteen white and fifteen black, upon a board marked as in the illustration.

The left hand half of the table, containing numbers 1 to 6 and 19 to 24, is called the *Inner Table* and the right hand half the *Outer Table*. The division between the inner and outer tables is called the *Bar.*

At the beginning of a game the men are placed as shown in the design. The player having the white men is stationed at the lower side of the table and the one having the black men at the upper side. The lower half of the inner table is the *Home Table* for the whites and the upper half is home table for the blacks.

The men of each side are moved from the opponent's home table around to player's own home table and then thrown off. The game is won by the player who first finishes throwing off all of his men. Two dice are used to determine the moves, each player in turn having one throw of the dice and moving any of his men as many points as the numbers on the dice indicate. After a player has all of his men in his home table he throws them off according to the numbers obtained by throws of the dice, the points in the home table being numbered from one to six. For example, if a player throws a four-three he may move one man four points and then three more or he may move one man four points and another one three. In making moves, the point to which a die number brings a man must be vacant, or have player's own men upon it, or have only one of opponent's men. If it has two or more of opponent's men it is closed and that move cannot be made. If only one man is on a point it is called a *Blot*, and if the opponent can just reach this point by a move he may capture this man, remove him and place him upon the bar. His owner must then, at his next turn to play, enter him in his opponent's home table upon a point corresponding to the number upon one of his dice; this he must do before moving another man. If, in this situation, the player whose man is on the bar throws a four-two and these two points of opponent's home table are closed (by having two or more of opponent's men upon them) player cannot play and opponent takes his turn.

If a player throws *Doublets*, he plays the throw twice; thus with double sixes a player may move one man twenty-four points or two men each twelve points, four men each six points, etc., but in such case each sixth point must be available (not closed). A player may pass over any number of men which may be upon intervening points between position of man played and point reached by the number upon the die, and a single man of opponent in this case is not captured.

After a player's men are all in his home table, he begins to throw off, which is done according to the numbers thrown by the dice. If he throws a six-one he may throw off one man from the six point and one from the one point. If he has no man on the one point he may move a man up one point, but if he has no man on the six point he may throw off a man from the highest point occupied. If, after a player begins to throw off, he is compelled to leave a blot and the opponent captures a man and places him upon the bar, this man must be entered in opponent's home table and carried around to home again before any more men may be thrown off.

If, when one player finishes, his opponent has taken off some men, a single game is won; if the opponent has not thrown off a single man, it is called a *Gammon* and counts as a double game, and if the opponent not only has not thrown off any men but still has a man in the inner table of the winner, it is a *Backgammon* and counts as a triple game.

The recent revival of the game has introduced a number of innovations which create additional interest when the game is played for stakes. Chief among these are the automatic and optional doubles and the Chouette (pronounced Shoe-et) or team play.

Automatic doubles. Each tie when throwing the dice for first play automatically doubles the stakes.

Optional doubles. At any time during the play, when either player thinks he is ahead, he may, after his opponent has completed his move and prior to throwing his own dice, double the original stake. If the opponent thinks his chance of success too slight, he refuses, forfeits the original stake and the game stops. Should he so desire, he may accept the double and the game goes on. The option of redoubling rests with the player who has last been doubled so that neither player may double twice in succession.

Chouette. This variation makes it possible for any number up to six to play the game. The players each throw two dice and the highest becomes the "Man in the Box" who plays alone against all the other players. The second highest becomes Captain of the team and the others are graded according to the numbers they cast, the third highest being second in command and so on.

The team members may consult as to plays and doubles but the captain's decision is final. If the Man in the Box proposes a double and one member of the team wishes to reject it despite the Captain's decision to accept, this team member may withdraw by paying his losses up to that time to the team. In this case the remaining members of the team assume the withdrawer's interest and win or lose more pro rata. If the Man in the Box wins he retains his position and is paid the accumulated stakes by each member of the team. The Captain of the defeated team goes to the lowest position on the team and each member moves up one place, the former second in command becoming Captain. If the Man in the Box loses, he pays each member of the team and goes to the foot of the team while the former Captain becomes the Man in the Box and the other players move up one position as before.

RUSSIAN BACKGAMMON

Here the men are not placed on the board before start-ing a game but are entered by throws of the dice. Both players enter their men in the same table and move around in the same direction, so that both have the same home ta-ble. After a player has entered some men he may, upon subsequent throws, move these men or enter new ones as he chooses. If a man is captured and placed upon the bar, he must be reentered before any man can be moved. If the first throw made by either player is a doublet, it is played just as in the ordinary game but, for any doublets thrown thereafter, the player plays the numbers doubled, then plays the numbers on the opposite sides of the dice doubled and then has a second throw.

SUGGESTIONS FOR GOOD PLAY

The object of the game being for a player to get his men home and thrown off before his opponent completes the same task, there are two things to keep in mind—pushing one's own men forward as rapidly as possible and hinder-ing the opponent's progress. In doing the former one should leave as few blots as possible so as to minimize the number of men which opponent may capture, and in doing the latter one should capture as many of opponent's men as possible and also should close as many points as possi-ble—especially in his home table. The point next to the bar just outside of the home table is called the *Bar Point* and this point upon both sides of the table should be closed at the first opportunity. Some of the best opening plays are as follows: (throws by the white—see diagram). With double sixes, move two men from point 1 to 7 and two from 12 to 18. With double ones, move three men from 17 to 18 and one of them to 19, or two from 17 to 18 and two from 19 to 20. This last leaves a blot but covers two valuable points. When leaving a blot is unavoidable, it should be covered at the first opportunity. With five-three, cover point 3 in the home table. With five-two or four-three, move one man from point 12 to 19. With six-five, move one man from point 1 to 12.

PING PONG

This is an indoor table game resembling tennis. It is played by two persons (singles) or by four (doubles). The regulation tournament table is 9x5 feet, with a line through the middle dividing it into right and left sides. An ordinary dining table is often used. The net stretches across the middle of the table and the players stand at each end. Serving and returning is done just as in tennis except that the served ball must strike the table upon the server's side first, and the ball may not be struck for returning on the fly. Scoring is done as in tennis, or the points may be counted up to 21 for game. If the latter method is used the serving passes from one side to the other after each five serves. If each side gets 20 points, the score becomes deuce as in tennis, and to win the game one side must win two points in succession; here the serving passes to the other side after each play. Only one ball is allowed in serving and if that does not strike in the proper court, the point is lost to the server.

EUCHRE

The game of Euchre is played with a deck of thirty-two cards, all below the sevens being deleted. In the four-hand game partners and the dealer are determined by cutting, the highest two playing as partners against the others and the highest being the first dealer.

The value of the cards is the same as at Auction Bridge, except that the Jack of trumps is called the Right Bower and is the highest trump; the Jack of the same color is called the Left Bower and is the second highest trump. For example, if Heart is the trump, the Jack of Hearts is the highest trump, the Jack of Diamonds comes next and then the Ace, King, Queen, ten, and so on down to the two of Hearts, following in their regular order. The Jacks of the opposite color rank no higher than at Auction Bridge.

In dealing, the dealer gives the first person to his left two cards and so on all around and then deals an additional three cards to each player in the same order. Regularity should be observed in dealing and no player should be given, in any round, more than the number of cards given to the first person. For instance, if the dealer begins by giving out two cards, he is not allowed to vary, so as to give another three and then two again but must continue as he began. This proper manner of dealing should be rigidly observed.

After five cards have thus been dealt to each player, the dealer turns up the top card on the pack, or *talon,* for the trump. After the first hand, the deal passes to each player in rotation to the left.

The game consists of five points. If all the tricks are taken by one side it constitutes what is called a *march* and counts two. It is necessary to take three tricks to count one, or *"make a point"* as it is called. Taking four tricks counts no more than three. If the player who determines the trump takes less than three tricks he is *"Euchred"* and the opponents score two points.

When the trump is turned, the first person to the left of the dealer looks at his cards, for the purpose of determining what he intends to do, whether to "pass" or "order the trump up"; and this, to a certain extent, will depend upon the strength of his hand. If he holds cards of sufficient value to secure three tricks, he will say, "I order it up," and the dealer is then obliged to take the card turned up, and discard one from his hand; and the card thus taken up becomes the trump. If the eldest hand has not enough strength to order it up, he will say, "I pass," and then the partner of the dealer has to determine whether he will "pass" or "assist." If he has enough, with the help of the card his partner has turned, to make three tricks, he will say, "I assist," and the card is taken up by dealer. If he passes, then it goes to the third hand, who may order up or pass. Should all the players pass, it becomes the dealer's privilege to announce what he will do, and if he thinks he can take three tricks, he will say, "I take it up," and immediately discards his weakest card, placing it under the remainder of the pack, and instead of the card thus rejected he takes that turned up, which becomes the trump. It is not considered *en regle* for the dealer to remove the trump card until after the first trick has been taken, unless he needs it to play. Should the dealer not be confident of winning three tricks, he says, "I turn it down," and at the same time places the turn-up card face down on the pack. Should all the players pass and the dealer turn down the trump card, the eldest hand is entitled to make trump what he chooses (excepting the suit already turned down). If the eldest hand is not strong enough in any suit, and does not wish to make the trump, he can pass again, and so it will go on in rotation, each one having an opportunity to make the trump in his regular turn, to the dealer. If all the players, including the dealer, decline the making of the trump, the deal is forfeited to the eldest hand. After the trump is determined and the dealer has discarded, the eldest hand opens the game and leads any card he chooses. The person playing the highest card takes the trick, and he in his turn is obliged to lead. In this manner the game proceeds until the five cards in each hand are exhausted. Players are required, under penalty of the loss of two points, to follow suit when possible. If, however, they cannot, they may discard or trump.

The three and four are used in keeping score. The face of the three being up, and the face of the four down on it, counts *one*, whether one, two or three pips are exposed; the face of the four being up, and the three over it, face down, counts *two*, no matter how many pips are shown; the face of the three uppermost counts *three*; and the face of the four uppermost counts *four*.

THE LAWS OF EUCHRE

SCORING

1. A game consists of five points. If the side who adopt, make or order up a trump, take—

    Five tricks, they score two points (called a *march*).

    Three tricks, they score one point.

    Four tricks count no more than three.

    If they fail to take three tricks they are euchred, and
      the opposing side scores two points.

2. When a player who plays alone takes—
    Five tricks, he scores four points.
    Three or four tricks, he scores one point.
    If he fails to take three tricks he is euchred, and the
    opposing side scores two points.

3. The penalty for a revoke takes precedence of all other scores.

4. An error in count can be rectified at any time before the next deal is completed.

5. A misdeal forfeits the deal, and the following are misdeals:

    A card too many or too few given to either player.
    Dealing the cards when the pack has not been properly
    cut; the claim for a misdeal in this case must be
    made prior to the trump card being turned, and
    before the adversaries look at their cards.

6. If, whilst dealing, a card be exposed by the dealer or partner, should neither of the adversaries have touched their cards, the latter may claim a new deal, but the deal is not lost.

7. If, during the deal, the dealer's partner touch any of his cards, the adversaries may do the same without losing their privilege of claiming a new deal should chance give them that option.

8. If an opponent displays a card dealt, the dealer may make a new deal, unless he or his partner has examined his own cards.

9. If a deal is made out of turn, it is good, provided it be not discovered before the dealer has discarded and the eldest hand has led.

10. If a card is faced in dealing, unless it be the trump card, a new deal may be demanded, but the right to deal is not lost.

11. If the pack is discovered to be defective, by reason of having more or less than thirty-two cards, the deal is void; but all the points before made are good.

12. The dealer, unless he turn down the trump, must discard one card from his hand and take up the trump card.

13. The discard is not complete until the dealer has placed the card under the pack; and if the eldest hand makes a lead before the discard is complete, he cannot take back the card thus led, but must let it remain. The dealer, however, may change the card he intended to discard and substitute another, or he may play alone, notwithstanding a card has been led. After the dealer has quitted the discard he cannot take it in hand again under any circumstances.

14. After the discard has been made it is customary for the dealer to let the trump card remain upon the talon until it is necessary to play it on a trick. If the trump card has been taken in hand, no player has a right to demand its denomination, but he may ask for the trump suit and the dealer must inform him.

15. Should a player play with more than five cards, or the dealer forget to discard and omit to declare the fact before three tricks have been turned, the party so offending is debarred from counting any points made in that deal. Under the above circumstances, should the adverse side win, they score all the points they make.

16. All exposed cards may be called, and the offending party compelled to lead or play the exposed card or cards when he can legally do so, but in no case can a card be called if a revoke is thereby caused. See Law 30. The following are exposed cards:—

Two or more cards played at once.

Should a player indicate that he holds a certain card in
his hand.

Any card dropped with its face upwards.

All cards exposed, whether by accident or otherwise,
so that an opponent can distinguish and name them.

17.   If any player lead out of turn, his adversaries may
demand of him to withdraw his card, and the lead may be
compelled from the right player, and the card improperly
led be treated as an exposed card.

18.   If any player lead out of turn and the mislead is
followed by the other three, the trick is completed and
stands good; but if only the second or the second and third
have played to the false lead, their cards, on discovery of
their mistake, are taken back, and there is no penalty
against any one except the original offender, whose card
becomes exposed.

19.   If any player play out of turn, his opponents may
compel him to withdraw his card, and the card improperly
played may be treated as an exposed card.

20.   If any player trump a card in error, and thereby
induce an opponent to play otherwise than he would have
done, the latter may take up his card without penalty, and
the trump so misplayed becomes an exposed card.

21.   If two cards be played, or if the player play twice
to the same trick, his opponent can elect which of the two
shall remain and belong to the trick; provided, however,
that no revoke be caused. (But if the trick should happen
to be turned with five cards in it, adversaries may claim a
new deal.)

22.   If a player, supposing that he can take every trick,
or for any other reason, throw down his cards upon the
table with their faces exposed, the adverse side may call

each and all of the cards so exposed, as they may deem most advantageous to their game, and the delinquent party must play the exposed cards accordingly.

THE REVOKE

23. When a revoke occurs, the adversaries are entitled to add two points to their score.

24. If a suit is led, and any one of the players having a card of the same suit shall play another suit to it—that constitutes a revoke. But if the error be discovered before the trick is quitted and the player having so played a wrong suit or his partner has played again, the penalty only amounts to the cards being treated as exposed.

25. When the player who has made a revoke corrects his error, his partner, if he has played, cannot change his card played, but the adversary may withdraw his card and play another.

26. When a revoke is claimed against adversaries, if they mix their cards, or throw them up, the revoke is taken for granted.

27. No party can claim a revoke after cutting for a new deal.

28. A revoke on both sides forfeits to neither; but a new deal must be had.

29. If a player makes a revoke, his side cannot count any points made in that hand.

30. A party refusing to play an exposed card on call forfeits two to his opponents, as in a revoke.

MAKING THE TRUMP AND PLAYING ALONE

31. Any player making a trump cannot change the suit after having once named it; and if he should, by error, name the suit previously turned down, he forfeits his right

to make the trump, and such privilege must pass to the next player.

32.   A player may only play alone when he adopts, orders up or makes a trump, or when his partner assists, or makes a trump. If a player who elects to play alone takes all five tricks he scores four points, if he takes three or four tricks he scores one point and if he takes less than three he is euchred and the opponents score two points.

33.   A player cannot play alone when he or his partner is ordered up by an opponent, or when the opposite side adopts or makes the trump.   Only those can play alone who have legally taken the responsibility of the trump and may be euchred; therefore, when one player elects to play alone, neither of his opponents may play alone against him.

34.   When a player having the right to play alone elects to do so, his partner cannot supersede him and play alone instead.

35.   When a player announces that he will play alone, his partner must place his cards upon the table, face downwards, and should the latter expose the face of any of his cards, either by accident or design, his opponents may compel him to play or not to play with his partner, at their option.

INTIMATION BETWEEN PARTNERS

36.   If a player indicates his hand by word or gesture to his partner, directs him how to play, even by telling him to follow the rules of the game, or in any way acts unfairly, the adversary scores one point.

37.   If a player, when they are at a bridge, calls the attention of his partner to the fact, so that the latter orders up, the latter forfeits the right to order up, and either of the opponents may play alone, if they choose so to do.

("What are trumps?" "Draw your card." "Can you not follow suit?" "I think there is a revoke?" The above remarks, or those analogous, are the only ones allowed to be used, and they only by the person whose turn it is to play.)

38. No player has a right to see any trick but the last one turned.

RULES FOR PLAYING EUCHRE

ON ADOPTING OR TAKING UP THE TRUMP

The question as to how much strength is required to take up the trump is a matter of considerable importance to a player. The purpose being to make a point, of course there must be a reasonable probability of taking three tricks, but it also depends, to a certain extent, upon the score. If the dealer should be three or four on the score, while the opponents are one or two, the deal might be passed by turning the trump down, and still the chances of gaining the game be not materially reduced; but if the position should be reversed, the dealer would be warranted in attempting the hazard upon a light hand, as the prospects of defeat with his making the trump would be no greater than if the opponents were allowed to make one to suit them. Of course, any player would know that his success would be certain if holding both bowers and the Ace. Anything less than these *might* be euchred, and here good judgment must be used. It is generally accepted as "sound doctrine" that three trumps—two of them being face cards supported by one side Ace—are sufficient to attempt a point. The player must note the state of the game, and act accordingly. If the game stand four and four, it is better for him to take up the trump on a small hand than to leave it for his adversaries to make, but if each side is three, he should be very careful of adopting the trump on a weak hand, because a euchre would put his opponents out.

No prudent player will order the trump up unless he holds enough to render his chances of success beyond reasonable doubt. There are times and positions of the game when, however, there would be no imprudence in ordering up on a light hand; for instance, supposing the game to stand four and four, the dealer turns the trump, and either the eldest or third hand has an ordinary good show of cards, with nothing better of another suit. In such a case it would be proper to order up, for should the trump be turned down, your chances of success would be lost, and in case you are euchred it would but give the game to those who would win it if allowed to make a different trump.

If the position of the player is eldest hand, and a suit should be turned in which he receives both bowers and another large trump, and he has also two cards of the corresponding suit in color, he should pass, because if the dealer's partner should assist, he would be able to euchre the opposing side, and if the trump were turned down, his hand would be just as good in the next suit; and having the first opportunity of making the trump, he could go it alone, with every probability of making the hand and scoring four.

As a general rule the eldest hand should not order up the trump unless he has good commanding cards, say right bower, King and ten of trumps, with an outside Ace, or left bower, King and two small trumps. The player at the right of the dealer should hold a very strong hand to order up the trump, because his partner has evinced weakness by passing, and if the opposing side turn down the trump, his partner has the first say to make a new one.

ON MAKING THE NEW TRUMP

If the dealer turns the trump down, the eldest hand has the privilege of making it what he pleases, and the rule to be generally followed is, if possible, to *Dutch* it, *i. e.*, to make it next in suit, or the same color as the trump turned. The reason for this is very evident. If Diamonds should be the trump turned, and the dealer refuse to take it up, it would be a reasonable supposition that neither of the bowers was in the hands of the opponents; for if the dealer's partner had held one of them, he would in all probability have assisted; and the fact of its being turned down by the dealer also indicates that he has neither of them. Then, in the absence of either bower in the opponents' hands, a weak hand could make the point in the same color. For reverse reasons, the partner of the dealer should cross the suit, and make it Clubs or Spades; as his partner, having evidenced weakness in the red suits by turning a red card down, it would be but fair to presume that his strength was in the black.

Be careful how you make the trump when your adversaries have scored three points, because a euchre would put them out, and, as a general rule, do not make or order up a trump when playing fourth hand.

ON ASSISTING

Two face cards are considered a good assisting hand; but where the game is very close, of course, it is advisable to assist, even upon a lighter hand; for if the game stands four all, the first hand will order up if the suit turned is the best in his hand, and, therefore, the fact of his passing would be an evidence of his weakness.

When assisted by your partner, and you hold a card next in denomination to the card turned up (whether higher or lower), play it as opportunity offers. For instance, if you turn up the Ace, and hold either the left bower or King, when a chance occurs play the bower or King, because your partner knows that you have the Ace remaining.

As a general rule, always assist when you can take two tricks.

ON THE LONE HAND

In order to avail yourself of the privilege of going alone, it is necessary that you should assume the responsibility of the trump; that is, you must adopt, order up, or make the trump; or your partner must assist, or make the trump. Should your partner announce that he will play alone you cannot supersede him and play alone yourself, but must place your cards upon the table, face downward, no matter how strong your hand may be. You must also bear in mind that, in order to avail yourself of the privilege of playing alone, it is necessary to declare your intention of doing so distinctly and in plain terms, thus: "I play alone"; if you fail to do this and the adverse side make a lead, you forfeit all claim to the privilege.

Some players have an absurd notion that one side may play alone against the other, and in case of the failure of the original player to take three tricks, that the adverse side may score four points. This is, however, directly opposed to the axiom in Euchre that only those can play alone that take the responsibility of the trump and incur the chance of being euchred.

In playing a lone hand it is always a great advantage to have the lead. The next advantage is to have the last play on the first trick; therefore, the eldest hand and the dealer may assume the responsibility of playing alone on weaker hands than either of the other players.

When your opponent is playing alone and trumps a suit you or your partner leads, be sure and throw away all cards of that suit upon his subsequent leads, provided you do not have to follow suit.

When opposing a lone hand and your partner throws away high cards of any particular suit, you may be sure he holds good cards in some other suit; you should, therefore, retain to the last the highest card of the suit he throws away (if you have it) in preference to any other card, unless it be an Ace of some suit.

THE BRIDGE

If one side has scored four and the other one, such position is called a "bridge," and the following rule should be observed:

To make the theory perfectly plain, we will suppose A and B to be playing against C and D, the former being four in the game and the latter but one. C having dealt, B first looks at his hand, and finds he has but one or two small trumps; in other words, a light hand. At this stage of the game it would be his policy to order up the trump, and submit to being euchred, in order to remove the possibility of C or D playing it alone; for if they should by good fortune happen to succeed, the score of four would give them the game; when, if it were ordered up, the most that could be done would be to get the euchre, and that giving but a score of two, the next deal, with its percentage, would in all probability give A and B enough to make their remaining point and go out. If, however, B should have enough to prevent a lone hand, he can pass as usual, and await the result. The right bower or left bower guarded is sufficient to block a lone hand.

The eldest hand is the only one who should order up at

3

the bridge, for if he passes his partner may rest assured that he holds commanding cards sufficient to prevent the adversaries making a lone hand. If, however, the eldest hand passes, and his partner is tolerably strong in trumps, the latter may then order up the trump to make a point and go out, for by the passing of the eldest hand his partner is informed that he holds one or more commanding trumps, and may, therefore, safely plan for the point and game.

The eldest hand should always order up at the bridge when not sure of a trick; the weaker his hand, the greater the necessity for doing so.

ON DISCARDING

When the dealer takes up the trump before the play begins, it is his duty to discard or reject a card from his hand, in lieu of the card taken up. We will suppose the ten of Hearts to be turned, and the dealer holds the right bower, with the Ace and nine of Clubs and King of Diamonds; the proper card to reject would be the King of Diamonds, for there would be no certainty of its taking a trick. The Ace might be held by the opponents, and by retaining the Ace and nine-spot of Clubs, the whole suit of Clubs might be exhausted by the Ace, and then the nine would be good; or, if the trump should be one of the red suits, and the dealer held three trumps and a seven of Spades and a seven of Hearts, it would be better to discard the Spade, for, as the dealer's strength was in the red suit, the probabilities would be that the other side would be correspondingly weak, and, therefore, the Heart would be better than the Spade. Where you have two of one suit and one of another to discard from, always discard the suit in which you have one card, for then you may have an opportunity to "ruff."

THE LEAD

We have seen that the game is opened by the eldest hand leading, and much depends upon this feature of the game.

Where a dealer has been assisted, it is a common practice to lead through the assisting hand, and frequently results favorably; for, in the event of the dealer having but the trump turned, a single lead of trumps exhausts his strength and places him at the mercy of a strong plain suit. It is not, however, always advisable to lead a trump, for if the eldest hand holds a tenace, his duty is to maneuver so as to secure two tricks; but this is only an exceptional case. The proper method of determining the nature of the lead is indicated by the quality of the hand and the purpose to be accomplished. The eldest hand, holding two Aces and a King with two small trumps, of course, would lead trump through an assisting hand, for the reason that the only hope of securing a euchre would be dependent upon the success of the plain suits, and they can be made available only after trumps have been exhausted.

Where the dealer takes the trump voluntarily, the eldest hand is, of course, upon the defensive, and to lead trump under such circumstances would be disastrous.

When your partner makes the trump or orders it up, lead him the *best* trump you hold.

When you hold the commanding cards they should be led to make the *march*; but if you are only strong enough to secure your point, side cards should be used; put the lowest on your partner's lead, if it be a commanding card; the highest on your adversary's.

When opposed to a lone hand, always lead the best card you have of a plain suit, so that the possibility of your partner's retaining a card of the same suit with yourself may be averted; particularly if it is a card of opposite color from the trump, for if a red card should be trump and an opponent played it alone, there would be more probability of his not having five red cards than of his holding that number, and the further chance that if he did hold five red cards, it would, in like proportion, reduce the probability of your partner having one of the same suit, and give him an opportunity to weaken your opponent's hand by trumping it.

The exception to the above rule is when you hold two or three cards of a suit, including Ace or King, and two small cards in other suits; in this case your best play would be to lead one of the latter and save your strong suit, for the reason that your partner may hold commanding cards in your weak suits, and thus you give him a chance to make a trick, and if this does not occur, you have your own strong suit in reserve, and may secure a trick with it later.

When playing a lone hand, always lead your commanding trump cards first, reserving your small trumps and plain suit for the closing leads. When you have exhausted your commanding trumps, having secured two tricks, and retain in your hand a small trump and two cards of a plain suit, lead the highest of the plain suit to make the third trick, then your trump. For instance, suppose Hearts are trumps, and you hold the right and left bowers and ten of trumps, and Ace and nine of Spades, lead your bowers, then the Ace of Spades, following with the ten of trumps and your nine of Spades. The reason for playing thus is obvious. You *may not* exhaust your adversaries' trumps by the first two leads, and if either of them were to retain a trump card superior to your ten, by leading the latter you would, in all probability, be euchred on a lone hand. For example, we will suppose one of your opponents holds the Queen, seven and eight of trumps, with a small Dia-

mond and Club, or two of either suit; he would play the
small trumps on your bowers, and if you led the ten of
trumps he would capture it with his Queen, and lead you
a suit you could not take. Your chance of escape from
such a dilemma would be very small. On the other hand,
if on your third lead you were to lead the Ace, you would
force your adversary to play his remaining trump and
allow you to win the point.

When you hold three small trumps and good plain suit
cards, and desire to euchre your opponents, lead a trump,
for when trumps are exhausted you may possibly make
your commanding cards win.

When you make the trump next in suit, always lead a
trump, unless you hold the tenace of right bower and
Ace, and even then it would be good policy to lead the
bower, if you hold strong plain suit cards.

When you hold two trumps, two cards of the same plain
suit and a single card, lead one of the two plain suit cards,
for you may win a trick by trumping the suit of which you
hold none, and then, by leading your second plain suit card,
you may force your opponents to trump, and thus weaken
them. With such a hand it would not be good play to lead
the single plain suit card, for you might have the good
fortune to throw away on your partner's trick and ruff the
same suit when led by your opponents.

When your partner has made or adopted the trump, it
is bad play to win the lead unless you have a hand sufficiently strong to play for a march.

If your partner assists you and has played a trump,
and you have won a trick, do not lead him a trump unless
you hold commanding cards and are pretty certain of making the odd trick or a march, for your partner may have
assisted on two trumps only, in which case such a lead

would draw his remaining trump, and, in all probability, prove fatal to his plans.

When you have lost the first two tricks and secured the third, if you hold a trump and a plain suit card, play the former, for in this position of the game it is your only chance to make or save a euchre. There are only two exceptions to this rule, viz.: when you have assisted your partner, or when he has adopted the trump and still retains the trump card in his hand. In the former instance you should lead the plain suit card, trusting to your partner to trump it; in the latter case, you should do the same unless your trump is superior to your partner's and your other card is an Ace or a King, in which case you should play trump and trust to the other card to win the fifth trick. The reason for this play is very manifest: if your opponents hold a better trump than you, it is impossible to prevent them winning the odd trick, and, therefore, the euchre or point; but if they hold a smaller trump, your lead exhausts it, and you may win the last trick with your other card. This position frequently occurs in the game, and we recommend it to the attention of the novice.

TRUMPS

In the game of Euchre nothing is more important than the judicious employment of trumps, and the successful issue of the game is, perhaps, more dependent upon a thorough knowledge of their power and use than all other points of the game combined.

If your partner adopts or makes the trump, and you hold the right or left bower alone, ruff with it as soon as you get the opportunity.

When playing second, be careful how you ruff a card of a small denomination the first time round, for it is an even chance that your partner will take the trick if you let it pass. When such a chance presents itself, throw away any single card lower than an Ace, so that you may ruff that suit when it is led.

When your partner assists and you hold a card next higher to the turn-up card, ruff with it when an opportunity occurs, for by so doing you convey valuable information to your partner.

When you are in the position of third player, ruff with high or medium trumps. This line of play forces the high trumps of the dealer, and thereby you weaken your adversaries.

CONCLUDING HINTS

Never lose sight of the state of the score. When you are four and four, adopt or make the trump upon a weak hand.

When the game stands three to three, hesitate before you adopt or make a trump upon a weak hand, for a euchre will put your adversaries out.

When you are one and your opponents have scored four, you can afford to try and make it alone upon a weaker hand than if the score were more favorable to you.

When you are eldest hand and the score stands four for you and one for your opponents, do not fail to order up the trump, to prevent them from going alone. Of course, you need not do this if you hold the right bower, or the left bower guarded.

Be very careful how you finesse; skillful players may attempt this in critical positions, but as a general rule the beginner should take a trick when he can.

When second hand, if compelled to follow suit, head the

trick, if possible; this greatly strengthens your partner's game.

EUCHRE WITH THE JOKER

When the "joker" is used it is the highest trump card, ranking above the right bower. If it should happen to be turned for trump, the dealer has the privilege of naming any suit he pleases for trump. In all other particulars the game is played in the same manner as the regular game of Euchre.

TWO-HAND AND THREE-HAND EUCHRE

The rules of the four-hand game apply to two or three-hand Euchre; the only difference being that in three-hand the march counts three in place of two.

In the three-hand game each one plays for himself, and is, therefore, opposed by two adversaries, so that the game requires closer attention and the exercise of more judgment than any of the other Euchre games.

In two-hand Euchre the player may stand upon a slight hand, but not so in the three-hand game; to stand or order up he must have a good hand, inasmuch as he has two hands combined against him, and should he be euchred, each adversary counts two.

Another important feature of the game is, that the play varies according to the score, for example: At the beginning of the game each player strives to make all he can for himself; at the first play the dealer makes a march and counts three; the next dealer makes one point, and the third dealer one; the first dealer again deals and turns down the trump, No. 2 passes and No. 3 makes the trump and a point; the game now stands thus:

Dealer No. 1...3 points.
  "   2...1 point.
  "   3...2 points.

No. 2 now has the deal, and should he be euchred, No. 1 wins the game; therefore, while No. 1 plays to win the game by a euchre, No. 3 plays to let the dealer make a point, which would make the game stand thus:

No. 1...3 points.
  "   2...2 points.
  "   3...2 points.

The deal is now with No. 3, and he will play to make a march and go out; No. 1 will oppose; and, if possible, euchre No. 3, which would, of course, put him out. It is, however, evidently the policy of No. 2 to prevent the euchre, and allow No. 3 to gain a point, that each may have another chance to win the game. No. 1 and No. 3 are now both three, and No. 1 deals, but not having a strong hand and fearing a euchre, he turns down the trump. No. 2 makes the trump and a point, his adversaries playing to prevent him making a march. Each player is now three, and No. 2 deals; but as all are anxious to win the game without dividing the honor or profit, the dealer is permitted to make a point, but not a march, if his opponents can prevent it.

No. 3 next strives to win by a march, but, as in the last case, his adversaries play to prevent him making more than one point, and the same strife occurs when No. 1 deals.

Now, as each player is four, the game must terminate with the deal, so that the dealer must either make his point or be euchred, in which case both his adversaries win, and therefore on the last deal both non-dealers play the strength of their combined game against the common enemy, and thus beat him if they can. The dealer, however, has a remedy against a defeat, which is in this: If, upon examining his hand, he believes he cannot make a point, he can pass, and thus throw the deal elsewhere, thus having one more chance to win. And the same policy may be pur- sued by each player, until the game is played out. If two players go out together in consequence of a euchre, the elder hand of the two wins.

SET-BACK EUCHRE

This game may be played by two or more persons, and is governed by the same rules as ordinary Euchre, except in the manner of counting. It is quite amusing and exciting, especially when played for money.

Suppose four persons sit down to play, and agree that the pool shall be one dollar; each one contributes twenty- five cents. At the beginning of the game each player is five, and now the struggle commences to wipe out these scores and thus win the game. Each player plays for him- self, and all are combined against him, who orders up or plays the hand. Should any one not win a single trick, he has one point added to his score, and whoever is euchred is obliged to put another quarter into the pool, and has two points added to his score.

The player who thinks he cannot take a trick has the right to throw up his hand, and thus save himself from being *set back*. The player who is the first to reduce his score to nothing wins the game and the pool.

A *march* counts from two to six points, corresponding with the whole number of players in the game.

The above is the game of Set-back Euchre pure and simple, but various modifications are frequently introduced. The following are the most popular of these:

After a trump is made, ordered up or taken up, should any player deem himself possessed of a sufficient force of trumps to make a march, he will say, "I declare,"—which signifies he will play to make all the tricks, and, if he is successful in making the march, he wins the game and pool, no matter how many points are scored against him. Should he, however, be unsuccessful in the undertaking, he forfeits double the number of points against him, and in addition must pay in the pool the penalty of a euchre. For instance, if a player stands with seven points to go, and declares without making the march, he must be "set back" to fourteen points, and pay a quarter to the pool. The player who declares to make a march has the privilege of the lead, and becomes eldest hand, unless he be the dealer; but if the dealer declares, he does not have that privilege. In some circles it is customary for the unsuccessful players to pay the winner of the pool a certain sum (previously agreed upon) for each point they have to go when the game is concluded; this is not, however, considered a rule to be strictly followed, but may be left to the option of the players.

Another variety of this game is played as follows: When a player adopting, making or ordering up the trump is euchred, he is set back two points, while his adversary scores two, as in the ordinary game.

SIXTY-SIX

This is a German game, but has gained much fame in the United States, from the fact that it is very scientific, and it may be considered in the first rank among games. It is usually played by two.

Twenty-four cards are used, viz.: The Ace, ten, King,

Queen, Jack and nine of each suit. The cards are valued in the order named above, trumps of course being the superior suit.

In cutting for deal, Ace is high and the ten next, and so on in accordance with their value in the game.

The cards are shuffled by the dealer and cut by the opponent. Six cards are then dealt to each player, three at a time, and the trump turned as in Euchre. Misdeals are dealt over again by the same dealer. A peculiar feature of the game is that the player who holds the nine of trumps may exchange it at any time (after he has taken a trick), at his option, for the trump card turned up.

The non-dealer (called *"Pone"*) leads first, but afterwards the winner of the trick has the lead. After each trick, each player takes a card from the top of the pack, the winner taking the first card and the loser the next; this continues until the pack is exhausted or one of the players closes or shuts down, as it is sometimes called.

The game is seven points, and they are made in the following manner: The player scoring sixty-six first is entitled to one point, but if he should score sixty-six before the other player has scored thirty-three, then he is entitled to two points, or if his opponent should not take a trick then he is allowed three points.

The cards taken in on tricks count as follows: Each Ace, eleven; each ten, ten; each King, four; each Queen, three; each Jack, two.

If, at any time after he has taken a trick, the player has a King and Queen in the same suit (called a marriage) in his hand, he may declare them by leading one of them out and showing the other; this entitles him to twenty points. If they are the King and Queen of trumps (called a royal marriage), they count forty.

The player who obtains sixty-six first announces the fact, and that closes the round; but if he should claim sixty-six and his cards do not show that number, he forfeits two points to his opponent.

THE RULES OF SIXTY-SIX

1. After the game is closed or shut down, no more cards can be drawn from the pack, and if the player who shut down fails to make sixty-six, his opponent scores two points.

2. If a player should shut down before his opponent has taken a trick, and then fails to make sixty-six, his opponent is entitled to three points.

3. Before the game is shut down and the pack is exhausted, neither player is compelled to follow suit, but is at liberty to play any card he pleases; but after the shut-down, each player must follow suit, if possible, but is not compelled to take each trick that he can. If he cannot follow suit he may discard or trump.

4. Players may examine the last trick taken, but no others.

5. When sixty-six is declared, all unemployed cards are void, and the round is ended.

6. If at the end of a round each player counts sixty-six points, neither scores; but the one who wins the next round is allowed one point in addition to what he may then make.

7. If a player should have dealt to him the Ace, ten, King and Queen of trumps he may lay down his hand and claim three points, as these cards count sixty-eight.

8. The discarding of the nine of trumps in order to take up the trump card must be done before the last card in the pack is drawn.

9. Marriages can be announced only when it is the announcer's lead.

10. Marriages can be announced after the shut-down or after the pack is exhausted.

THREE-HAND SIXTY-SIX

The same as the two-hand game. Dealer takes no cards, the two other players only participating in the play. Dealer scores as many points as are won on his deal by either of the players. If neither score, by reason of neither reaching 66, or both reaching 66 or more and failing to announce it, dealer scores 1 point and active players nothing.

Game.—Seven points. A dealer cannot score enough to win game. His 7th point must be won when he is active player.

FOUR-HAND SIXTY-SIX

Use 32-card pack (A, K, Q, J, 10, 9, 8, and 7 of each suit).

Eight cards are dealt to each player—three, then two, then three, in rotation to the left, beginning with eldest hand. Last card is turned for trump and belongs to dealer.

Eldest hand leads, and each succeeding player in turn must not only follow suit, but must win the trick if possible. Having no cards of suit led, player must trump or overtrump if he can, and must win partner's trick if possible.

There are no marriages, but scoring points for cards are same as in two-hand, and winner of last trick scores 10 points. After hand is played out, side counting 66 or more, but less than 100, scores 1 game point; over 100 less than 130, 2 points; if they take every trick (130), 3 points. If both sides have 65, neither scores, and 1 point is added to the score of winners of next hand.

Game.—7 points. In some localities the ten of trumps counts 1 game point for side winning it, in addition to its value as a scoring card. If one side has 6 game points and wins ten of trumps on a trick, such side scores game immediately.

AUCTION SIXTY-SIX

Instead of turning up the trump, as in the ordinary game of Sixty-six, it is bid for. The short pack, 24 cards, is used, all below the nine being deleted. There are four players, who cut for partners, the highest two pairing against the lowest two, partners sitting opposite each other. The highest cut deals the first hand. Six cards are given to each player, three at a time. No trump is turned.

The player to the left of the dealer has the first bid, or may pass. He may bid that he will play, that he will make 90, or 100, or 120, or that he will win every trick. The next player must bid higher or pass, there is no limit to the number of bids each may make. The highest bidder names the trump.

The eldest hand leads. Marriages are counted when it is the player's turn to lead, one of the marriage cards being led, the other shown. The highest bidder and his partner score 1, if they make 66 and bid less than 90. They get 2 points for reaching 90 before their opponents get to 66 if they bid 90. They get 4 points if they bid and make 100; and 5 points if they bid and make all the tricks. Twenty points is game. Failure to make the bid loses what should have been made had bid been successful.

One may bid and play a lone hand. If he succeeds he wins double. If he loses he loses double.

SPOIL FIVE

This game may be played by from two to ten players as individuals (best five-hand or six-hand), with a deck of 52 cards.

Ace of Hearts is always third best trump. As trumps, the cards of the four suits rank as follows: Spades and Clubs, 5 (high), J, A Hearts, A, K, Q, 2, 3, 4, 6, 7, 8, 9, to 10 (low). Diamonds, 5 (high), J, A Hearts, A, K, Q, 10, 9, 8, 7, 6, 4, 3, to 2 (low). Hearts, 5 (high), J, A, K, Q, 10, 9, 8, 7, 6, 4, 3, 2 (low).

As plain suits, the cards rank as follows: Spades and Clubs, K (high), Q, J, A, 2, 3, 4, 5, 6, 7, 8, 9, 10 (low). Diamonds, K (high), Q, J, 10, 9, 8, 7, 6, 5, 4, 3, 2 to A (low). Hearts, K (high), Q, J, 10, 9, 8, 7, 6, 5, 4, 3, to 2 (low).

Instead of cutting, any player deals cards, one at a time, face up, around in rotation to the left, beginning with player next to him; first player receiving a Jack deals. Any player may shuffle cards, dealer last, and player to dealer's right cuts, leaving at least five cards in each packet.

Deal five cards to each player—three, then two, or two, then three, in rotation to the left, beginning with eldest hand. After each player has received five cards, the next card is turned for trump. If pack is found to be imperfect, or any but the trump card found faced in pack, same dealer deals again. Too many or too few cards dealt; cards exposed by dealer; failure to have cards cut, or to deal same number of cards to each player on same round; dealer counting cards on the table or in remainder of the pack, are misdeals, and next player on dealer's left deals.

Robbing the Trump.—Player holding Ace of suit turned for trump may, when it is his turn to play, exchange any card in his hand for card turned, if he wishes; if not, he must request dealer to turn down trump card, thus announcing that he holds Ace, otherwise he loses right to exchange for trump card, and his Ace becomes lowest trump, even if it be the Ace of Hearts. If Ace is turned, dealer may discard at once and take Ace into his hand after first trick. Eldest hand should ask dealer to do this before leading, but if dealer does not want Ace, he may play with his original hand, announcing this intention.

The Play.—The object of the game is to take tricks. Eldest hand leads any card. Players in turn, if able to follow suit, must either do so or trump. Should a player hold no card of suit led, he may either throw off a card of another suit, .or trump. Highest card played of suit led wins trick, unless trumped, when highest trump played wins.

Reneging.—Holding either five or Jack of trumps or Ace of Hearts, with no smaller trumps, when a trump lower. than the one held is *led*, player need not follow suit, even though a higher card than the one he holds falls on the lead.

Irregularities.—A hand discovered in play to have too many or too few cards, must be discarded, face down, and its holder forfeits his interest in pool for that hand, the others playing without him. Player retains any tricks he takes previous to discovery that his hand is incorrect.

Player taking turned trump when he does not hold Ace; exposing a card (except to lead or play to trick) after any player has taken two tricks; or throwing off when he should have followed suit, must discard his hand, face down, and forfeit his interest in that pool, on that and subsequent deals until pool is won. If not won on that hand, he must add to pool after each deal just as though he were eligible to win.

Scoring.—Each player begins with an equal number of counters. Each player puts an equal number of counters in pool, and if pool is not won on first deal, each dealer in turn adds another counter. After pool is won, each player puts up equal number of counters for new pool.

Player who takes three tricks and immediately abandons balance of his hand, wins the pool. Should he continue to play, and take all five tricks, he wins pool, and in addition each player must give him one counter. Should he continue after taking three tricks, and fail to take all five, he loses pool. Pool then goes to next player winning three or five tricks.

Game.—First player losing all his counters loses game; or first player winning an agreed number of counters wins the game.

FORTY-FIVE

This is a variation of Spoil Five and may be played by two players as individuals or by four or six as partners (two against two and three against three, respectively). Game is scored by points; side taking three or four tricks scores 5 points; five tricks, 10 points. Sometimes each trick counts 5 points, and score of side taking fewest tricks is deducted from that of side taking most tricks. Thus three tricks count 5; four tricks, 15; five tricks, 25 points. 45 points is game.

AUCTION PITCH

Auction Pitch is played with a pack of fifty-two cards, which rank as at Auction Bridge, and by any number of persons from four to eight.

The deal is determined by cutting; the player cutting the highest card deals. Ace is high.

After the deal has been determined, and the cards have been shuffled and cut by the player to the right of the dealer, the dealer delivers six cards to each player, three at a time, in rotation, beginning with the player to his left. No trump is turned. After the first hand has been played, the deal passes in rotation to the left.

After the cards have been dealt, the eldest hand (the player to the left of the dealer) proceeds to sell the privilege of pitching the trump.

Each player in turn has the right to make one bid, but no more.

The bidding proceeds in rotation, beginning with the player to the left of the eldest hand. The eldest hand has the last say, and may either sell to the highest bidder, or decline to sell, and pitch the trump himself.

If the seller declines to entertain the highest bid, and pitches the trump himself, he is entitled, if successful, to score all the points he may make; but if he fails to make as many points as the highest number offered, he must be set back just that number of points and he cannot score anything he may have made during the play of that hand.

A player whose bid has been accepted may score not only the number of points he bid, if he makes them, but also any points he may make in excess thereof.

If a player buys the privilege of pitching the trump and fails to make or save the necessary number of points he must be set back the number of points he bid, and he cannot score anything he may have made during the play of that hand.

The seller, when he accepts a bid, scores the points at once, and before a card is led.

If no bid is made, the seller must pitch the trump himself.

The game is seven or ten points, as agreed. All points a player may make are deducted from his score. All points a player may be set back are added to his score. The player whose score is first reduced to nothing wins the game.

The points rank and are scored in the following order of precedence:

1. *High* (the highest trump out) counts one. 2. *Low* (the lowest trump out) counts one. 3. *Jack* (the Jack of trumps) counts one. 4. *Game* counts one.

Low scores for the player who originally held it. *Jack* may be taken with any superior trump, and scores for the player who wins the trick containing it. *Game* counts for player whose cards, taken in tricks won by him, figure highest; tens counting 10 each, Aces 4, Kings 3, Queens 2, Jacks 1.

In the event of a tie in counting game, that point is not scored by either party.

PLAYING THE HAND

After it has been determined who is to pitch the trump, the player having that privilege must lead a card of the suit he makes trump.

The highest card of the suit led wins the trick, and the winner of the trick has the next lead.

After the first trick it is not compulsory to lead a trump.

Each player must follow suit if he can, unless he choose to trump. If he has no card of the suit led, he is not compelled to trump, but may play a card of any suit he chooses.

The playing proceeds in this way until all the cards are played out. After the hand is played the scores are made, and a new deal ensues; this is continued until some player wins the game.

If a player make a revoke he is debarred from scoring any point he may have made in the play of the hand; and in addition the revoking player must be set-back the highest number of points that was bid (in the hand) for the privilege of pitching the trump.

Any loss an innocent player may have sustained by reason of the revoke, if claimed, must be rectified and made good, provided the same can be clearly demonstrated by subsequent examination of the tricks.

In all other particulars this game is governed by the laws of Seven-up.

SMUDGE

A variety of Auction Pitch, bidding to the board, in which a player making four points, after having bid four, wins the game if he was not in the hole when he made the bid.

SEVEN-UP
(All-Fours—Old Sledge)

This game, usually played by two and sometimes by three, as individuals, or by four as partners (two against two), with a full pack, was originally known as All-Fours,

and derived that name from the four chances for each of
which a point is scored, namely: *high*, the best trump out;
low, the smallest trump dealt; *Jack*, the Jack of trumps;
game, counted from such of the following cards as the respective players have in their tricks, viz.: every Ace is
counted as 4; King, 3; Queen, 2; Jack, 1; and ten, 10. *Low*
is always scored by the person to whom it was dealt; but
Jack being the property of whoever can win or save it,
the possessor is permitted to revoke and trump with that
card, and when turned up as trump the dealer scores; it is
also allowable for the player who lays down a high or low
trump to inquire at the time whether the same be high
or low.

After cutting for deal, at which the highest card wins,
six cards are to be given to each player, either by three
or one at a time, and the next turned up for trump; then
if the eldest does not like his card, he may, for once in a
hand, say, "I beg," when the dealer must either give a point
or three more cards to each, and turn up the next for
trump; but if that should prove of the same suit as the
first turned up, three cards more are to be given, and
so on till a different suit occurs.   The cards rank as at
Auction Bridge, and each player should always strive to
secure his own tens and face cards, and to take those of
the adversary.   Seven or ten points form the game, which
may be set down on a score sheet, though a very customary
method is to draw two cards from the pack, and lay them
one on the other, so as to exhibit only the number of spots
the player has gained.

When the dealer shows any of his adversary's cards a
new deal may be demanded, but in showing his own he
must abide by the same.

If discovered, previous to playing, that too many cards

are given to either player, a new deal may be claimed, or the extra cards drawn out by the opponent; but should even a single card have been played, there must be another deal.

CALIFORNIA JACK

A variation of Seven-up for two or four players. Deal same as Seven-up, and turn remainder of pack face up. Top card indicates trump suit (or cards may be cut for trump suit before the deal). Eldest hand leads, and winner of first trick takes the top card from pack, and each player to left in turn takes one card. Winner of one trick leads to next, etc., until cards in pack and hands are exhausted. Points count same as in Seven-up, except that *low* counts for player or side winning it in a trick. Ten points is game.

SHASTA SAM

A variation of California Jack in which the pack remains face down instead of face up. The trump is determined by cutting before the deal.

PEDRO SANCHO

The game of Pedro Sancho is played the same as Auction Pitch or All-Fours, with the following exceptions:

1. The five of trumps is called Pedro, and counts five in the score.

2. The nine of trumps is called Sancho, and counts nine in the score.

3. It is possible to hold eighteen points in one hand, and the points score and take precedence in the following order, viz.: 1st, high; 2d, low; 3d, Jack; 4th, game, one point each; 5th, Pedro, five points; 6th, Sancho, nine points. (Game counts one point for player whose cards, taken in tricks

won by him, figure highest; tens counting 10 each, Aces 4, Kings 3, Queens 2, Jacks 1.)

4. Pedro and Sancho, like Jack and game, are not sure cards; they may be respectively captured by any trump of a higher denomination, and count in the score of the winner of the tricks containing them.

5. The dealer sells the trump, not the eldest hand, as in Auction Pitch.

6. The bids may pass around the board one or more times, until all the players are satisfied. For instance: after all the players (once around) have bid or refused, they may again, in turn, supersede their former bids; and this process may be repeated until the highest possible bid that can be obtained has been made, and accepted or rejected by the dealer.

7. The game is won by the player who first scores fifty points.

In scoring, each player commences with fifty points (or more, if previously agreed). All points made are deducted from the player's score; any accepted bid not accomplished is added to his score. The player whose score is first reduced to nothing wins the game.

The game is usually kept by a scorer, chosen by mutual agreement. It is his business to see that the points claimed by any player are in accordance with the cards held by him; he must also declare the state of the game, when requested to do so by any of the players.

A player whose bid has been accepted is permitted to score not only the amount of the bid he has made, but also any points he may succeed in making in excess of his bid.

If the dealer refuses to entertain the highest bid, he is entitled to score all the points he makes; but if he fails to make as much as the highest bid offered, he is set back just that number of points.

The first object for a player to attain in this game is, of course, to make points for his own score; but his next endeavor should be to do all in his power to set back the player who is striving to secure the amount of his bid; in doing this, however, strict attention must be paid to the state of the score, and the play regulated in accordance with it. Thus, it is good policy, when a player holds points which he finds he cannot make, to play them, if possible, into the hands of the one whose score is lowest. It is even better to let these points go to the bidder, if his score is low, than to permit them to fall to another player whose score already stands high.

If two players have already reduced their score to two, and one of them has made high, game, Pedro and Sancho, the other player could go out before him with low and Jack.

The foregoing is the method usually adopted for playing the game of Pedro Sancho. There are, however, a few modifications which find favor in some localities. These are as follows:

1. When four play, the four threes may be discarded from the pack, and twelve cards dealt to each player, so that all the cards are in play. For eight players, six cards to each will produce the same result. With less than four play, nine or twelve cards may be dealt to each, as agreed upon, to increase the chances of counting-cards being out.

2. The deuce only is low, and is not a sure card, but counts for the taker instead of the holder. If the deuce of trumps has not been dealt, no point can be scored for low.

3. Game is represented solely by the ten of trumps,

which can be captured by any higher trump. If the ten has not been dealt, no one can score the one point for game.

4. The player who has the pitch can only, if successful, score the amount of his bid, the other players scoring at the close of the round any points each has made.

5. The game is also played without Sancho, making the score only nine points, and game twenty-one points. This variety is generally known as "Pedro."

DOM PEDRO

Dom Pedro (or Snoozer) is the same as Pedro Sancho with the joker (called Dom Pedro or Snoozer) added to the pack. The joker ranks below the deuce of trumps in play and counts 15 points for the taker of the trick in which it is played. It does not score low, but is a trump and wins over any card in plain suits. The game is 50 or 100 points.

DRAW POKER

Draw Poker is played with a pack of fifty-two cards, and by any number of persons from two to six.

Before the dealer begins to deal the cards, the player next to his left, who is called the *ante-man* or *age*, must deposit in the pool an *ante* not exceeding one-half the limit previously agreed upon. This is called a blind.

The deal is performed by giving five cards to each player, one at a time, beginning with the player to the left of the dealer.

GOING IN ON THE ORIGINAL HAND

After the cards have been dealt the players look at their

hands, and each one in rotation, beginning with the player to the left of the *age*, determines whether he will *go in* or not. Any player who decides to go in, that is, to play for the pool, or *"pot,"* must put into the pool double the amount of the ante, except the age, who contributes the same amount as his original ante. This makes the blind good, and all the players interested in that hand will have contributed alike.

Those who decline to play throw their cards, face downward, upon the table in front of the next dealer.

Any player when it is his turn, and after making the ante good, may *raise, i.e.*, increase the ante any amount within the limit of the game; the next player, after making good the ante and raise, may then also raise it any amount within the limit; and so on. Each player, as he makes good and equals the other players who are in before him, may thus increase the ante if he chooses, compelling the others to equal that increase or abandon their share of the pool.

Each player who raises the ante must do so in rotation, going round to the left, and any player who remains in to play must put in the pool as much as will make his stake equal to such increase, or abandon all he has already contributed to the pool.

THE STRADDLE

Another feature that may be introduced when betting upon the original hand is the straddle. The straddle is nothing more than a double blind. For example:

A, B, C, D and E play. A deals. B, the age, antes one chip. C can straddle B's ante by putting in the pool two chips, provided he does so before the cards are cut for the deal. D may double the straddle, *i.e.*, straddle C, and so on up to the age, provided the bets do not exceed the limit. In the above instance, supposing C only to straddle, it would cost D, E and A each four chips to go in, and it would cost B three and C two chips. Each straddle costs double the preceding one.

The straddle gives a player the first opportunity to be the last in before the draw; that is, the player to the left of the last straddler, after looking at his hand, and before the draw, must be the first to declare whether he will make good the straddle, and so on, in rotation, up to the player who made the last straddle. After the draw, the player to the left of the age must make the first bet, provided he remains in. A good player very rarely straddles.

FILLING THE HANDS

When all are in who intend to play, each player has the right to draw any number of cards he chooses, from one to five, or he can retain his cards as originally dealt to him. If a player draws cards, he must discard a like number from his hand previous to drawing, and the rejected cards must be placed face downward upon the table near the next dealer.

The dealer asks each player in rotation, beginning with the age, how many cards he wants, and when the player has discarded he gives the number requested from the top of the pack. When the other hands have been helped, the dealer, if he has gone in and wants cards, helps himself last.

BETTING, RAISING AND CALLING

When all the hands are filled, the player to the left of the age has the first say, and he must either bet or retire from the game, forfeiting what he has already staked. The same with all the other players, in rotation, up to the age. When a player makes a bet, the next player must either see him, *i.e.*, put in the pool an equal amount, or go better, *i.e.*, make the previous bet good, and raise it any amount not exceeding the limit; or he must pass out. This continues either until some one player drives all the others out of the game and takes the pool without showing his hand or until all the other players who remain in see the last raise (no one going better) and call the player who made it. In this event, *i.e.*, when a call is made, the players remaining in all show their hands, and the strongest hand takes the pool.

The following is an example illustrating the mode of betting before and after the draw: The limit is thirty chips, and A, B, C, D and E are the players. A deals. B, the age, antes one chip; C goes in and puts up two chips; D makes good and raises ten chips, putting in twelve chips; E passes out of the game; A makes good, sees D's raise, putting in twelve chips; B makes good, sees D's raise, and goes five chips better, this costing him sixteen chips; C passes out and abandons the two chips he has already put in; D sees B's raise, and bets the limit better, contributing thirty-five chips; A sees D, and deposits thirty-five chips; B also sees D, and puts thirty chips in the pool. A, B and D now each have forty-seven chips in the pool, which, together with the two chips abandoned by C, make a total of one hundred and forty-three chips.

After the hands are filled, B being the age, and C having passed out, it becomes D's *say, i.e.*, D's turn to reclare what he will do. D determines to stake five chips; A sees D's bet and goes thirty chips better, and puts up thirty-five chips; B sees A, and deposits thirty-five chips; D makes good, putting up thirty chips and *calls* A.

Each of the players now has eighty-two chips in the pool, which, including the two chips which C forfeited, makes a total of two hundred and forty-eight chips. They show their hands, and A, having the best hand, captures the pool.

Suppose that instead of B and D calling A, they had passed out. Then A would have taken the pool without showing his hand.

If all the players pass, up to the age, the latter takes the pool, and the deal ends.

THE OLD-FASHIONED GAME

The foregoing is a description of what is called modern Draw Poker, and is the game now almost universally played in this country; but some old-fashioned players, who object to a compulsory blind, which the ante of the age really is, prefer the old game of Draw Poker, which differs from the modern game in the following particulars:

1. The dealer opens the hand by putting up a fixed ante before dealing, which is not, in the strict sense of the term, a bet or a blind.

2. The age alone has the privilege of going a blind, provided he does so before the cards are cut for the deal, but this is optional, and not compulsory.

3. Previous to the draw any player may pass and afterwards come in again, provided no bet or blind has been made before he passes.

4. If, previous to the draw, all the players, including the dealer, pass without making a bet, the hand is ended, and the eldest hand puts up an ante and deals. This contingency is not likely to occur very often.

VALUES OF THE HANDS

The values of the hands are as follows, commencing with the lowest:

1. *One Pair.*—(Accompanied by three cards of different denominations.) If two players each hold a pair, the highest pair wins; if the two are similar, the highest remaining card wins.

2. *Two Pairs.*—(Accompanied by a card of another denomination.) If two players each hold two pairs, the highest pairs win.

3. *Triplets.*—(That is, three cards of the same denomination, not accompanied by a pair.) The highest triplets win. Triplets beat two pairs.

4. *A Straight.*—(That is, a sequence of five cards not all of the same suit.) An Ace may either begin or end a straight. For example: Ace (highest), King, Queen, Jack, ten, is a straight, and the highest straight. Five, four, three, two, Ace (lowest) is a straight, and the lowest straight. An Ace cannot occupy an intermediate position, thus: Queen, King, Ace, two, three, is not a straight. If more than one player hold a straight, the straight headed by the highest card wins. A straight will beat triplets.

Straights are not always played; it should therefore be determined whether they are to be admitted at the commencement of the game.

5. *A Flush.*—(That is, five cards of the same suit not in sequence.) If more than one player holds a flush, the flush containing the highest card wins; if the highest cards tie, the next highest cards in these two hands win, and so on. A flush will beat a straight, and consequently triplets.

6. *A Full.*—(That is, three cards of the same denomination and a pair.) If more than one player holds a full, the highest triplets win. A full will beat a flush.

7. *Fours.*—(That is, four cards of the same denomination, accompanied by any other card.) If more than one player

holds fours, the highest fours win. When straights are not played, fours beat a straight flush.

8. *A Straight Flush.*—(That is, a sequence of five cards, all of the same suit.) If more than one player holds a straight flush, the winning hand is determined in the same manner as the straight, which see. When straights are not played, the straight flush does not rank higher than a common flush, but when straights are played, it is the highest hand that can be held, and beats four of a kind.

When none of the foregoing hands are shown, the highest card wins; if these tie, the next highest in these two hands, and so on.

If, upon a *call* for a show of cards, it occurs that two or more players interested in the call hold hands identical in value, and those hands are the best out, the players thus tied must divide the pool equally.

TECHNICAL TERMS USED IN POKER

Age or Eldest Hand.—The player immediately at the left of the dealer.

Ante.—The stake deposited in the pool by the age at the beginning of the game.

Blaze.—This hand consists of five face cards, and when it is played, beats two pairs.

Blind.—The ante deposited by the age previous to the deal. The blind may be doubled by the player to the left of the age, and the next player to the left may at his option *straddle* this bet; and so on, including the dealer, each player doubling. The player to the left of the age alone has the privilege of the first straddle, and if he decline to straddle, it debars any other player coming after him from doing so. (See Rule 30.) To make a blind good costs double the amount of the ante, and to make a straddle good costs four times the amount of the ante. Each succeeding straddle costs double the preceding one.

Bluff.—Playing one's hand in such fashion as to make other players believe it is better than it is, so that they shall refuse to see your bet and you will take the pot without having to show your hand.

Call.—When a player who remains in does not wish to see and go better, he may see and call, and then all those playing show their hands, and the highest hand wins the pool.

Chips.—Ivory or bone tokens, representing a fixed, agreed value in money.

Chipping, or to Chip.—Synonymous with betting. Thus a player instead of saying, "I bet," may say, "I chip," so much.

Discard.—To take from your hand the number of cards you intend to draw and place them on the table, near the next dealer, face downward.

Draw.—After discarding one or more cards, to receive a corresponding number from the dealer.

Eldest Hand, or Age.—The player immediately at the left of the dealer.

Fill.—To match or strengthen the cards to which you draw.

Foul Hand.—A hand composed of more or less than five cards.

Freeze-Out.—In Freeze-out Poker each player exposes an equal amount at the beginning of the game, which cannot be added to from any source other than winnings from other players. No player can retire with any of this stake until the close of the game or the hour fixed for its close. No player can be deprived of a call if he puts up all his money, and no player, when his money is exhausted, can

4

borrow or continue in the game on credit under any circumstances.

Going Better.—When any player makes a bet it is the privilege of the next player to the left to raise him, that is, after making good the amount already bet by his adversary, to make a still higher bet. In such a case it is usual to say, "I see you and go (so much) better," naming the extra sum bet.

Going In.—Making good the ante of the age and the straddles (if any), for the privilege of drawing cards and playing for the pool.

Jack-Pots.—This is a Western modification introduced into the game, and is fully explained further on.

Limit.—A condition made at the beginning of a game, limiting the amount of any single bet or raise.

Making Good.—Depositing in the pool an amount equal to any bet previously made. This is done previous to raising or calling a player, and is sometimes called seeing a bet.

Original Hand.—The first five cards dealt to any player.

Pat Hand.—An original hand not likely to be improved by drawing, such as a full, straight, flush, or pairs.

Pass.—"I pass" is a term used in Draw Poker to signify that a player throws up his hand and retires from the game.

Pot.—The pool, or amount to be played for.

Raising a Bet.—The same as "going better."

Say.—When it is the turn of any player to declare what he will do, whether he will bet or pass his hand, it is said to be his say.

Seeing a Bet.—The same as making good.

Straddle.—See *Blind.*

Table Stakes.—A table stake simply means that each player places his stake where it may be seen, and that a player cannot be raised more than he has upon the table; but at any time between deals he may increase his stake from his pocket, or he may put up any article for convenience' sake, say a knife, and state that he makes his stake as large as any other player's, and he is then liable to be raised to any amount equal to the stake of any other player, and must make good with cash. When playing table stakes, if a player has no money on the table, he must put up or declare his stake previous to raising his hand, and, failing to do this, he must stand out of the game for that hand.

RULES OF DRAW POKER

CUTTING AND DEALING

1. The deal is determined by throwing around one card to each player, and the player who gets the highest card deals.

2. In throwing for the deal, the Ace is high. Ties are determined by cutting.

3. The cards must be shuffled above the table; each player has a right to shuffle the cards, the dealer last.

4. The player to the right of the dealer must cut the cards.

5. The dealer must give each player one card at a time, in rotation, beginning to his left, and in this order he must deliver five cards to each player.

6. If the dealer deals without having the pack properly cut, or if a card is faced in the pack, there must be a new deal. The cards are re-shuffled and re-cut; and the dealer deals again.

7. If a card be accidently exposed by the dealer while in

the act of dealing, the player to whom such card is dealt must accept it as though it had not been exposed. (See Rule 16.) This rule does not apply when a card is faced in the pack.

8. If the dealer gives to himself, or either of the other players, more or less than five cards, and the player receiving such a number of cards discovers and announces the fact before he raises his hand, it is a misdeal. The cards are re-shuffled and re-cut, and the dealer deals again.

9. If the dealer gives to himself, or either of the other players, more or less than five cards, and the player receiving such improper number of cards lifts his hand before he announces the fact, no misdeal occurs, and he must retire from that game for that hand.

10. After the first hand the deal proceeds in rotation, to the left.

DISCARDING AND DRAWING

11. After the deal has been completed, each player who remains in the game may discard from his hand as many cards as he chooses, or his whole hand, and call upon the dealer to give him a like number from the top of those remaining in the pack. The eldest hand must discard first, and so in regular rotation round to the dealer, who discards last; and all must discard before any player is helped. (For the sake of convenience, each player should throw his discarded cards face downward upon the table near the next dealer.)

12. Any player, after having asked for fresh cards, must take the exact number called for; and after cards have once been discarded, they must not again be taken in hand.

13. Any player, previous to raising his hand or making a bet, may demand of the dealer how many cards he drew,

and the latter must reply correctly. By raising his hand or making a bet, the player forfeits the right to inquire and removes the obligation to answer.

14. Should the dealer give any player more cards than the latter has demanded, and the player discover and announce the fact before raising his cards, the dealer must withdraw the superfluous cards and restore them to the pack. But if the player raises the cards before informing the dealer of the mistake, he must retire from the game during that hand.

15. Should the dealer give any player fewer cards than the latter has discarded, and the player discover and announce the fact previous to lifting the cards, the dealer must give the player from the pack sufficient cards to make the whole number correspond with the number originally demanded. If the player raises the cards before making the demand for more, he must retire from the game during that hand.

16. If a player discards and draws fresh cards to his hand, and while serving him the dealer exposes one or more of the cards, the dealer must place the exposed cards upon the bottom of the pack, and give the player a corresponding number from the top of the pack after all the other active players have been served. (See Rule 8.)

BETTING, CALLING AND SHOWING

17. In opening the pool before the cards are dealt, the age makes the first ante, which must not exceed one-half the limit. After the cards are dealt, every player in his proper turn, beginning with the player to the left of the age, must make the ante good by depositing double the amount in the pool, or retire from the game for that hand. (This opening bet of the age is simply a compulsory blind.

Many poker players consider this objectionable and prefer the old-fashioned game, as follows: 1. The dealer antes a fixed sum previous to dealing, which is not a bet or a blind. 2. The age may go a blind, but this is optional. 3. Previous to the draw, any player may pass and come in again, provided no bet or blind has been made before he passes.)

18. After the cards have been dealt, any player in his proper turn, beginning with the player to the left of the age, after making good the age's ante, may raise the same any amount not exceeding the limit of the game.

19. After the hands are filled, any player who remains in the game may, in his proper turn, beginning with the player to the left of the age, bet or raise the pool any amount not exceeding the limit of the game.

20. After the draw has been made, the eldest hand or age has the privilege of deferring his say until after all the other players have made their bets or passed. The age is the last player to declare whether he will play or pass. If, however, the age pass out of the game before the draw, then the next player to his left (in play), after the draw, must make the first bet, or failing to bet, must pass out. The privileges of the age cannot be transferred.

21. If a player in his regular turn bets or raises a bet any amount not exceeding the limit of the game, his adversaries must either call him, go better, or retire from the game for that hand. When a player makes a bet he must deposit the amount in the pool.

22. If a player makes good or sees a bet, and calls for a show of hands, each player must show his entire hand to the board, the caller last, and the best poker hand wins the pool.

23. If a player bets or raises a bet, and no other player

goes better or calls him, he wins the pool, and cannot be compelled to show his hand.

24. Upon a show of hands, if a player miscalls his hand, he does not lose the pool for that reason, for every hand shows for itself.

25. If a player passes or throws up his hand, he passes out of the game, and cannot, under any circumstances whatever, participate further in that game.

26. Any player betting with more or less than five cards in his hand loses the pool, unless his opponents all throw up their hands before discovering the foul hand. If only one player is betting against the foul hand, that player is entitled to the ante and all the money bet; but if there are more than one betting against him, then the best hand among his opponents is entitled to the pool.

27. If a player makes a bet and an adversary raises him, and the player who made the previous bet has not money sufficient to see the raise, he can put up all the funds he may have and call for a show for that amount.

28. None but the eldest hand (age) has the privilege of going a blind. The party next to the left of the eldest hand may double the blind, and the next player straddle it, the next double the straddle, and so on, but the amount of the straddle, when good, must not exceed the limit of the game.

29. A player cannot straddle a blind and raise it at the same time, nor can any player raise a blind before the cards are dealt.

30. If the player to the left of the age declines to straddle a blind, he debars any other player from doing so.

JACK-POTS

The Jack-pot is a modification introduced in the game of Draw Poker and is played as follows:

When all the players pass up to the blind hand, the latter allows his blind to remain in the pot, and each of the other players deposits a similar amount. The blind now deals, and any player, in his regular turn, may open or break the pot, provided he holds a pair of Jacks or better; but a player is not compelled to do so, this being entirely optional.

Each player in turn, commencing with the one at the left of the dealer, declares whether he can or will open the pot; if he declines to open he says: "I pass." If he has the requisite hand and elects to open, he says: "I open."

If no player opens the pot, then each player deposits in the pool the same amount that was previously contributed or such amount as may be agreed upon, and the deal passes to the next player. The same performance ensues until some player holds the necessary cards and is willing to break the pot.

A player may break the pot for any amount within the limits of the game, and each player in turn must make the bet good, raise it, or pass out.

After all the players who determine to go in have made good, and the hands have been filled, the player who opened the pot makes the first bet.

If all pass up to the player who broke the pot, the latter takes the pool and can only be compelled to show the Jacks, or better, necessary to break the pot.

The opener should place his discard face down under the chips in the pool. This precaution is taken because in some cases the opener wishes to split his openers by discarding one and drawing, for instance, to a four flush. In this case his final hand will not contain legal openers and he must produce them by showing his discard. By always discarding in this manner, the opener is enabled to conceal the fact when he desires to split his openers.

When a player breaks the pot without holding the requisite cards to do so, he must deposit in the pool, as penalty, twice the amount of his original bet. (The amount of penalty for such an error should preferably be mutually agreed upon before opening the game. The above penalty seems light enough, considering the injustice that an error of this kind might work on the rest of the players. It has been suggested that ten times the original ante would not be an excessive penalty.)

If no player come in except the one who broke the pot on an insufficient hand, a new hand must be dealt and the penalty added to the pot.

If one or more players participate in the call when such an error as the foregoing occurs, the player holding the best hand outside the delinquent player takes the pool; or if a player drives the original breaker and all others out, then the pool must go to him.

Progressive Jack-pots are played as follows: When, after a deal, no one opens the game, the players each place another chip in the pool, new hands are dealt, etc., as before described, and no player can, under the second deal, open with less than Queens or better. If a third deal becomes necessary, it requires Kings or better to break the pot; and should it come to a fourth deal, it takes Aces or better, and so remains for any subsequent deals, until some player can and will break the pot.

STRAIGHT POKER

Draw Poker rules govern in this game in regard to cards, preliminaries, values of hands, foul hands, and limits.

Each player antes an equal amount. The dealer serves

each player with five cards, dealing as in Draw Poker. There is no draw.

Beginning at dealer's left, each player in turn either passes or bets. He may pass and hold his hand till a bet is made, and then in his next turn may bet. If he passes after a bet is made, he must discard his hand.

When a bet is made, the next player, and the others in turn, either pass, stay (bet an equal amount), or raise, till all who stay have an equal amount in the pool. Then on the show-down the highest hand takes the pool. If there is a tie, the pool is divided. If any player makes a bet that no other player will see, the pot goes to him.

STUD POKER

Draw Poker rules govern in this game in regard to cards, preliminaries, values of hands and limits.

Before the deal, the player on the dealer's left may, if he desires, put up a blind. The dealer serves one card, face down, to each player around to the left. Each player in turn must then decide after receiving his card, which he looks at, whether to pass, stay or raise. If he passes, he throws his one card in the discard pile and is out for that deal. If he stays, he puts up double the blind, at the same time raising (within the limit) if he so desires. The betting then proceeds as in Draw Poker until all players have either passed or seen all raises, after which the second round is served, face up.

If there has been no blind, the dealer serves two rounds before betting begins, first round face down, second round face up. The player receiving the highest card on this round must then bet or pass, when the others in turn pass, stay (bet an equal amount) or raise as before. If two or more cards of the same denomination are high, the player receiving the first of them makes the first bet.

The dealing continues until each active player has received five cards, one face down, four face up.

After each round the betting follows as described, the player having the highest cards showing betting first on each round. If he prefers, he may pass after the first round, when the next player may begin the betting, and all must pass out or bet an equal amount. If at any time any player makes a bet that no other player will see he takes the pot, and deals the next hand.

If two or more players stay to the finish, the highest hand takes the pot. If there is a tie, the pot must be divided.

If the dealer exposes a card too soon—_i.e._, if, before betting is concluded on a round, he begins serving another, the card or cards so shown must be thrown in the discard, and the dealer should be made to pay a forfeit, to be agreed upon beforehand.

WHISKEY POKER

Dealer serves five cards, face down, one at a time, to each player in the game, including himself, and to an extra hand in the middle of the table, called the _"widow."_ He must serve all the other players in turn, around to the left, then to the widow, then himself last.

Any player who is willing to play his hand as it is signifies it by knocking on the table.

Each player, beginning on dealer's left, may knock, pass, or take the widow. If any player knocks on the first round, the widow is turned face up on the table. The next player, and all the others in turn, except the one who knocked, may each draw one card from the widow, at the same time replacing it with a card from his hand. Or any player in his turn, at any time in the game, may discard his entire hand and take the entire widow in its place.

If any player takes the widow before it has been turned over, he does not expose it, but must place his own cards on the table face up. The other players may then draw in turn, till some one knocks.

If all pass on the first round, the dealer, after passing, turns the widow face up, and the game proceeds.

After one knocks, the others may have one more draw from the widow in turn, or may retain their hands without drawing. No player can draw after he has knocked.

After the knock, and the final round of draws, all hands must be shown. The highest takes the pot if a pot has been made; or the lowest pays the forfeit agreed upon beforehand.

DEUCES WILD

This variation of Poker is popular wherever players of average ability wish to neutralize the technical knowledge of values possessed by the old-school players, or where it is desirable to add a little excitement to the game.

The Pack.—Any of the standard poker packs may be used; 52 cards, with or without the joker, or the short pack of 44 cards, with or without the joker, but the cards deleted from the short pack must be the 3's and 4's, leaving in the deuces.

The Deuces.—These four cards may be called anything the holder of one or more of them pleases, the same privilege being accorded to the joker, if it is in the pack. Two Aces and a deuce may be called three Aces. The 10, 8, 6 of Hearts and two deuces may be called three 10's, three 8's, three 6's, or a straight, or a straight flush.

Blind and Ante.—The dealer puts up the amount agreed upon for the blind, and every pot is a jack, but there is no opening qualification required. Each player in turn to the left of the dealer may open it by putting up an ante that is double the amount of the dealer's blind, and may raise it to any amount within the limit agreed upon for betting. As soon as any player opens by putting up an ante, each player in turn to the left, including those who previously passed, may come in.

The Betting.—The first player who puts up an ante, called the "opener," must make the first bet, and each player in turn to the left must call, raise, or pass out. In some places the opener is allowed to *"breathe,"* and each player to the left can do the same, until a bet is made. If none is made, all who have drawn cards show their hands for the pool, no player being allowed to make a bet after all have breathed.

Calling and Showing.—Before laying his cards on the table, when a call is made, each player must distinctly announce what he has, and his hand must be taken at this valuation, provided it is in the cards. This is very important because of the many mistakes made in the valuation of a hand when the deuces are a part of it.

For instance, a player goes in on two deuces and a Queen, which he intends calling three Queens, and draws a pair of eights. In the call he claims a Queen full, and is beaten by four treys. What he actually had was four eights. A player calls his hand four sixes, and lays down three deuces and the six and three of Clubs. What he really had was a straight flush 7 high.

Rank of Hands.—Five of a kind is the highest hand and, since the joker is higher than an Ace, four deuces and the joker make the highest possible hand. A straight flush comes next, then four of a kind, a full house, a flush, triplets, two pairs and one pair. In case of ties, the natural cards are better than combinations made with the deuces or joker, because of the greater difficulty of getting them.

Three actual Kings will beat a King and two deuces. Two sixes and a deuce will beat a six and two deuces. Any straight or flush made without a deuce or joker will beat one made with any of those artificial fillers. This is because there are more artificial cards than natural ones in each denomination.

The deal passes to the left, and all the laws for the regular game of Poker govern any irregularities.

MISTIGRIS

This game is Draw Poker, the only difference being that it is played with 53 cards, the joker being added to the regular pack. The joker counts for any card the player who holds it may desire. Thus he may hold five of a kind. This hand beats a royal flush. Otherwise Draw Poker rules govern.

THE DELETED PACK

Among the many devices to get the so-called scientific player away from his poker probabilities is the deleted pack. This consists in taking out the deuces and treys, sometimes the fours also. The principal change this makes is in the odds on the draw. An open-end straight is just as easy to fill as ever; but there are only ten cards in the suit to fill flushes. The hands naturally run larger, owing to the smaller pack. This game may be combined with the joker or the wild widow; or with deuces wild, if the treys, fours and fives are thrown out.

FREAK HANDS

In some localities, notably in the South, certain freak hands are played in connection with any form of Poker. A *blaze* is any five face cards, and beats two pairs but loses to three of a kind. A *tiger* is 7 high and 2 low, without a pair, sequence, or flush. It ranks between a straight and a flush. A *Dutch straight* or *skip* is a sequence of all even or all odd cards, such as 4, 6, 8, 10, Q. It beats two pairs and a blaze. A *round the corner straight* might be Q, K, A, 2, 3. It beats three of a kind but loses to a regular straight.

PEEK POKER

There are two forms of Peek Poker; seven cards being dealt to each player, or eight. With seven cards, the first two are dealt face down, and the remaining five face up. With eight cards, the last is also face down. In all other particulars Peek Poker is the same as Stud Poker.

THE WILD WIDOW

This is a modification of the variety of Poker known as "Deuces Wild," described on a previous page.

The game is practically Draw Poker except that after the fourth card has been dealt to each player, including the dealer, one card is dealt to the table, face up, and remains there. The fifth card is then given to each player, face down, to complete their hands.

The three cards of the same denomination as the widow are then running wild and any player holding one or more of them may call it or them when he pleases. Five of a kind is the best possible hand. Suppose the widow is an 8, and a player holds an 8 with three tens and a six. He can call his hand four tens or a ten full on sixes. He must call his hand before showing it, and he cannot change his call after his hand is laid down.

The Wild Widow is sometimes played with the joker in the pack, so that there shall be four cards running wild. In some places it is also the rule to lay the hand down and let the cards speak for themselves, instead of making the player say just what he has, or how he uses his wild cards. It is also insisted in some circles that one must have a pair of Jacks or better to open.

CASSINO

Cassino is played by four people, either each for himself or two against two, or by three or two.

The points are thus calculated:

The Big Cassino (ten of Diamonds)................ 2 points
Little Cassino (the deuce of Spades)................ 1   "
The four Aces, one point each........................... 4   "
The greatest number of Spades....................... 1   "
The greatest number of cards........................... 3   "
A sweep before the end of the game when any
    player can match all on the board................. 1   "

By agreement sweeps may not be counted.

There are two ways to settle: 1st. Each deal is a game in itself, the player, or side having the most points wins, or the majority of the 11 points wins. 2nd. 21 points is game. If two players reach 21 on the same deal, the points score out in the following order: Cards, Spades, Big Cassino, Little Cassino, Aces and sweeps. If the Aces have to decide it, they score in the order of Spades, Clubs, Hearts and Diamonds.

The Deal is determined by cutting. High deals, Ace being high. Four cards are dealt to each player, two or one at a time in rotation to the left, and four cards are dealt to the table face up, just before the dealer helps himself.

The talon is placed face down on the table, and after the first round of four cards has been played, four more are dealt to each player, but none to the table, this continuing until all have been dealt out. The deal passes to the left.

If, after the four cards are dealt to the table, a card is exposed in dealing, or one is found faced in the pack, player to whom it falls may refuse it and be supplied from top of pack. Should the exposure of a card occur on the last round of the deal, dealer must take exposed card, and player whose hand is short may draw from dealer's hand.

If wrong number of cards is given to any player after the first round, the error must be corrected by drawing from the pack and dealer cannot count anything on that hand of four cards.

The Play.—Each player, beginning with eldest hand, may make any of the following plays:

1. Take in a combination, *i.e.*, if he holds a card in his hand of the same denomination as one on the table, he may play his card and take in the two. He may also take in any other cards the sum of which equals the denomination of the one he plays; thus, a nine will take all the nines on the table and also an eight and Ace, seven and two, etc.

2. He may *build* a combination of two or more cards, by adding a card from his hand to one or more cards on the board, if the sum of such cards equals another card he holds in his hand. He can take in the build with such card on his next turn to play, provided no other player has taken it with another card of the same denomination or built higher on it. Thus, if a five is on the board and he holds a nine and four, he can build his four on the five and take it with his nine on his next turn; provided no player has built it higher or taken it in with another nine.

3. He may *call* a combination; thus, if he holds two fours, and a third four, or a three and an Ace, or two two's are on the board, he may play one of his fours on the board, calling it "fours," and take them on his next turn; provided no other player takes it away from him with a four. A *build* can be built higher, but a *call* cannot, since the call contains more than one combination.

4. A sweep is taking in every card on the table at once. Sweeps are noted by facing one card of the combination in which the sweep is made. If player cannot make any combination, he plays a single card to the table. After pack is exhausted, player taking last combination takes in all the cards remaining on the board, but this does not constitute a sweep, unless he can take all the cards by combination as above.

Notes.—A player cannot raise his own build, unless he has the cards to take in either the first or the second build.

A player can, if possible, make a second build or a call, or take in a combination, or capture another's build, before taking in his first build; otherwise he must take in his first build at his next turn to play.

Cards once taken in cannot be examined, except the last combination won; nor points nor cards counted until all the cards have been played. A mistake cannot be corrected after another combination has been taken in.

A card played out of turn must be withdrawn and laid to one side until the player's correct turn to play, when he must play it to the table. Player in error cannot combine it or win any combination of cards with it. Any cards taken in with it by offending player must be restored to the table.

Builds may be raised with cards from the hand only;

never with cards from the board. Builder or caller must name the denomination of the build or call, otherwise any other player may separate and use such cards of it as he chooses.

A player taking in a card not belonging to his combination or build must restore it and all other cards in the combination or build to the table, and his own card is laid out separately from the others. If the combination was his own, the cards composing it must be separated; if an adversary's, the combination must be left intact. A player taking in a combination with a wrong card or taking in a wrong combination or card not belonging to him must be challenged, and the error proved before the next combination is taken in. If a player makes a build or a combination and has not in his hand the proper card to take it, he must, upon discovery of the error, restore the cards of such combination to the table. Opponents' cards played subsequent to the error may be taken back and different cards played if opponents choose. If the erroneous build or combination has been taken by another player, there is no penalty nor any remedy.

Rules for Playing Cassino

The principal objects are to remember what has been played; when no pairs or combinations can be made, to clear the hand of face cards, which cannot be combined and are only of service in pairing or in gaining the final sweep; and if no face cards are left, to play any small ones, except Aces, as thereby combinations are often prevented.

In making pairs and combinations a preference should be given to Spades, because of their value in the scoring.

When three Aces are out, take the first opportunity to play the fourth, as it then cannot pair; but when there is another Ace remaining, it is better even to play the Little Cassino, that can only make one point, than to risk the Ace, which may be paired by the opponent and make a difference of two points; and if Big Cassino and an Ace be on the board prefer the Ace, as it may be paired or combined, but Big Cassino can only be paired.

Do not neglect sweeping the board when opportunity offers; always prefer taking up the card laid down by the opponent, also as many as possible with one, endeavoring likewise to win the last cards or final sweep.

In the last hand dealt it is well sometimes, especially if you are the last to play, to hold a face card to take the last trick, as it may decide the cards.

While Big or Little Cassino is in, avoid playing either a ten or a deuce.

When you hold a pair, lay down one of them, unless when there is a similar card on the table and the fourth not yet out.

Attend to the adversaries' score, and, if possible, prevent them from saving their lurch, even though you otherwise seemingly get less yourself, particularly if you can hinder them from clearing the board.

At the commencement of a game, combine all the cards possible, for that is more difficult than pairing; but when combinations cannot be made, do not fail to take a pair.

ROYAL CASSINO

The rules of Cassino apply. In this form of the game, however, each Jack is considered an eleven-spot, each Queen a twelve-spot, each King a thirteen-spot, and Aces either ones or fourteens, as players may elect. These cards can be built into combinations with spot cards, making a much more scientific game. Count as in Cassino. A still better

and more scientific game of Royal Cassino is played by us·
ing packs containing eleven and twelve spots of each suit.
This makes Jacks thirteens, Queens fourteens, Kings fifteens, and Aces ones or sixteens. The number of combina·
tions possible is thus greatly increased and interest added.

ROYAL DRAW CASSINO

The same as Royal Cassino, except that after the first
four cards are dealt to players and board, remainder of
the pack is placed face downward on the table, and each
player, after playing a card from his hand, draws the top
card from the pack, thus restoring the number of cards in
his hand to four. This is continued until pack is exhausted,
when hands are played out, and count made in the regular
manner. If a player fails to draw in proper turn he cannot
correct the error until his next turn to draw, when he must
draw two cards.

SPADE CASSINO

The same as Royal Draw Cassino, except that each card
of Spade suit counts 1 point for game. Ace, Jack and
deuce of Spades count 2 each—1 point as Ace and Jack
and Little Cassino respectively, and 1 each as a Spade.
Sixty-one points constitute a game. A cribbage board is
used for scoring, and points are scored as made. The only
thing which remains to be counted at end of play, therefore,
is cards.

VINGT-UN (Twenty-one)

Vingt-Un, or Twenty-One, may be played by two or more
people. It is essentially a family game, and when played as
such the stakes are usually represented by counters, which

may be of any value. It is common to limit the stakes
to be laid to ten or twelve counters. As the deal is advantageous and often continues long with the same person,
it is usual to determine it at the commencement by the first
Ace turned up, or any other mode that may be agreed
upon.

The deal usually passes to the left, each player dealing
one round in turn. Sometimes, however, it is retained by
the person who commences until a natural twenty-one occurs, when it passes to the next in rotation. (The old mode
of play, however, is that in the case of a natural twenty-one
the deal passes to the holder, and many still adhere to this
custom. This item of the game must, therefore, be regulated by the custom of the table, or be previously agreed
upon.) The pony, or youngest hand, should collect the cards
that have been played, and shuffle them together ready for
the dealer against the period when he shall have distributed
the whole pack.

The object of the game is to make twenty-one with the
cards received. An Ace may be counted 1 or 11, each face
card counts 10 and lower cards count their numerical
value.

The dealer begins by giving one card, face downward, to
each player, including himself. After the first card has been
dealt round, each places his stake upon it (which may, if
he chooses, be as low as a single counter), and the dealer,
upon the stakes being all laid, and before proceeding with
the deal, looks at his own card, and if he thinks proper
(having perhaps an Ace, ten, or face card), he may double
the stakes, which he announces by crying "Double."

He then distributes a second card to each, and lastly
to himself. Should he chance to have a natural twenty-one
he declares it at once, before any more cards are dealt, and

collects the stakes (which, by a twenty-one, are doubled);
but should he have drawn less than twenty-one, the game
proceed thus: The dealer inquires of each player in rotation, beginning with the eldest hand on the left, whether he
stands, or wishes another card, which, if required, must be
given from the top (face upward) of the pack, and afterwards another, or more, if requested, till the points of
the additional card or cards, added to those dealt, exceed
or make twenty-one exactly, or such a number less than
twenty-one as the player may choose to stand upon; but
when the points exceed twenty-one, the player is said to
have overdrawn, and his cards are to be thrown up forthwith, and the stake laid on them paid to the dealer. When
the deal has gone around the table in this manner, the
dealer turns up his own cards to the view of the company,
and should he have any number of points between, say, from
17 to 20, he usually "stands," that is, pits his cards against
the other players. Those under his number, as well as ties,
pay; those above it receive. (Ties are the principal advantage of the dealer.) If the dealer should have only 14 or
15 points in his first hand, the chances would be against
him were he to stand on so small a number. He would,
therefore, draw another card, and should this be a very low
one (an Ace or a deuce) and he have reason to suppose, by
the extra cards dealt round, that he had to contest high
numbers, he would draw again, and if he obtained 19 or 20
points would then probably win on more than he loses, the
average of chances being in his favor; if by drawing he
should happen to make up twenty-one, he would receive
double from all, except from the ties and those who had
already thrown up; if more than twenty-one, he would have
to pay all who stand, paying the twenty-ones double.

Should either the dealer or a player happen to turn up

two cards of the same denomination, for instance, two Aces, deuces, or any other number, or two Kings, two Queens, etc., he would have the choice of going on both, and should the next card he draws be a triplicate, he may go on all three. If the cards happen to be Aces, which count either as 1 or 11, at the option of the player, and if by great luck he should then successively draw three tens or face cards, thus making three natural twenty-ones, he would obtain double stakes upon each, therefore six times as much as the stakes placed on the various hands, and should he, on laying his first card, have cried "double," the stakes payable would, in such case, be twice doubled, therefore, upon the three cards twelve-fold. This is an extreme case, cited merely to show the nature of the game. It commonly happens, however, that when either dealer or player "goes" on several cards, he loses on one or more, and thus neutralizes his gains. Players, as already intimated, have the same right of "going" on several cards as the dealer.

When any player has a twenty-one, and the dealer not, then the player wins double stakes from him; in other cases, except when a natural twenty-one happens, the dealer pays single stakes to all whose numbers under twenty-one are higher than his own, and receives from those who have lower numbers; players who have similar numbers to the dealer pay; and when the dealer draws more than twenty-one, he overdraws, and has to pay all who have not thrown up.

Twenty-one, whenever dealt in the first two cards, is styled a natural twenty-one, and should be declared immediately.

One of the first thoughts of the dealer, after the cards have been cut, should be to look for Brulet, which is a natural twenty-one formed by the bottom and top card, when they happen to be an Ace and a "ten" card. The card or cards looked at must be thrown out, and mixed with those collected by the pony. Brulet either clears the board of the stakes laid (usually one or two counters levied on each player, at the commencement of every game, and collected into a tray) or takes the amount of the limit from each, as may be agreed.

The odds of this game merely depend upon the average quantity of cards likely to come under or exceed 21; for example, if those in hand make 14 exactly, it is 7 to 6 that the one next drawn does not make the number of points above 21, but if the points be 15, it is 7 to 6 against that hand; yet it would not, therefore, always be prudent to stand at 15, for as the Ace may be calculated both ways, it is rather above an even bet that the adversary's two first cards amount to more than 14. A natural twenty-one may be expected once in 7 deals when two, and twice in 7 when four, people play, and so on according to the number of players.

MACAO

A variation of Twenty-One, only one card being dealt. Tens and face cards do not count; Aces count one. Nine is number to be reached instead of 21. A player receiving nine in the first deal is paid three times amount of his wager; an eight, twice the amount; or a seven the amount he has staked. The dealer, if he receives a nine, eight or seven on the deal, is paid by each player three times, twice, or once the amount of such player's stake. Otherwise, the game is played on same principle as Twenty-One.

FARMER

Use full pack, with the eights and the sixes of Diamonds, Clubs and Spades discarded. Spot cards count at their numerical values, face cards 10, and Aces 1. Each player places one chip in center of table, forming the Farm (or pool). This is sold to highest bidder, who must deposit in the Farm as many chips as he bid. He then becomes dealer and banker. One card is dealt to each player, and each must draw one card, and may draw more, if desired, as in Twenty-One, the object being, however, to reach 16 points, instead of 21. If a player overdraws, he does not announce it until the hands are exposed. Any player having exactly 16 wins the Farm and all it contains. If two or more players have 16, the one holding the six of Hearts wins; or if no one has this card, the 16 made with fewest cards wins. If this is a tie, eldest hand wins. If no one has exactly 16, the Farmer still remains in possession of the Farm, and thus holds it, deal after deal, until some one wins it by holding exactly 16.

Whether Farm changes hands or not, after hands are exposed, all who have overdrawn pay dealer one chip for each point (according to the count given above) they hold over 16. These chips are the Farmer's own property. Those holding less than 16 pay nothing to dealer, but the one nearest to 16 receives one chip from each of the other players. Ties are decided by the possession of the six of Hearts, fewest cards, or the eldest hand, as above. When the Farm is won, it is emptied by the winner, and a new pool is formed and sold as before.

SEVEN AND ONE-HALF

A variety of Twenty-One played with 40 cards (the 8's,

9's and 10's of each suit being discarded). Any number may play. Cards have no relative rank, but their counting value is as follows: face cards, one-half point each, spot cards counting their numerical values, Aces 1, deuces 2, etc. The object of the game is to hold cards the collective numerical value of which most nearly approaches seven and one-half, without passing that number.

The first dealer may be determined by cutting. Dealer gives each player one card, dealing to the left. After examining his card and before any further cards are served by the dealer, each player bets any amount within the limit fixed at the beginning of the game. As all bets are made after the player has seen his card, the dealer may, after examining his card, and before serving any of the players, require all players to double their bets. There is no redouble.

After all bets are made, the eldest hand may stand or draw cards, as he may elect. Cards may be drawn until he is satisfied, or the collective numerical value of the hand exceeds seven and one-half. A player who overdraws must announce the fact at once, abandon the hand and pay his stake to the dealer. All cards drawn are served face up. The remaining players are served in a similar manner. The dealer then turns his card face up and either draws or announces that he will stand. Should he elect to stand, he takes all bets from players having an *equal* or less number of points in their hands and pays those having a greater amount. Should he overdraw or "break," he must pay all players who have not previously overdrawn.

Should any player draw exactly seven and one-half, he must announce the fact at once and expose his entire hand. Should the dealer not draw exactly seven and one-half, after serving the remaining players, he must pay to each player drawing seven and one-half double the amount of their stake. Should the dealer draw exactly seven and one-half, he collects double the stake of each player who has not previously overdrawn, regardless of whether or not other players may hold hands of similar value.

Splits.—Should the first card drawn by a player be of the same value as the original card served him and their combined numerical value *not exceed* seven and one-half, he may "split" the pair, betting on the second card an amount equal to the original bet. Cards are served to either hand first, but one hand must break or be satisfied before cards are served to the second. The first card served to either card of the split pair is served *face down*. Should the first card served to either of the split pair be of the same value as the split, a third hand may be formed, etc. For example: The first card served a player is an Ace. He bets two chips and asks for a card. This card proves to be an Ace and he announces a split, betting two chips on the second Ace. He then draws to the first hand again and receives a third Ace. Another split is announced and two chips bet on the third hand. He then draws to each hand separately until satisfied or until he overdraws.

Change of Deal.—The first player to the dealer's left to expose seven and one-half, when the dealer fails to draw a similar hand, takes the deal. If more than one seven and one-half is turned, each player holding such hand has the option of dealing, should those ahead of him decline the deal. Should all decline, the deal remains unchanged, but the dealer must pay double on these hands, even though he retains the deal. In some localities a player who does not desire to deal when he has the opportunity, may dispose of the deal to another player, or he may pool his chips with another player. In this case only one card is served to both players pooling their chips. When the deal is lost, the chips in the pool are equally divided.

Misdeal.—There is no misdeal, but a player is not compelled to accept a card exposed during the deal.

BACCARAT

This is another variety of Twenty-One, one player being the banker, the others, from three to eleven, the punters. Three packs of cards are shuffled together and used as one. The face cards and tens count nothing; all spot cards, including the Ace, reckon at their face value. The object is to secure cards whose total numerical value most closely approaches eight or nine. An eight made with two cards is better than a nine made with three.

Players make their bets on the right or left of the table, any amounts they please, before the deal begins. The banker lays the cards before him, face down, and slips off the top card, giving it to the player on his right, face down. Then he gives a card to the player on his left and then one to himself. This is repeated and then the three players examine their two cards.

If any of the three has eight or nine he shows it at once. If the banker has eight or nine and neither punter has as much, the banker wins everything on the table. If either player has more than the banker, he wins. If equal, it is a stand-off. All the bets made on the side of the table on which the player sits must be paid or lost according to the success or failure of the player holding cards who sits on that side.

If no one has eight or nine the banker must offer a card, face down, to the player on his right. If he refuses it, it is offered to the player on the left, and if he refuses it, the banker must take it. If the player on the right takes it, the one on the left may ask for one, but the banker is ·not obliged to take a card if his offer is accepted by either punter although he may take one if he desires. Cards so drawn are at once turned face up. Each player may draw only one card. A player cannot go over nine. If he has a six and draws a seven his count would not be thirteen, but three, because all tens are counted nothing.

CHEMIN DE FER

This is a variation of Baccarat in which six packs of cards are used, all shuffled together. As soon as the first banker loses a deal, the player to his left takes the bank and the deal, and retains it until he loses. The banker in each deal gives cards only to the player on his right and to himself, so that the banker must win or lose each time he deals. The player to the right of the banker has a right to go banco, which is a challenge to play for the entire capital in the bank at one deal. This takes precedence of all other bets. If the player refuses, the one on his right again may go banco, and so on in order.

SPECULATION

This is a lively round game that several may play, using a complete pack of 52 cards, with counters, on which such a value is fixed as the company agree. The highest trump in each deal wins the pool. After determining the deal, the dealer pools six counters, and every other player four; next three cards are given to each, one at a time, and another turned up for trump.

If the turned trump is an Ace, the dealer takes the pool and the deal passes to the left. If it is a face card the dealer offers it for sale and may sell it to the highest bidder or refuse to sell. Each player's cards are placed in front of him face down and after the ownership of the turned up trump is decided the eldest player turns up his top card. If it is a higher trump than the dealer's trump card, its owner may sell or keep it. The next player then turns up his top card and this continues around the table. The one having the highest trump by purchase or otherwise, leaves it face up on his other cards, which are not turned up unless another player turns a higher trump. After all of the cards are exposed the one holding the highest trump wins the pool.

LOO

Loo, or Lue, subdivided into limited and unlimited Loo, is played two ways, either with five and three cards, dealt from the whole pack, either first three and then two, or one at a time. From three to eight persons may play together, but five or six makes the best game.

After cards have been dealt to each player another is turned up for trump; the Jack of Clubs is the highest card and styled Pam; the Ace of trumps is next in value, and the rest in succession, as at Whist. Each player has the liberty of changing for others from the pack all or any of the five cards dealt, or of throwing up the hand in order to escape being looed. Those who play their cards either with or without changing, and do not gain a trick, are looed; as is likewise the case with all who are playing, when a flush or flushes occur, and each, except any player holding Pam or an inferior flush, is required to deposit a stake to be given to the person who sweeps the board, or divided among the winners at the ensuing deal, according to the tricks which may then be made. In limited five-card Loo the penalty for being looed is always three or six counters, but in the unlimited game each person looed must pay a sum equal to what happens to be on the table at the time. Five cards of a suit, or four with Pam, compose a flush, which sweeps the board, and loos all those playing. If several players hold flushes the elder hand (the player nearer to the dealer's left) wins. When the Ace of trumps is led, it is usual to say, "Pam be civil," the holder of which last-mentioned card is then expected to let the Ace pass, if he can do so without revoking.

When Loo is played with three cards, they are dealt one at a time, Pam is omitted, and the cards are not exchanged nor permitted to be thrown up.

In different companies these games are frequently played with a few trifling variations.

One of the most usual in three-card Loo is the laying out of two or three extra hands, which are called Misses. These may be exchanged with their own hands by any of the players, the eldest hand having the first choice, and the others according to their turn, the dealer being last. It commonly happens that the first two or three players avail themselves of their option, so that it rarely comes round to the dealer. The Miss, which is to be taken at a venture, without previous inspection, must be played.

LOTTERY

Of the minor games of cards, Lottery is without doubt one of the most agreeable when there are a great number of players; for it may be played by ten, twelve or more, but not well with less than four or five players. Two entire packs of cards are employed, one of which serves for the tricks, and the other for the lots or prizes. Each player should take a certain number of counters, more or less, that and their value depending on the will of the players. These points being settled, every one puts up as many counters as he desires for his stake, and these, being collected into a box or purse on the middle of the table, compose the fund of the Lottery.

The players being all ranged round the table, two of them take each a pack of cards, and as it is of no importance who deals, there being no advantage in being eldest or youngest, the cards are commonly presented in compliment to some two of the players. The dealers, after shuffling the cards, have them cut by their right-hand neighbors, and one of them deals a card to each player; all these cards are to remain face down and are called the *lots*; each player then places on his lot as many counters as he thinks proper; it is well, however, to have them vary from each other so that there may be as few as possible of the same value. The lots being thus prized, the player who has the other pack deals likewise to each player one card, which are called the *tickets*; each player having received his ticket card, the lots are then turned, and each looks to see whether his ticket answers to any of the lots; for example, if any of the lots are the Jack of Clubs, the Queen of Hearts, the Ace of Spades, the eight of Clubs, the six of Diamonds, the four of Hearts, the three of Spades or the two of Diamonds, the player whose card corresponds to any of these takes up the lot and the counters which were upon it.

The two dealers then collect those cards that belong to their respective packs, and after having shuffled them, deal again in the same manner as before, the lots being laid down and drawn by the tickets, in the manner we have just mentioned.

If the party should last too long, instead of giving only one card to each for his ticket, you may give two, three, or even four, one after the other, according as you would have the party continue. Increasing the value of the lots likewise helps greatly to shorten the party.

Another method is, to take at random three cards out of one of the packs, and place them, face downward, on a board or in a bowl on the table for the prizes; then every player purchases from the other pack any number of cards for tickets as may be most agreeable, paying a fixed sum or certain quantity of counters for each, which sums or counters are put in different proportions on the three prizes to be gained by those who happen to have purchased corresponding cards, and such that happen not to be drawn are continued till the next deal.

This game may be played with a single pack by separating it into two divisions, each containing a red and black suit.

COMMERCE

There are two distinct methods of playing this game, the new and the old mode. The new way is played by any number of persons, from three to twelve, with a complete pack of 52 cards. Every player has a certain quantity of counters on which a fixed value is put, and each, at every fresh deal, lays down one for the stake. Sometimes the game is continued until, or finished when, one of the players has lost all the counters given at the commencement; or it is sometimes decided to fix the duration to a determinate number of times that the deal passes completely round.

After determining the deal, the dealer, styled also the banker, shuffles the pack, which is then cut by the right-hand player. Three cards, either altogether or one by one, are given to each person, beginning on the left-hand.

The object of the game is to get one of the three following combinations which are valued in the order given—1st, three of a kind; 2nd, a sequence; 3rd, a flush.

After the cards have been dealt round, the banker inquires, "Who will trade?" which the players, beginning with the eldest hand, answer by saying, "For ready money," or "I barter." Trading for money is giving a card and a counter to the banker, who places the card under the stock or remainder of the pack, and returns in lieu thereof another card from the top. The counter is profit to the banker, who consequently trades with the stock free from expense. Barter is exchanging a card without pay with the next right-hand player, which must not be refused; and so on, the players trade around the table in turn, till one of them obtains the object aimed at, and thereby stops the

Commerce; then all show their hands, and the highest three of a kind, sequence or flush wins the pool. The player who first gains a counting combination should show it immediately, and he wins the pool unless another player has a higher combination. If any one chooses to stand on the hand dealt, and show it without trading, none of the junior players can trade that deal, and if the eldest hand stands, then of course no person can trade.

Whenever the banker does not gain the pool, he is to pay a counter to that player who obtains the same, and if the banker possesses a counting combination but does not win the pool, because another player has a better hand, then he is to give a counter to each player.

The game by the old method is won by the same combinations as those just described but the dealing is different. In addition to giving each player three cards, three are turned face up on the table and should these three be such as the dealer approves of, he may, previous to looking at the hand dealt to himself, take them up in lieu of his own, but then he must abide by the same, and cannot afterwards exchange any during that deal. All the players, beginning with the eldest hand, may in rotation change any card or cards in their possession for such as lie turned up on the table, striving thereby to make counting combinations, and so on round again and again, till all have refused to change; but every person once standing cannot change again that deal. Finally the hands are all shown, and the possessor of the highest combination, or the eldest hand if there are more than one of the same value, takes the sum agreed upon out of the pool, and the person having the worst hand puts one counter therein, called "going up."

BLIND HOOKEY

This is purely a game of chance, without any limit as to the number of players, but is best suited to a party of four, six or ten. Each player cuts for the deal, and the highest deals. The pack, being then shuffled by the player on the dealer's right hand, may be again shuffled by the dealer himself, and, being cut by the right-hand player, is placed by the dealer before the player on his left hand. This player cuts a parcel for himself, consisting of not less than four cards, nor of more than shall allow an equal number at least to all the players, and lays them before him with the faces downward. All the players having done the same, and a small parcel being left for the dealer, he also lays it before him, face downward. Each player then places upon the parcel of cards before him the stake which he is inclined to wager. The dealer then turns up his parcel, and the others do the same, in order towards the left, each exposing the bottom card. Those players turning up higher cards than the dealer win their wagers and those turning up lower ones lose to the dealer, but should the card "tie," the dealer wins, which is a considerable advantage.

MATRIMONY

Matrimony may be played by any number of persons from five to fourteen. It is composed of five chances, usually marked on a board or sheet of paper, as follows:

133

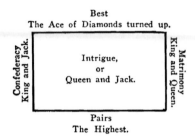

Best
The Ace of Diamonds turned up.

Confederacy
King and Jack.

Intrigue,
or
Queen and Jack.

Matrimony
King and Queen.

Pairs
The Highest.

The Ace of Diamonds turned up takes the whole pool, but when in hand ranks only as any other Ace.

The game is generally played with counters, and the dealer stakes what he pleases on each or any chance, the other players depositing each the same quantity, minus one, distributed among the 5 chances any way desired; that is, when the dealer stakes twelve, the rest of the company lay down eleven each. After this, one card is dealt round to every one, beginning on the left, then to each, another card turned up, and he who happens to get the Ace of Diamonds sweeps all; if it is not turned up, then each player shows his hand, and any of them having matrimony, intrigue, etc., takes the counters on that point; when two or more people happen to have similar combinations, the eldest hand has the preference; and should any chance not be gained, it stands over to the next deal.

PIQUET

The game of Piquet is played by two persons with thirty-two cards, namely, Ace, King, Queen, Jack, ten, nine, eight, and seven of each suit, and these cards rank according to the succession in which they are here placed. Having cut for deal the dealer shuffles the cards and his opponent cuts them, after which he deals twelve cards to each player, two at a time. This leaves eight cards, called the *"stock,"* which are placed face down between the two players.

In *Rubicon Piquet,* which is the more popular game, instead of playing 100 points, six deals constitute a game, and at the end of these six deals the scores are added up, the lower being deducted from the higher and 100 points added to the difference. If either or both players fail to reach 100 points in the six deals, the one having the higher score is the winner and he adds to his score the points made by the loser instead of deducting them.

The various scoring combinations are as follows, and they are counted in the following order:—

1st. Carte-blanche.
2nd. The Point.
3rd. Sequences.
4th. Fours or Threes.
5th. Repic.
6th. Points for Leading to or winning tricks.
7th. Pic.
8th. Cards.
9th. Capot.
10th. Lurch.

These will be explained in order and the values given.

Carte-Blanche.—A player has Carte-blanche when his hand does not contain a face card. It counts 10 and, if held by pone, should be announced immediately after taking up and sorting the hand. If held by Dealer it is not declared until pone has discarded.

The Point.—The player who has the longest suit wins

the Point. If both players have suits of equal length the winner is the one having the largest count. An Ace is eleven, each face card ten and the spot cards count their numerical value. The value of the Point is the number of cards in the suit.

Sequences.—A sequence is composed of three or more consecutive cards of the same suit. The longest sequence wins and, if each player has one of the same length, the one with the higher cards wins. Sequences of three or four count one for each card. Those of five or more add ten so that one of six cards counts sixteen, etc. The player having the best sequence can count any others which he has, but his opponent counts none.

Fours or Threes.—Any four of a kind better than nines counts fourteen and any such three of a kind counts three. The player having the highest fours may count any other fours or threes but his opponent counts none. If neither player has a four, the one having the highest three may count any other threes but his opponent counts none.

Before describing the other scoring points the manner of playing will be given.

After the deal and the declaration of Carte-blanche (if either player holds it) pone discards and draws from the stock. He must discard at least one card and may not discard more than five, drawing as many as he discards. The five top cards of the stock are called his and he has a right to look at any of them which he does not draw, but in drawing he must distinctly announce how many he is taking.

The dealer then discards and draws from the stock. If pone has taken all of his five, dealer can only exchange three because that is all that remain in the stock but if pone has left any of his five, declarer must take them before taking any of the last three, in other words, declarer must draw from the top of the stock. If declarer leaves any cards in the stock he has a right to look at them but if he does so pone may also look at them *after* he has made the first lead.

Dealer is not obliged to draw any unless he wishes them.

After discarding and drawing each player must have twelve cards and then pone announces any scoring combinations that he holds, beginning with the Point, the suit of which is not mentioned but only the length. The sequences are defined by the number of cards and the highest, as, "sequence of six to the King" and the fours and threes in the same way, "four Kings" or "three Queens."

To each of these declarations as they are made in regular order, the dealer must reply *"good," "equal"* or *"not good."* If pone announces a five card suit for Point and dealer has one of the same length he says "equal" and pone then gives the count of his five cards "50" and if dealer's count is less than this he says "good."

As each of pone's declarations is admitted by dealer to be good he announces his accumulated score as for example: His point is 50, score 5; his sequence of five to an Ace, good, 15, makes 20; his three Aces are good, counting 3, makes 23, to which he may add any lower sequences or threes.

Pone having finished his declarations, and announced their value in points, leads any card that he desires. If this card is a ten or better he is entitled to one point for the lead, whether or not he wins the trick, and he adds this point to his score, making 24.

An example of scoring two hands will perhaps make this

clearer. Pone after drawing holds:—

S—A-K-Q-J-7; H—A-K-Q; D—A-K-Q; C—A.

He announces: "Five-card suit." "Equal." He gives value, "48." "Not Good." "Sequence of four to the Ace." "Not good." "Four Aces." "Good" which allows him to count his three Kings and three Queens. The one four and the two threes count 20, and upon leading one of the Aces he announces "21."

The dealer, before playing to the trick, proceeds to claim the count for his combinations, holding the following hand:—

H—J-10-9-8; D—J-10-9;   C—K-Q-J-10-9.

The Point is worth 5; the three sequences, 15, 4, and 3 making a total of 27. His three Jacks and three tens are shut out by higher combinations in pone's hand. Having claimed these 27 points, and their correctness having been admitted by pone, the dealer plays to the first lead. If either player forgets to declare anything before he plays, the count is lost.

We can now more easily describe the remaining counts.

Repic.—If either player is able to reach 30 points by declarations without his opponent holding any combinations over him he adds 60 to his score calling 90 in place of 30. The important thing to remember about Repic is that the declarations always count in regular order, Carte-blanche, then the Point, sequences and fours or threes. Pone cannot make Repic if the dealer has a Carte-blanche or the Point but if neither one has a Carte-blanche and they are tied for the Point, pone may have a Repic. Suppose pone holds the following cards:—

S—Q; H—K-Q-J-10-9; D—A-Q-9; C—A-K-Q.

If the Hearts are admitted good for the Point they must

also be good for a five-card sequence and these two count 20. The three-card sequence in Clubs counts 3, making 23. The four Queens must be good because dealer could not have four Kings or Aces. This adds 14 making a total of 37 and 60 are added for Repic making 97 altogether, to which he will add one by leading a card higher than a nine. Again suppose pone held the following cards:—

S—A-K-10; H—A-K-Q-J-8; D—A-K; C—A-K.

If his Hearts are good for Point that and his four Aces and four Kings will make him 33; but dealer has a five-card sequence, the count for which comes in order before fours and therefore prevents pone's making Repic. Suppose with these cards pone was told that the score for Point was even, he would count 29 for his two fours and the first lead. In this case dealer might have a six-card sequence in Diamonds and a five-card one in Clubs, counting 31, and these would give him Repic or 91 because sequences score before fours.

Pic.—If either player can make 30 points by declarations and play combined, before his opponent scores anything, 30 are added for the Pic. Pic can never be made by dealer unless pone leads a card smaller than a nine because a higher lead gives him a point. To illustrate the Pic, suppose pone has the following:—

S—K; H—A-9; D—K-Q-J-10-9; C—A-K-Q-J.

If the Diamond suit is good for the Point it must also be good for a five-card sequence, which makes the Club four-card sequence good and the three Kings must be good. These count 5, 15, 4 and 3 making 27, and by leading out the Ace, King, Queen of Clubs he scores 3 more making 30, and adding 30 for Pic he has 60.

Any lead which is above a nine spot counts one and if the opponent wins the trick he counts one but if the leader of such a high card wins the trick he counts only one, not two. A player must follow suit when possible but does not need to take the trick unless he wishes to do so.

The last trick counts one, in addition to the count for winning it with a card better than a nine.

Cards and Capot.—If either player wins more than six tricks he adds 10 to his score for Cards and if either one wins all twelve tricks he scores 40 points for Capot, but this 40 includes the one point for the last trick and the 10 for the odd trick.

Lurch.—If one player reaches 100 points before his opponent has 50, it is a Lurch and counts a double game.

SUGGESTIONS FOR GOOD PLAY

The discarding is the most difficult part of the game and a player must decide what combinations he will try to fill. As a rule the Point is the first thing to try for because that will prevent a Pic or Repic by opponent and this is especially the thing to do if the cards in the long suit are in sequence, as it gives the double advantage of winning the Point and obtaining a high sequence. Cards is also a valuable point to strive for, which means that the highest cards should be kept and a player's best judgment is needed to decide what cards to discard holding these two objects in view. Trying to fill low sequences or low fours or threes is not nearly so apt to be profitable as if the cards held to be drawn to are high ones because, if you do fill, your opponent is apt to have something better and render yours worthless.

THREE-HANDED PIQUET

In this game ten cards are dealt to each player leaving two for the stock which may be drawn by the dealer only, who discards if he takes them. The eldest hand declares first. He makes Repic and counts 90 if he can reach 20 without playing a card, or he makes Pic (60) if he can count 20 in hand and play under the same conditions as in the two-hand game. The majority of tricks count 10; if it is a tie, each counts 5. Capot counts 40 if all of the tricks are taken by one player but if two take them all they count 20 each.

FOUR-HANDED PIQUET

All the cards are dealt out, two and three at a time, each player receiving eight. The eldest hand declares first by announcing everything which he has and then leading a card. Suppose the cards are distributed as follows, S being the dealer:—

S—K-Q-J-10
D—J-10-9-8

	N.	
S—A; H—A; D—A-Q C—A-Q-J-10	W. S.	E.
		H—K-Q-J; D—K-7 C—K-9-8

S—9-8-7; C—7
H—10-9-8-7

W. announces a four-card Point of 41, sequence of three to the Queen, four Aces and adds "I lead a Club." If second hand admits all of these to be good he says nothing but plays a card; here, however, N. would announce two sequences four to the King (which would nullify W's three-card sequence) and four to the Jack and would play a Spade, having no Club. E. would then announce three Kings (made good because of his partner's four Aces) but his sequence is shut out by N's better one: The dealer,

S, then declares four to the ten and a sequence of three to the nine.

W. in taking the first trick would announce the total score for his side as 22 (4 for the Point, 14 for four Aces, 3 for Kings and 1 for the lead). In playing the hand out W-E make a Capot and the adversaries score 15 for their three sequences of four and one of three.

Pic and Repic are scored the same as in the three-handed game and if two partners each hold Carte-blanche they are entitled to 90 points for Repic, no matter what the opponents held, because Carte-blanche takes precedence of all other scores.

ECARTE

Ecarté is played by two persons with a pack of thirty-two cards, the deuce, three, four, five and six of each suit being deleted. The King is the highest card; the Ace ranks next after the Jack.

Five points scored are game, unless there be any mutual agreement to the contrary.

Whoever wins three tricks scores one point; whoever wins all the tricks scores two. This is called, in French, making the *"vole."*

Only two points can be scored in a single deal, unless one of the parties hold or turn up the King of trumps.

It may be either played in games or rubbers. A rubber consists in winning two games out of three.

It is usual to have two packs of cards, used alternately; to prevent mixing them, the backs should be of different colors.

First cut for deal. Highest deals and pone cuts, leaving

at least five cards in each packet. There is a slight advantage in dealing, because the King turned up scores a point.

ON DEALING—THE PLAY

The cards are dealt by two and three or by three and two. Five are given to each player, and the eleventh is turned up for trump.

A trump is superior to every other card of a different suit.

The residue of the pack (Fr. *talon*) is placed on the right of the dealer, and the écart (or cards rejected) on the left, both to avoid confusion and to show, if forgotten, which player was dealer.

The King of trumps counts as one point in favor of the person either turning it up or holding it.

It is not sufficient that the holder of the King mark it; he ought to distinctly announce that he has the King. If the holder is pone, he ought to make this announcement before he leads his first card, except when he plays King first, and in that case it is allowable to announce it *after* it is on the table, but *before* it is covered by the adversary's card. This rule is only applicable to pone; the dealer should invariably announce the King just before covering pone's first card, otherwise he cannot score it; for his own interest he ought not to announce it until just after the opponent's first card is played.

When pone is not satisfied with his hand, he proposes to take other cards, saying, "I throw out," or "I propose"; the dealer accepts or refuses, according to whether satisfied or not with what he holds; if he accept, he gives as many cards as his adversary requires, and then serves himself with as many as he may want.

Whoever plays without changing cards, or refuses to change cards, loses two points if he does not make three tricks; and making them, scores one.

When a proposition is once made or refused, there can be no retracting; also, when once a certain number of cards are asked for, that number can neither be diminished nor increased.

If, after the second time of giving cards, pone still wishes to propose, he has the power of so doing; likewise after the third, and so on until the pack is exhausted; but the dealer in refusing no longer loses two points if he does not make three tricks.

When, after having changed several times, pone proposes again, without paying attention as to whether sufficient cards remain or not, and the dealer accepts, the former takes as many cards as he needs even though he may take them all and if there do not remain as many as dealer wanted he must be content with what there are, and if he has discarded more than remain in the pack he must fill his hand from the discard.

Each player, previously to receiving fresh cards, puts his discard on one side, and, once this discard is made, he can no longer touch it. Should either happen to look at the rejected cards, even his own, not only is it forbidden to retake them, but he is obliged to play with his cards on the table, being supposed to have cognizance of his adversary's discard.

It is obligatory to play the suit announced: thus any one calling "Club," and playing Spade or any other suit, is obliged, if the adversary desire, to retake his card and to play the suit announced; if he has none the adversary can call a suit.

If, however, the adversary deem the card played more favorable to him than the suit announced, he has the right to prevent its being taken back.

Whoever from mistake, or otherwise, announces "the King," and has it not, loses one point independently of the result of that deal; that is to say, instead of marking the King thus falsely announced, the adversary marks it unless the mistake is declared previously to a card being played. It is easy to see the necessity of this forfeit, since a ruse of this nature might cause the other player to lose the point or miss the vole from not daring to lead trumps, thinking the King to be in his adversary's hand.

It is not allowable to look at the adversary's tricks, under penalty of playing with cards on table.

Whoever through error, or purposely, throws his cards on the table, loses one point, if he has already made a trick, and two points if he has not.

ON REVOKING OR UNDERFORCING

It is forbidden to either revoke or underforce. This latter term means answering a card with one of the same suit, but inferior value to those remaining in hand; for instance, putting the nine of Clubs on the ten, having the Ace in hand.

When a player revokes or underforces, he is obliged to retake his card, and the hand is played over again; but a player committing this fault does not score if he makes the point, and scores only one if he makes the vole.

ON MISDEALING

When the dealer turns up two or more cards instead of one, pone has the right to pick out that which ought to be the trump, or to put aside the cards thus exposed and take the next remaining on the pack for trump, or to recom-

mence the hand, taking the deal; but he has only this last
choice provided he has not seen his hand.

When the dealer shows or turns up one or more cards of
his adversary's hand, he must finish dealing, and the adversary has then the choice of recommencing the hand,
taking the deal, or counting the deal good.

If the cards exposed belong to the dealer, neither party
has the choice of recommencing the deal, the fault being
the dealer's and advantageous to the player who has seen
them. ·

If, however, this happen after the discarding, the player
who has exposed the cards can only require another or
others, but cannot recommence the deal.

If the dealer gives one or more cards too many, pone
has the right either to look at his hand and throw out the
extra cards, first showing them to the dealer, or to recommence the hand, taking to himself the deal.

If he has given too few, pone has the right to take the
number wanting from the talon or residue of the pack,
without, however, changing the trump, or to recommence,
taking the deal.

If, the dealer has·dealt himself too many cards, the adversary has a right either to pick out at hazard the extra
cards, or to recommence the hand, taking the deal.

If the dealer deals himself too few cards, the adversary
has a right either to make him take the number wanting
from the talon, or recommence the hand, taking the deal.

If one of the two players, having too many or too few
cards, should discard without giving notice to his adversary, and if the latter should perceive it, the player who thus
makes ·a false discard loses two points and the right of
marking the King, if he had turned it up.

ON MISDEALING AFTER CHANGING CARDS

If the dealer gives more or less cards than asked for, he loses the point and the right of marking the King if he has it in his hand, but not if he has turned it up, the turn-up being anterior to the misdeal.

If the dealer deals himself more cards than he has thrown out, he loses the point and the right of marking the King if he has it in his hand.

If he deals himself fewer, he completes his hand from the first cards of the talon, since they are his by right.

If he only perceives it when he has played, pone counts as tricks those cards which dealer cannot play to.

If, however, the fault is not the dealer's, as in the case where pone has asked for more or less cards than he has thrown out, then pone loses one point and the right of marking the King. But if he has too few cards he may mark it, for the simple reason that, holding the King with too few cards, he would of course have equally held it if he had asked for his proper number.

Whoever (after having changed cards) holds more than five, loses a point and the right to score the King.

ON THE PRINCIPLES

The following are the fundamental principles of this game:

As five cards are dealt to each, and one turned up, it is evident that a player, after having looked at his hand, has a knowledge of six cards, and that there remain twenty-six unknown to him, viz., twenty-one in the talon and five in his adversary's hand, making altogether thirty-two, of which number the pack is composed.

It is then on the six known and the twenty-six unknown cards that he must base his calculations.

For example: if in the six known cards there are two of the same suit turned up (or trumps) there remain six trumps in the twenty-six unknown.

Hence, if in the twenty-six unknown there are six trumps, or rather less than a quarter, it is probable that in the adversary's five cards there is, at most, but one trump, since one is also a trifle less than the quarter of five.

This principle is the basis of all; and in order to place it in a more obvious light, we have given in the following table the number of the principal combinations of twenty-six cards, calculated mathematically.

Twenty-six cards can form 65,780 combinations of five cards, or, in other words, 65,780 different hands of five cards each.

	IF IN THE SIX KNOWN CARDS						
	there is not one Club	there is one Club	there are two Clubs	there are three Clubs	there are four Clubs	there are five Clubs	there are six Clubs
The science of combinations teaches that the number of hands of five cards which will be without a Club, in the twenty-six unknown cards, is..................	8568	11628	15504	20349	26334	33649	42504
With one Club............	24480	27132	29070	29925	29260	26565	21252
With two Clubs..........	23848	20349	17100	13300	9240	5313	2024
With three Clubs........	8568	5985	3800	2100	924	253	....
With four Clubs..........	1260	665	300	105	22	....	....
With five Clubs............	56	21	6	1	....	....	....
Total....................	65780	65780	65780	65780	65780	65780	65780

To point out the method of using this table,—suppose the player has but one Club in the hand first dealt him, and that the trump card is also a Club, making *two known* Clubs, and that it is desired to ascertain what are the chances of probability which can also give two or more to the adversary.

It will be seen in the third column that of the 65,780 hands which the twenty-six unknown cards can form, there are:—

Without one Club 15,504
With one Club 29,070

Total of hands which have not two Clubs....   44,574
Hands with two Clubs 17,100
  "   "   three Clubs 3,800
  "   "   four Clubs 300
  "   "   five Clubs 6

Total of hands which have two or more Clubs   21,206

Total of hands which twenty-six cards can form   65,780

From these combinations we may draw the conclusion that a player can risk with probability of success a first hand which ought to win the point if it does not encounter two trumps in that of his adversary, since the odds are 44,574 against 21,206, or, reduced to simple terms, a little more than 2 to 1, that two Clubs will not be found in the adversary's first hand.

The Kings being superior cards, and that turned up of double importance (as the King gives one point, moreover as a trump taking any other trump), it is an interesting inquiry how many, according to the doctrine of chances, there are likely to be in the adversary's hand after the cards have been distributed to each of the players and the trump ascertained.

To resolve this question we have compiled the following table:

	IF IN THE SIX KNOWN CARDS				
	there is not one King	there is one King	there are two Kings	there are three Kings	there are four Kings
The number of hands without a King in the 26 unknown cards is	26334	33649	42504	53130	65780
With one King	29260	26565	21252	12650	....
With two Kings	9240	5313	2024	....	....
With three Kings	924	253	....	....	....
With four Kings	22	....	....	....	....
Total	65780	65780	65780	65780	65780

Hence, if there were one King in the six known cards, it would be seen in the second column that in 65,780 different hands which the adversary can have there will be 33,649, that is to say, more than half, which are without Kings, and consequently it is probable that he has no King in his hand.

This rule about Kings applies also to Queens, Jacks, etc.

This same table serves to ascertain the probability of finding the King of trumps in the adversary's hand; it is sufficient to glance down the fourth column, where it is seen that when one King only fixes the attention, there are 12,650 games that contain it, and that there are 53,130 which do not.

Consequently the odds are 53,130 against 12,650, or, in simple terms, 21 against 5, that the adversary has not the King of trumps, first hand.

It will perhaps be noticed that the first three columns of the last table are the same as the last three of the preceding table; this arises from the circumstance that when there are four, five or six Clubs known, and there consequently remain four, three or two in the twenty-six unknown cards, the case as to the probability of finding four Clubs is exactly similar to that of finding four Kings.

ON THE METHOD OF PLAYING

When a player holds three cards (including the King of trumps) which insure the point, he ought always to propose, if the two cards are not sufficiently strong to give reasonable expectation of the vole.

When pone has hopes of making the vole, and the adversary cannot answer a lead of trumps, it is better to play a King if single, and then to continue trump; because, the system of the game being to play double cards (*i.e.*, two or more of a suit), if the adversary is dubious which to retain, he will by preference keep the suit in which he was attacked. If the player is engaged with an adversary who is acquainted with this ruse, it may be still advantageous to act in a similar manner, but in an inverse sense; that is to say, equally play the King, although guarded, before continuing trump, because, imagining that it is done to induce him to keep the suit of the King already played, he will part with it more readily than any other suit.

When pone expects to make the vole, and has not trumps sufficiently strong to begin by playing them, he must be careful to keep changing his suit in order not to be ruffed, and to be able to make a trump, whatever it may be, at the fourth card after having secured the point.

When pone has made two tricks, and remains with the Queen of trumps and two small ones, knowing the King to be in the adversary's hand, he ought to lead one of the small trumps, and wait with the Queen guarded. Nothing could prevent his making the odd trick even against King twice guarded.

When there is a fear lest the adversary should make the vole, and pone has only one trump and four weak cards, without any hope of making the point, he must play his strongest single card, in order to get a chance of employing his trump in case the suit of his single card should be led up to him.

When the game is three against four, and the player who is four makes his adversary play, or plays himself without changing, the one who is at three, if he have the King, would do well not to announce it, in order to draw his antagonist into the error of leading trump to pass* his good cards, and be taken by the King which he did not expect, thus losing the point which he would perhaps have won had he known that the King was in the adversary's hand: in this case it is of less consequence for the player who is at three to announce his King and mark it, inasmuch as he gains two points, that is, the game, if he make three tricks, his adversary having played, or forced him to play, without changing.

HANDS TO BE PLAYED WITHOUT PROPOSING

These are termed *"jeux de regles."* No hand ought to be played without proposing, except when the odds are 2 to 1 that pone make three tricks, for the risk is 2 to 1 against him if he do not make them, except the cases where the adversary is at four, because as he then wants but one point to win, the risk is no longer 2 to 1, and by playing without a change the chance of giving him the King is avoided.

On this principle all *jeux de regles* are played without changing (although there are a few which can scarcely count in their favor 2 to 1).

*(Note. To *pass* a card means to lead it and make a trick with it, without its being taken by a higher of the same suit or ruffed.)

The following are *jeux de regles*: all those hands which cannot fail making three tricks, except from finding two trumps (first hand) in the adversary's hand.

Example 1.—A has one trump, no matter how small, a three-card sequence to a King, and a small card of either remaining suit; the odds are more than 2 to 1 that he wins the point (the probability is demonstrated in the first table). Begin with the King and continue the suit, if not ruffed, until you are ruffed; if it happens at the second card, your trump will bring you back to your suit and enable you to make the third trick.

Example 2.—Two trumps, a Queen with one guard, and a small card. This hand ought always to be risked by pone, although the odds are scarcely 2 to 1. If the trumps are small, begin by playing the single card, being certain, if it is taken, the adversary will not return the suit, and that he will prefer playing a King if he has one; should it be of that suit to which you hold Queen and one, you make her, later, with the two trumps, supposing he has not superior ones. But if one of the two trumps is strong, for instance, the Queen or the Jack, you must then begin with the plain Queen; because you hope, if she is ruffed, to regain the lead with one of your trumps, and then make a trick with your Jack or Queen of trumps, in order to pass the second card of the suit which has been ruffed.

Example 3.—Two trumps, a Jack and Ace of another suit, and another Jack. Begin with the guarded Jack; if it passes, and the trumps are in sequence and pretty high, risk one; if that makes, play the other, and then your Ace, etc. Generally speaking, a player ought to commence with a card which is guarded, except when he fears the vole or when he can only hope for the point by being played up to.

Example 4.—Two Kings, and. Queen with one guard. As necessarily one King is guarded, begin with this; if it makes a trick, continue the suit; should it be ruffed, the chance remains of regaining the lead through the other King, or through the Queen, and returning afterwards to the suit of the King first played.

Example 5.—One trump, a single King, and a Queen twice guarded. Commence with the Queen, if she passes, continue the suit; if she is ruffed, immediately you regain the lead, again play the suit of the Queen that has been ruffed.

Example 6.—One trump, and King with three. If your trump happens to be the Queen, play her; for the odds are 21 to 5, that is, rather more than 4 to 1, that the King is not in the adversary's hand, more than 2 to 1 that he has not two trumps, and 55,594 to 10,186, or more than 5 to 1, that he has not two cards of the suit of which you hold King and three others; but it is especially necessary when you are at three, and your adversary four, that you should not hesitate playing the hand in this manner. For in every other position probabilities which would appear only to offer favorable chances, isolated, present also the contrary when united: for, firstly, you may encounter the King of trumps and then probably lose two points; you would likewise lose if you encountered two cards of the suit of which you hold the King; and if the adversary is enabled to take, you might equally lose against an adversary who has no trump; whilst by beginning with the King you can win against an adversary who has two trumps, if, after having ruffed, he should lead trump in order to pass a King.

Example 7.—Two trumps, and three cards of a suit. This is a very strong hand, and ought always to be risked by the player. Having the lead, you commence with the highest card of your suit; if it is ruffed, your adversary must have three trumps in order to get the point.

Example 8.—All hands which require only two cards to be discarded. In this class are found those *jeux de regles* of which we have spoken, where the odds are not 2 to 1 that they will win the point; and yet they are played, because in two cards a player has much less chance of drawing advantageously than has his adversary in the five which he perhaps requires, and amongst which he may find the King; hence there are very few hands and very few cases wherein a player ought to change for two cards only.

If you play with two trumps and a King unguarded, begin with a low card and never with a King, in order to avoid getting it ruffed; but on the contrary, to be enabled to regain the lead with one trump, play the other to protect the King, and then pass it.

Holding three trumps, especially when in sequence, it is almost always the game to lead trump, no matter how inferior they may be.

There are so very few hands which can be counted more advantageously to be led up to than to lead, that we will not mention them; with such sort of hands, never refuse to change once and never accede to it a second time.

HANDS WHICH WIN OR LOSE THE POINT, ACCORDING TO THE MANNER IN WHICH PLAYED

Example.—Suppose a Club the trump. The dealer has the Ace of trumps, King and nine of Diamonds, Jack and nine of Spades. Pone has Queen of trumps, Queen of Spades, Ace of Hearts, eight and seven of Diamonds. The right game of pone is to lead his eight of Diamonds, as it is guarded by the seven; if the dealer take with the nine, he ought to lose the point, and if he take with the King,

he ought to win it; because, taking with the King, he
intimates that he has no other Diamond, and as he is certain
that the adversary led the strongest of his suit he runs
no risk in employing the ruse; then he plays his Jack of
Spades, which is also his guarded card; pone takes with
the Queen, and then leads Queen of trumps, in order to
pass his seven of Diamonds, which he imagines to be a
sure card, the eight having brought out the King, and he
loses the point; whereas if the dealer, who took with the
King, had taken with nine, pone, after having played the
Queen of trumps, would have preferred endeavoring to
pass his Ace of Hearts, which had but three cards superior
to it, rather than his seven of Diamonds, which had five,
and he would thus have gained the point.

As it is necessary to make three tricks in order to win
the point, it often happens that after having trumped once
it is advisable to lead trumps, in order to pass a King or
some high card; again, there are cases where this would
be bad play, as is demonstrated by the following example:

Suppose a Spade the trump card; pone has the Jack and
ten of trumps, the King of Clubs and the King of Diamonds
once guarded, the dealer has Queen and nine of trumps,
Jack and ten of Hearts and seven of Diamonds.

Should pone not find the King of trumps in his adversary's hand, he has a game which warrants his hoping to
make the vole; he ought then to commence by playing his
King single, in preference to his guarded King; having more
chances of escaping the ruff with it than with that which
is guarded, and of being able afterwards to win a trick with
a lead from the Jack of trumps, having only to fear the
Queen (if the dealer has not announced the King), and
endeavor to get the vole; the right play therefore is, to
commence with the King of Clubs; if the dealer trumps

it, adieu to all hopes of the vole:—there only remains to
secure the point; the dealer then leads the Jack of Hearts,
which pone takes with his ten of trumps; and *now* comes
the nicety: he loses the point if he leads Jack of trumps in
order to pass his King of Diamonds,—whereas he gains it
if he plays his King first. For if he leads his Jack of trumps,
the dealer takes it with the Queen, and makes his second
Heart, whereas, had he played his King of Diamonds, it
would have been answered with the seven;—he plays Diamonds again—the ten,—the adversary is obliged to trump
with Queen and then play his ten of Hearts, which pone
takes by ruffing it with the Jack of trumps, thus making
the third trick.

We have given one reason why it was preferable to play
the King of Clubs rather than that which was guarded;
we may add another which confirms the rule that a single
King ought to be played first; which is, that if the adversary, with two Diamonds to the Queen and two Clubs
to the Queen, has any hesitation which suit to keep, he will
prefer keeping the Queen of Clubs, which is his suit first
attacked, to keeping the Queen of Diamonds.

Final Example.—Be particular to hold your cards well
up, so that none can see them but yourself, for fear of any
indiscreet exclamations on the part of onlookers,—as the
following *coup* is not so easy that it can be learned by every
player. The object is to win the point with a hand which
would infallibly lose if it were played naturally, that is
to say, without *finesse*.

Suppose a Heart the trump. Pone has the King, Ace and
ten of trumps, the King of Diamonds and the King of
Spades. The dealer has the Queen, Jack and seven of
trumps, the eight and seven of Clubs. Pone would feel
almost sure of making the vole if to his King of trumps,

with which he ought to open the game, he sees fall the
Queen; and yet this would cause him to lose the point,
if the dealer is sufficiently adroit to throw her away, instead
of the seven, on the King; because pone would then continue leading trumps, by playing his Ace, and the dealer
would take it with his Jack, and then play his eight of
Clubs, which pone would ruff with his ten of trumps and
play one of his Kings; the dealer would ruff this with his
seven of trumps, and then pass his second Club; pone, having no more trumps to ruff with, loses the point; whereas
had the dealer thrown the seven instead of the Queen of
trumps on the King, pone, fearful of meeting the Queen
and Jack of trumps accompanied by Clubs, would not have
continued leading trumps, but played one of his Kings, and
would necessarily have won the point.

POOL ECARTE

Pool Ecarté is played by three, each player putting up a
certain number of counters for pool. The players cut, and
the highest two play as in the regular game. The loser of
the first game puts as many counters into the pool as he
put up originally and drops out in favor of the odd player
(called *rentrant*). This continues until one player wins
two successive games, when he takes the pool. A new
pool is then made up and played. Odd player must not
advise either player on first hand of any pool, but after
that he may, as he then has an interest in the pool.

CRIBBAGE

Cribbage is a game played by two persons with a complete pack of 52 cards, which rank from King (high) to

Ace (low). We shall commence by treating of the five-card game, which, besides being the parent stem, affords the greatest scope for the exercise of skill. Sixty-one points constitute the game. These points are scored on a Cribbage board, of which a representation is appended. It has, as will be seen, four rows of holes, 30 holes to a row and one extra hole at each end between the double rows (called *home* or *game* holes).

The board is placed between the players. It is a matter of indifference how the end of the board from which you commence is placed; but both players commence at the same end, each beginning at an outside edge (A or B) and passing along it to the top, then down the inside row to game. To mark the game, each player has two pegs; if the first score be two, stick a peg in the second hole, and when next it becomes your turn to mark, place the second peg in the number that gives the points you have to mark, counting from your first peg. When you have to mark a third score, take out the back peg, and reckon from the foremost, which must never be disturbed during the progress of the game, the scores being invariably marked by the hindmost peg of the two. Thus, the foremost peg always keeping its hole, the players can detect the amount that is marked, and check each other's score. To avoid confusion it is usual for the pegs of each player to be of different colors, although the one player never in any way touches his adversary's half of the board. If a Cribbage board is not available, each player may use a piece of paper or cardboard marked thus:

Units	1	2	3	4	5	6	7	8	9	10
Tens	1		2		3		4		5	6

Two small markers are used for counting in each row. If 121 points are played to a game, the lower row may be continued to 12.

All the Kings, Queens, Jacks and tens count ten each; the rest of the cards according to their numerical value. The points which count for the game are made by fifteens, sequences, flushes, pairs, etc. The board being duly prepared, the players cut for the deal, the highest card winning the cut. If you play games, you must cut at the termination of each; not so when playing rubbers. The opponent of the dealer then shuffles the pack, the dealer being entitled to do so the last.

The first move is the marking of three holes, by the player who loses the deal, as a recompense for the adversary's advantage. Five cards are then dealt with the faces downward, one at a time to each player, the rest of the pack being placed face downward on the table. The players then gather up their cards, and, each having taken out two, they are placed by themselves on the table, with the faces down. These four cards are what is called the "crib," which becomes the property of the dealer. Each player having put out his two crib cards, which of course have not been seen by his adversary, pone cuts the remainder of the pack, and the dealer turns up the top card.

The game commences by pone leading and announcing the nature of his card. Suppose it is a King, he calls "ten"; the dealer, replying with an "eight," cries "eighteen," as the amount of the ten and eight. His opponent plays again, and announces the increased aggregate, and thus the play proceeds till the whole amount reaches exactly thirty-one, or as near it, without exceeding, as can possibly be accomplished by the cards in either hand. He who makes up thirty-one scores two or he who comes nearest to it that the cards permit, scores one; the remaining cards in hand, if any, are thrown up.

The better to convey a view of a hand in process of being played, let us suppose the pone plays a three, and calls "three"; the dealer then puts on a "ten" card, and cries "thirteen," upon this pone plays another "ten" card, and exclaims "twenty-three"; dealer rejoins with a five, and proclaims the total, "twenty-eight." Pone, finding his third or last card will not come within the prescribed limits of thirty-one, declares his inability to play by the word "go." Should the dealer also be unable to play under thirty-one, he scores one for the go and one for the last play and the remaining cards are thrown down. If dealer's remaining card is an Ace or Deuce, he plays it and scores the same two points, while if his last card is a three, he plays it making thirty-one and scores two points for making thirty-one.

The points which each player has made during the playing out of the hand, having been all scored at the time they were gained, and the deal being finished, each player now counts his hand, and marks that number of points towards game to which he is entitled. Pone counts first; and, having marked his gains, if any, on the board, the dealer in his turn counts—first, his hand, and then his crib, for the crib belongs to the dealer.

Another deal then takes place, and is conducted in a similar manner; and so on, until either one of the players has completed the required number of sixty-one, when he is

6

proclaimed the victor, and the game is finished.

WHAT YOU MARK AT CRIBBAGE

Points in *play* can only be made in the following ways:

By fifteens; by sequences; by pairs; by pairs-royal; by double pairs-royal; by the Jack being turned up; by making thirty-one, or the nearest number to it.

Points on counting the hand and crib, after the hand is played out, are made in the following ways:

By fifteens; by sequences; by flushes; by pairs; by pairs-royal; by double pairs-royal, and by the Jack being of the same suit as the card turned up.

Fifteens.—As often as you make the number fifteen in playing, you score two. ·The leader, for instance, plays an eight, you put a seven down, cry "fifteen," and straightway you score two points. The result is the same whenever you make fifteen, whether in one or more leads or rounds. The hand being played, you now set about summing it up, taking two points for every fifteen you can make by means of counting the cards together. The turn-up, or "start" card, is common property, and available to both players in computing their hands, and to crib also. All this is wholly without reference to anything that occurred while the hands were being played; and by whatever combination fifteen can be made out of the cards as above enumerated, two points are added to the score. Should you hold King, Jack and a five, you count two fifteens; should a "ten" card turn up, you score three "twos," that is to say, a third for the combination of your five with such "ten" card; and if, instead of being a "ten" card, the turn-up should be a five, you count eight, having four fifteens on the cards. The dealer calculates the crib for fifteens, in the same manner that he does his hand, and uses the turn-up with both, that is separately; he cannot combine his hand with his crib.

Thirty-one.—Every time you make this amount in the course of the game you score two.

End-hole.—If neither player makes exactly thirty-one, he who plays the card that makes the nearest number to it, without exceeding it, scores one; this is "one for the go."

Pair or Pairs.—Every pair made in the play or the hand counts two points. To pair is to play a card of the same denomination. If a "ten" card be played, and you can play a similar "ten" card next, without exceeding thirty-one, it is a pair, and counts two. But in these pairs all "ten" cards do not count alike. It must be King for King, Queen for Queen, and so forth. At the end of the deal you take the turn-up card to assist you in pairing, and count two for each pair made by its assistance.

Pair-Royal, or Proil.—This consists of three cards of a kind, held either in the hand or crib, or occurring in the course of the game, as three Kings, three Aces, three nines, etc. It scores six. Thus, if the leader play a six, you put another six down and score two for the pair; he then returns a six, makes a pair-royal, and counts six points. If you have a pair-royal in your hand or your crib, you also score six for it; and should you only hold a pair, and turn up the third, it reckons also for six. It is needless to say these combinations do not count for points when other cards have been played between them.

Double Pair-Royal.—Four cards of a kind make this combination, for which the score is twelve, alike whether made in play or in the hand or in the crib. The turn-up card reckons with hand and crib in this as in every other case. Moreover, should your opponent have made a pair-royal, by playing a third of a kind, you are entitled to the double pair-royal if you answer him with a fourth.

In taking six for a pair-royal, or twelve for a double

pair-royal, you are not to suppose that the six and the twelve are merely increased numbers, bestowed as premiums for such combinations of the cards, and settled by arbitrary arrangement, independent of the rule that two points are allowed for every pair. A pair counts two, and the same principle, applied to a pair-royal, produces six; because, as a pair-royal contains three distinct pairs you score two for each pair. Place, for instance, three sixes in a row on the table, and mark them 1, 2 and 3, thus:

1	2	3
Six	Six	Six

Here Nos. 1 and 2 form the first pair, Nos. 1 and 3 the second pair, and Nos. 2 and 3 the third pair, without the same two cards having ever been counted more than once together.

Having analyzed this example, there will be little difficulty in ascertaining the number of pairs to be found by taking a double pair-royal. The readiest way to attain demonstration is to place the four sixes in a row on the table, as you did the three sixes, and number them 1, 2, 3 and 4, thus:

1	2	3	4
Six	Six	Six	Six

Nos. 1 and 2 taken together form a pair,
and yield two points 2
— 1 and 3 form the second pair, and give
two more 2
— 1 and 4 form the third pair 2
— 2 and 3 form the fourth pair 2
— 2 and 4 form the fifth pair 2
— 3 and 4 form the sixth pair 2

Total.................. 12

Thus we have six distinct pairs in a double pair-royal, which, of course, are thereby entitled to twelve points. Observe, that in making these points, although we reckon the cards over and over again, they always unite in different associations, and the same two cards are never counted twice together.

Sequences.—These consist of three or more cards following in successive order, whether of the same suit or otherwise. He who holds them scores one point for every card in the combination, whether it take place in playing or in counting the hand or crib. But there cannot be a sequence under three cards. As in certain other cases, the face cards, King, Queen and Jack, rank in sequence after their usual classification as to rank, and not all alike as "ten" cards. To form a sequence in play, it matters not which of the cards is played first or last, provided the sequence can be produced by a transposition of the order in which they fell. Thus you lead the five of hearts, your adversary returns the three of Diamonds, you then play the four of any suit, and score three for the sequence; he then plays six, and makes four, and so on, as long as the continuous sequence can be made.

In counting your sequences at the close of the deal, you use the card turned up along with your hand and crib, and count them every way possible. A single example of this will here suffice:

Suppose the crib to consist of two Kings (Clubs and Diamonds), and two Queens (Hearts and Spades), the Jack of Spades being the card turned up—how many can you take for sequences?

Twelve, being four sequences of three each; to be computed by counting the Jack with the Kings and Queens, ringing the changes on the latter somewhat in a similar manner to the mode in which you formed a double pair-royal. To simplify this, take the Jack, the two Queens, and the two Kings, and spread them before you; when they will count thus:

Jack with Queen of Hearts and King of Clubs 3
Jack with Queen of Spades and King of Clubs 3
Jack with Queen of Hearts and King of Dia-
    monds 3
Jack with Queen of Spades and King of Dia-
    monds 3
                                                                    —
Points for the four sequences............................ 12

The Jack.—If you hold a Jack of the same suit as the card turned up you are entitled to one point, which you take on counting your hand. Should there be, in the crib, the Jack of the suit turned up, the dealer, to whom the crib belongs, takes one point on counting his crib. In the euphonious phraseology of some Cribbage players, this is termed "one for his nob."

Should the turn-up card itself be a Jack, the dealer immediately scores two points, which, by way of antithesis with "his nob," is called "two for his heels."

A Flush.—A flush cannot happen in play, but occurs only in computing the hand or crib. A flush is when four or more cards in hand, or crib, are of the same suit, in which case you are allowed to score one point for every card of which the flush is composed. Thus, if your hand comprise four Hearts, you will take, on scoring for your hand, four for the flush in Hearts; and should the turn-up card chance to be also a Heart, you will add another point for that, making five. You are not permitted, however, to reckon a flush in the crib unless the cards of which the crib is composed are of the same suit as the card turned up. It is essential to recollect the difference between a flush in the hand and a flush in the crib.

In counting the hand and crib after the deal, pone counts first. It will facilitate your counting if you sum up the points to which you are entitled in the following order: fifteens; sequences; flushes; pairs, pairs-royal or double pairs-royal; the point for the Jack. Counting the hand or crib is technicaly termed "showing." Thus pone is said to have "the first show," a point of immense importance at the final stage of the game; since he may thus be enabled just to "show out," and consequently win the game, while the dealer may hold in his hand and crib points enough to make him more than out, but altogether useless, since he has not the first show.

Pone having summed up his score, under the observation of his opponent, the latter then performs the same operation as to his own hand. He then turns up crib, and scores all to which it may entitle him.

THE LAWS OF CRIBBAGE

1. In single games there must be a fresh cut for each game; but not so when rubbers are played. The highest card wins the cut; when both players cut alike, it is a tie and there must be another cut.

2. In cutting for the deal, not less than four cards should be removed, and not more than half the pack, that a fair and proper cut may remain for him who cuts last.

3. The cards are to be dealt out one by one, and they must not be touched till the deal has been completed.

4. The dealer may expose his own cards in dealing, but if he shows one of his adversary's the latter scores two points and may demand a new deal, provided he does so before turning his cards. When a faced card occurs in

dealing there must be a new deal, including all the formalities of cutting, shuffling, etc.

5. If the dealer misdeals without being aware of it till one of the hands has been taken up, the opponent may score two, and the cards must be dealt over again. Should his adversary expose a card during the progress of the deal, the dealer may deal over again if he pleases, provided he has not seen his hand.

6. Though both players have the privilege of shuffling the pack previous to the cards being dealt, the dealer has the right to do so last.

7. Should the dealer give his adversary more than five cards, pone may mark two points, and there must be a new deal; but in such a case pone must discover the error before he takes up his cards, or he cannot claim the two, though there must still be a new deal. Should the dealer, in dealing, give himself more than five cards, his adversary may mark two points, and either call a new deal or draw the extra card or cards from the hand of his opponent. Should the dealer give to either player less than five cards there must be a new deal; and should the dealer deal two cards at once to either player, there must be a new deal, unless his adversary consents to his withdrawing the surplus card, in which case it must be placed on the top of the pack.

8. Should either player find that his adversary has more than five cards in his hand, he can claim two points and a new deal.

9. Should the pack being dealt from be touched previous to being cut for the "start," the player so offending forfeits two points.

10. In cutting for the start pone must remove at least three cards and leave not less than four behind.

11. Should the dealer turn up a Jack, and neglect scoring

the two points for such Jack until he has played his first card, he cannot take the two points. (He is, however, in time to take the two points after his adversary has played his first card; a distinction of some consequence.)

12. Pone must discard for the crib first. A card once so laid out cannot be taken up again. Either player confusing his cards with the crib forfeits two points, and his opponent may claim a new deal. The dealer alone is entitled to touch the crib, but he may not do so until he takes it up to count it.

13. He who takes more points than he is entitled to, when counting his hand or crib, or scoring for a penalty, may be put back as many points as he has over-scored, and then his adversary may add the same amount to his own score.

14. No penalty attaches to a neglect of scoring points to which the player is entitled.

15. One player cannot demand of another his aid to make out a score. Suppose K to say to L, "Am I not twelve?"—L replies properly enough, "I shall neither tell you, nor shall I pass my opinion on the subject. If you take more than you ought, I shall take you down."

16. If one player touches the pegs of his adversary, save to correct an error of the score, he shall forfeit two points. If a player touches his own pegs, save when he has a right to score, he forfeits two points. When both pegs have been displaced by accident, the opposite player must be allowed to restore them to their places; or in the event of being refused, he can claim the game. When the foremost peg has been displaced by any chance, it must be put into the hole behind the back peg of the player to whom it belongs.

17. He who scores, as won, a game that he has not won, forfeits it.

18. A player who detects his adversary with more or

fewer cards in his hand than he has a right to can score two points and call a new deal.

19. When the "lurch" has been agreed to between the players at the commencement of a game, it counts as a double game; it consists in one player having marked sixty-one before the other has scored thirty-one.

20. When scoring points, if the pegs are quitted, that score cannot be altered. If two cards are played, and any points remain uncounted, they become forfeited. Should a player put his cards away without pegging for them, he forfeits any points he might have claimed for hand or crib.

21. When a card that may legally be played has been shown, it cannot be recalled. If it cannot be played according to the laws of the game, no penalty attaches to the exposure.

22. If a player neglects to play, when he can come in under thirty-one, his opponent may score two.

23. In counting a hand or crib, it must be plainly set out, and remain till the other side fully understands the nature of the claim made on account of it.

24. There is no penalty for a number called in mistake in the progress of the game.

25. The three points given pone may be claimed by him during any part of the game; but if his adversary be permitted to score his sixty-one points, it is then too late, for the game is at an end.

26. If either player refuses to pay a penalty that he has incurred by infringing the rules of play, his adversary may claim the game.

27. Bystanders shall not in any way interfere with the progress of the game.

ON DISCARDING FOR THE CRIB

How to discard in the best manner for the crib is one

of the most scientific parts of the game and consequently one of the most important.

When pone is discarding for dealer's crib he should lay out such cards as are likely to be of the least possible advantage in the production of scoring combinations, but when dealer is discarding to his own crib he should lay out good cards favoring the interests of his crib, even in preference to those of his own hand.

The five is the most useful card, since it makes fifteen equally with any one of the "ten" cards, of which there are sixteen in the pack. Fives must therefore be in general the most desirable cards to lay out to your own crib, and the least desirable (for you) to lay out to your adversary. To discard a pair of any cards, again, is mostly bad play, unless it is for your own crib; and cards which follow each other in order, as a three and four, or nine and ten, being likely to be brought in for sequences, are generally bad cards to lay out in the case of its being your adversary's crib. Suppose you discard, to your opponent's crib, two Hearts, when you might with equal propriety have laid out a Heart and a Club instead—you here give him the chance, however remote you may fancy it, of making a flush in his crib, which could not be effected by him had you laid out the Heart and Club.

To lay out cards, purposely, which are disadvantageous for the crib, is called in the "Cribbage dialect" of our ancestors "balking" or "bilking" the crib.

The least likely cards to count for points in the crib, and therefore generally the best to discard for your adversary, are Kings; since a sequence can only be made up to or, as it may be termed, on one side of them, and cannot be carried beyond them. A King is therefore a greater balk in the crib than the Queen. So, again of an Ace—a sequence can only be made from it, and not up to it; and an Ace is, therefore, frequently a great balk to a crib; though in discarding an Ace some judgment is required to be exercised, being often a good card to hold for play and forming a component part of fifteen, particularly when combined with sixes, sevens and eights, or with fours and "ten" cards.

The cards, then, best adapted to balk an antagonist's crib are: a King with a ten, nine, eight, seven, six or Ace; a Queen with a nine, eight, seven, six or Ace, or cards equally distinct, or far off, and therefore certain not to be united in sequence by meeting with any other cards whatever. Of course, particular hands require particular play, and general principles must give way before exceptions. "Circumstances alter cases."

Never lay out a Jack for your adversary's crib, if you can avoid it; as the probability of the turn-up card being of the same suit as the Jack is 3 to 1 against it. Consequently, it is only 3 to 1 but the retaining of such Jack in your hand gains you a point, whereas, should you discard it to your opponent's crib, it is only 3 to 1 against the chance of its making him a point; hence the probable difference of losing a point by throwing out your Jack is only 3 to 2⅓ or 9 to 7,—that is to say, in laying out a Jack for your antagonist's crib—sixteen times—you give away just seven points, it being only 9 to 7 but you give away a point every time you play in this manner, and every single point is of consequence if contending against a good player. There may, of course, occur exceptions to this and every other rule.

The cards which are usually the best to lay out for your own crib are two fives, five and six, five and a "ten" card, three and two, seven and eight, four and one, nine and six, and similar couples. If you have no similar cards to lay out, put down as close cards as you can, because by this means you have the greater chance of either being assisted by the cards laid out by your adversary or by the turn-up; and further, you should uniformly lay out two cards of the same suit for our own crib, in preference, other things being equal, to two other cards of the same kind that are of different suits, as this gives you the probable chance of flushing your crib; whereas, should you lay out two cards of different suits, all gain under the head of a flush is at once destroyed. It is usually good play to retain a sequence in hand, in preference to cards less closely connected, more especially should such sequence be a flush. Since the probable chance of points from the crib is about twenty per cent over the hand, it is your best play to favor your crib at the expense of your hand.

In general, whenever you are able to hold a pair-royal in hand, you should lay out the other two cards, both for your own and your adversary's crib; some few cases, however, excepted. For example, should you hold a pair-royal of any description, along with two fives, it would be highly dangerous to give your antagonist the brace of fives, unless in such a situation of the game that your pair-royal would put you out, having the first show, or else that your adversary is so nearly home himself that the contents of the crib are wholly unimportant. Many other cards are very hazardous to lay out to your adversary's crib, even though you may hold a pair-royal; such as two and three, five and six, seven and eight, and five and a "ten" card; therefore should you have such cards combined together, you must pay particular regard to the stage of the game. This caution equally applies to many other cards, and particularly when, the game being nearly over, it happens to be your own deal, and that your opponent is nearly home, or within a moderate show-out. Here special care should be taken to retain in hand cards which may enable you to play "off," or wide of your adversary, and thus prevent his forming any sequence or pair-royal in the play of the cards. In similar positions you should endeavor, also, to keep cards that will enable you to have a good chance of winning the end-hole, which frequently saves a game.

GENERAL DIRECTIONS FOR PLAYING THE GAME SCIENTIFICALLY

To gain the end-hole, or point nearest to thirty-one, is, among professed players, justly esteemed a considerable advantage, and should be proportionately kept in view. By attaining the end-hole yourself you not only score a point, but save a difference of two points by snatching it from your opponent. In playing for this there is much scope for judgment.

Should you hold a three and a two, it is frequently the best play to lead off the three, on the chance of your adversary's playing a "ten" card (of which never forget that there are sixteen), making thirteen, when your two "drops in," and produces two points for the fifteen. The same principle applies to the leading from a four and an Ace, and has this additional advantage, that should you thus succeed in forming fifteen, your opponent can form no sequence from your cards.

Remember that when your adversary leads a seven or eight, should you make fifteen, you give him a chance of coming in with a six or a nine, and thus gaining three holes against you. Sometimes this would even tend to your advantage, by allowing of your rejoinder with a fourth card in sequence. For instance, your opponent leads an eight, and you make fifteen by playing a seven; he plays a six, making twenty-one, and scores three for the sequence; but having a nine, you play it, and score four for a sequence or, having a ten, you score two for 31. In all such cases, play to the state of the game; for what would be at one time correct would be, at another, the worst possible play.

To lead from a pair is usually good; because, should your opponent pair you, you form a pair-royal, making six holes: while the chance of his rejoining with a fourth is too small to be taken into consideration. It would rarely, though, be correct to lead from a pair of fives.

When your adversary leads a card which you can pair it is usually better to make fifteen, in preference, should you be able to, as you will naturally suspect he wishes you to pair him, in order to make a pair-royal himself. But here, as elsewhere, your chief guide is the relative state of the scores.

When you can possibly help it, do not, in play, make the number twenty-one; for your antagonist is then likely to come in with a "ten" card.

Should you hold a nine and three, it is good play to lead the three; because, should it be paired, you form fifteen by playing the nine. The same applies to the holding of a four and a seven, in which case, should your four be paired, you make fifteen with the seven.

The following style of play facilitates your obtaining frequently the end-hole: Should you hold two low cards and one high card, lead from the former; but should you hold one low card and two high cards, lead from the latter. Like other general directions, all this is subject to contingencies.

Holding a ten and five, and two holes being at the moment an object of great importance, lead the "ten" card, in hopes of your adversary's making fifteen, when you can pair his five.

When compelled to lead from a sequence of three cards, play the lowest or highest, in preference to the middle card.
In laying out your own crib, if you hold a pair of fives, and no "ten" card, discard them both. Bear in mind that of all the "ten" cards the Jack is of the most importance and that those cards which tell best in counting the hand are not always the best for playing.

If in play you throw down a four, making the number twenty-seven, your adversary has the chance of pairing your four and of making at the same time thirty-one. If you make twenty-eight with a three, you incur the same risk. These apparent trifles must be studied, and you should be constantly on the watch to grasp them for yourself, should your antagonist leave an opening.

As the dealer plays last, his chances are greater than those of the leader for making the end-hole. The dealer has also in his favor the chance of gaining the two points by lifting a Jack.

The phrase "playing off" is used to denote playing cards which are wide apart, in contradistinction to its reverse, termed "playing on." Thus, should your opponent lead a four, and you answer with a two, three, five or six, you "play on"; because you give him the option of making a sequence, should he hold the fitting card. But if, in answer to his four, you play a high card, you "play off," since he can have no card capable of forming a sequence. Whether to play "off" or "on" is half the battle, and depends entirely, should you hold the option, on the relative state of the scores.

It is frequently your game to allow your adversary to form a sequence, in order to come in yourself for a longer one. To tempt him to this, play a card close to his, instead of playing off. Suppose you hold a three, four and five, and your opponent leads a seven; in this case, should it be to your interest to bestow a certain number of points in order to realize the same amount for yourself, you play the five; for if he answers with a six, marking three, you play your four, and score four.

ODDS OF THE GAME

The chances of points in a hand are calculated at more than 4 and under 5; and those to be gained in play are reckoned 2 to the dealer and 1 to the adversary, making in all about 6, on the average, throughout the game; and the probability of those in the crib are estimated at 5; so that each player ought to make 16 in two deals, and onward in the same proportion to the end of the game; by which it appears that the first dealer has rather the advantage, supposing the cards to run equal and the players to be likewise equally matched in skill. By attending to the above calculation any player may judge whether he is at home or not, and thereby play his game accordingly, either by making a push when he is behind and holds good cards, or by endeavoring to balk the opponent when his hand proves indifferent.

SIX-CARD CRIBBAGE

This game is also played with the whole pack, but both in skill and scientific arrangement it is vastly inferior to that played with five cards. Still it is a pleasant resource in a dull hour, and abounds with amusing points and combinations, without taxing the mind much. It is played on the same board, and according to the principal portion of the rules of the preceding game. Its leading peculiarities may be thus summed up.

The dealer gives six cards to each player. Two of these are laid out for the crib, and four retained for the hand. The deal and the "start" card are the same as at the five-card game; also it has the same scoring combinations. The game is 61 or 121. Pone, however, is not allowed any points at the beginning. At the six-card game, the cards are not thrown down after reaching 31 but are all played out, beginning at one again, giving more chance for points from "go," and the last card played scores a point unless it makes 31.

As all the cards must be played out, should one party have exhausted his hand, and his adversary have yet two cards, the latter are to be played, and should they yield any advantage, it must be taken. For instance, C has played out his four cards, and D, having two left (an eight and seven), calls fifteen as he throws them down, and marks three points; two for the fifteen, and one for the last card. Again, should D's two cards have been a pair (threes for instance), he marks two for the pair and a third point for the last card. Speculating on this and other probabilities, you will always endeavor, when you are last player, to retain as close cards as possible, for this will frequently enable you to make three or four points by playing your last two cards, when you would otherwise make but a single point. But this demands further illustration as it is of paramount importance. For example:

Suppose you hold for the last two cards a seven and eight, and that your adversary has only one card remaining in his hand, the probable chance of its being either a six or a nine (in either of which cases you come in for four points) is eleven to two; therefore it is only eleven to two but you gain three points by this play, exclusive of the end-hole; whereas, were you to retain as your last two cards a seven with a ten, or any two cards similarly wide apart, you have no chance to score more for them than the end-hole, as there is no probability of their coming in for any sequence; or if you can retain a pair of any kind for the last two cards (your adversary having only one card, and he being the first player), you by this means make a certainty of two points, exclusive of the end-hole. Again, if dealer makes 28 with his second card and pone says "go," and dealer's two remaining cards are a two and an Ace, he would play the two calling "30," when pone would have to say "go" again and dealer's Ace will be played for 31. This gives him 4 points, one each for the two "go's" and two for the 31.

The calculations for discarding at the five-card game are, for the most part, applicable to this. Still there is not quite so much temptation to sacrifice the hand for the sake of the crib, as they now both contain the same number of cards. At this game the hand scores more than the crib, as there is one player always on the lookout to balk crib, while so many points being open to the play offers a greater inducement to keep together a good hand. As soon as thirty-one, or the number nearest to it, is made in playing the hand, the cards should be turned down, that no confusion may come of their being mixed with the succeeding cards, and the remaining cards played beginning at one again.

As before explained, in speaking of Five-card Cribbage, your mode of conduct must be governed uniformly by the state of your game. Play to your score and put the final result partially out of view. Whether it is your policy to play "on" or "off" must be ever the question in making up your judgment.

On an average, a hand ought to yield about seven, and a crib five points. It is useful to remember this in discarding, and to note the difference between the odds of seven to five in favor of the hand here and the superiority of the crib to the hand at Five-card Cribbage.

The average number of points to be made each time by play is from four to five. The dealer has the advantage here because he plays last. Pasquin considered that you were only entitled to twenty-five points for three shows and play, and that the dealer is at home if, when he makes his second deal, he is twenty-five points up the board, or, when he deals for the third time, within eleven holes of the game. The present system of calculation is to allow twenty-nine instead of twenty-five holes for the three shows, and to consider that at the end of the second round each player is at home at twenty-nine holes.

As you are on a parity at starting, being both at home, you will play with moderate caution your first hand, taking fair risks, but not running into wide speculations. On taking up your second hand, you will adapt your play to the relative scores and will play "on" or "off" according to the dictates of policy. The same rule will govern your conduct during the remainder of the game; and should your adversary have gained the preference, or should you be more than home, both cases must be taken into consideration in playing your hand. If your cards present a flattering prospect, and you are by no means home, it is your duty to make a push, in order to regain the lead by running; whereas, should your adversary be better planted than you, and should you take up bad cards, it will be the best play to keep off and only endeavor to stop your antagonist as much as possible, and thereby have a probable chance of winning the game through his not being able to make his points.

As so many points are to be gained in play by the formation of long sequences you will frequently find it advantageous, having eligible cards for the purpose in view, to lead or play so as to tempt your adversary to form a short sequence, in order that you may come for a longer. This opportunity is particularly to be sought for when a few holes are essential to your game, though gained at any risk. If you hold, as leader, a one, two, three and four, the best card to lead is the four, since, if paired, you answer with the Ace, and your adversary's second card may not form a fifteen.

THREE-HAND CRIBBAGE

The game of Three-hand Cribbage is not often played. The board is of a triangular shape, to contain three sets of holes of sixty each, with the sixty-first or game hole. Each of the three players is furnished separately with pegs, and scores his game in the usual manner.

Three-hand Cribbage is subject to the same laws as the other species of the game. The calculations as to discarding and playing are very similar, but it must be remembered that, as all three are independent, and fight for themselves alone, you have two antagonists instead of one.

Five cards compose the deal. They are delivered separately, and after dealing the fifteenth, another, or sixteenth, card is dealt from the pack to constitute the foundation of the crib. To this each of the three players adds one card, and the crib therefore consists of four cards, while each individual remains with four cards in hand. The deal and crib are originally cut for, and afterwards pass alternately.

It is obvious that you will be even, if you gain only one game out of three, since the winner receives a double stake, which is furnished by the two losers to him who first attains the sixty-first hole. It has been computed that he who has the second deal has rather the best chance of victory, but there seems very little difference.

Occasionally, at this game, some amusement arises from the complicated sequences formed in play, but ordinarily it is a poor-enough affair. It will frequently happen that one of the three players runs ahead of the two others so fast that it becomes their interest to form a temporary league of union against him. In this case they will strive all they can to favor each other and regain the lost ground; and in general players will do well not to lose sight of this principle, but to prefer favoring the more backward of the adversaries to giving the chance of a single point to the other.

FOUR-HAND CRIBBAGE

The game of Four-hand Cribbage is played by four persons, in partnership of two and two, each sitting opposite to his partner. Rubbers or single games are played as desired. Sixty-one generally constitutes the game, but it is not unusual to agree, in preference, to go twice round the board, making the number of game 121.

At the commencement of the sitting it is decided which two of the four players shall have the management of the score, and the board is placed between them. The other two are not allowed to touch the board or pegs, though each may prompt his partner and point out any omissions or irregularities he may discover in the computation. The laws which govern Five-card Cribbage are equally applicable here as to the mode of marking holes, deficiencies in the counting, the taking of too many points, etc. He who marks has a troublesome task, arising from the constant vigilance requisite to be exercised in order not to omit scoring points made by his partner; his own gains he seldom forgets to take. He who does not mark should acquire the habit of seeing that his partner marks the full number he requires. Partners may assist each other in counting their hands or cribs, their interests being so completely identified.

It is most usual to play rubbers, and to cut for partners every rubber. The highest two and lowest two play together. The Ace is always lowest.

The deal and crib pass alternately round the table from right to left. The usual laws of Cribbage regulate the act of dealing, as to exposing cards, and so forth; and no one is suffered to touch his hand until the deal is complete. Before dealing, the cards must be cut in the ordinary way by your right-hand antagonist.

The dealer delivers five cards to each, in the usual mode, from right to left, one card at a time. The remainder of the pack he places on his left hand. Each person then lays out one card for the crib, which is the property of the dealer. The left-hand adversary must discard first, and so round the table, the dealer laying out last. There is no advantage in this, but such is the custom.

As there is but one card to be laid out from the five received by each player, there is seldom much difficulty in making up your choice. Fives are the best cards to give your own crib, and you will never, therefore, give them to your antagonists. Low cards are generally best for the crib, and Kings or Aces the worst. Aces sometimes tell to great advantage in the play at this game. When your partner has to deal, the crib, being equally your own as if you had it in your proper possession, must be favored in the same way. Before discarding, always consider with whom the deal stands.

When all have discarded for the crib, the pack is cut for the start-card. This cut is made by your left-hand adversary's lifting the pack, when you, as dealer, take off the

top card. Observe that it is the left-hand adversary who
cuts this time, whereas, in cutting the cards to you at the
commencement of the deal, it is your right-hand adversary
who performs the operation.

Having thus cut the turn-up card, the player on the left
hand of the dealer leads first, the player to his left following, and so on round the table, till the whole of the sixteen
cards are played out. Fifteens, sequences, pairs, etc., count
in the usual way for those who obtain them. Should either
player be unable to come in under thirty-one, he declares
it to be "a go," and the right of play devolves on his left-
hand neighbor. No small cards must be kept up which
would come in, under a penalty. Thus should A play an Ace,
making the number twenty-eight, and should each of the
other three pass it without playing, not having cards low
enough to come in, on its coming round to A he must play
if he can under thirty-one.

Example:

B plays an Ace and makes thirty. Neither of the other
three can come in, and, on the turn to play coming round
again to B, he plays another Ace, and marks four points,
two for the pair of Aces, and two for the thirty-one.

Many similar examples might be adduced, and there frequently arise difficult and complicated cases of sequences
made this way out of low cards. Indeed, the playing out
of the hand requires constant watchfulness on all sides,
much more so than in Six-card Cribbage. So many points
are made by play in Four-hand Cribbage that it is essential
to play as much as possible to the points or stages of the
game, sufficient data respecting which will be presently
given.

In leading, great care is necessary, not only at first
starting, but after every "rest," or thirty-one. A five is a

bad lead, because the chances of a ten succeeding it are so numerous; and an Ace is seldom a good lead, since, should the second player play what is highly probable, a "ten" card, your partner cannot pair him without making the ominous number of twenty-one, a number equally bad at every description of Cribbage, since the next player has thus so good a chance of converting it, by another "ten" card, into thirty-one. A nine, again, is a bad lead, for should your left-hand adversary make fifteen with a six, he cannot be paired by your partner without making twenty-one. Bear this constantly in mind, and when possible to avoid it by equally good play, never either make the number twenty-one yourself nor lead so as to compel your partner to do so. Threes or fours form safe leads.

The second player will observe caution in pairing a card so as not to give away the chance of six for a paltry couple, unless, from some collateral reasons, he may consider it a safe pair, as in the case of the turn-up's being a similar card, his holding a third of the same in his hand, having seen one of the same already dropped, and so on. The same care must be shown in not playing closely on, unless compelled by the cards. Suppose your right-hand adversary leads a three, it is obvious that, if you reply with two or four, you give your left-hand antagonist a good chance of forming a sequence, which he could not do had you played off. On the other hand, there frequently arise cases in which you feel justified in playing "on," purposely to tempt your adversary to form the sequence, in order to give your partner the chance of coming in for a still longer one. In many situations a few holes may be of paramount value, gained at any risk. If the second player can make fifteen, it is generally better play than pairing the card led. Towards the end of the game it is sometimes important to retain cards all wide apart, when the object is merely to prevent your antagonist from making points in play; but as you only discard one card, you have little chance of assorting your hand as you could wish.

The third player should aim at making the number below twenty-one, in order to give his partner a good chance of gaining the end-hole for the "go," or the two for thirty-one.

The dealer, knowing he will have to play last the first round, will sometimes find it advantageous to hold Aces, or low cards, for the purpose, particularly when it is essential to score a few holes in play or when the only chance of game arises from the possibility of playing out. If holding Aces, it is frequently better play, when you have the option, to make twenty-seven or twenty-eight, rather than thirty, in order to have a chance of bringing in your Aces, which sometimes yield a heavy amount of points at that stage of the computation. When it is certain that the game will be decided in the course of the playing out of the hand, without coming to your show, you will keep good cards for playing at all hazards.

When the hand is played out, the different amounts are pegged, the crib being taken last. He who led off must score first, and so on round to the dealer. Each calls the number to which he considers himself entitled, and watches to see that they are scored properly, while at the same time he does not fail to scan his adversaries' cards with an observant eye, to see that, through mistake, they do not take more than their due.

The number of points to be expected, on an average, from each hand, is seven, and from the crib about four to five. From the play it is computed that each of the four players should make five points every time. Reasoning on this data, the leader's side are at home at the close of the first round should they have obtained nineteen or twenty points, and the dealers are home at the end of the first round should they have acquired twenty-three or twenty-four. At the finish of the second round, with their average number, each set of players would be forty-two to forty-three. At the close of the third round, the leaders should be just out, or else the dealers will win. You must not, however, suppose there is any advantage to be gained from not having originally the deal; the chances are so various that the players start fully equal, no matter whether with or without the deal. From the above calculation, the game, going only once round the board, should be over in three rounds, both sides having a crib inclusive. Those who have not the first deal have the original chance of winning, if they can keep it, by holding average cards throughout the game. Should they fail in making this good, the dealers (those who dealt originally are here signified) will generally sweep all, having their second crib, and first show afterwards. It is quite as likely as not that the leaders will fail in holding "their own." They should, therefore, observe moderate caution in the first hand, but under this head it is needless to say more to either side than to impress it upon them again and again to become thoroughly acquainted with the number of points which form medium hands, as well as the different stages of the game, and play accordingly. Moderate attention is all that is required to play Four-hand Cribbage well. It is a pleasant, lively game, and when well conducted yields considerable amusement. Good Cribbage is always preferable to bad Auction Bridge.

FAN TAN

The Pack.—Full pack of 52 cards.

Number of Players.—Any number may play—best six or seven-hand.

Rank of Cards.—A (low) to K (high).

Cutting.—Cut for deal; high deals, Ace being lowest card.

Shuffling.—Any player may shuffle cards, dealer last, and player to dealer's right cuts, leaving at least five cards in each packet.

Dealing.—One card at a time to each player in rotation, beginning with player next to dealer on the left, until all cards are dealt. Deal passes to the left.

Object of the Game.—To get rid of all cards in the hand before other players have done so.

The Play.—Each player is provided with an equal number of chips or counters. Eldest hand (player to dealer's left) plays a seven face up on the table. If he has no seven, he puts one chip into the pool. Next player then plays a seven, or if eldest hand has played a seven, next player may play a six or an eight of the same suit. Each player in turn then plays a card (either seven or a card next in sequence and suit to the one last played). Sixes are placed on one side of the sevens and eights on the other. Fives are played on sixes and build down to Aces, and nines are played on eights and build up to Kings. (See diagram.)

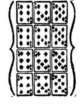

On each eight, build up: Nine, ten, Jack, Queen and King—following suit.

On each six, build down: Five, four, three, two and Ace—following suit.

Should any player be unable to play at his proper turn he must add one chip to the pool. First player getting rid of all his cards wins the pool. Each player with cards remaining in his hand must pay the winner one chip for each card he has left.

Should a player fail to play when possible, he forfeits three chips. If he overlooks the play of a seven, he forfeits 5 chips each to the holder of the six and eight of that suit.

In the two-hand game cards are dealt as though three were playing, the third hand remaining face downward on the table. In case either player cannot play at his proper turn he must draw the top card from the extra hand. If still unable to play he must forfeit a chip and draw again.

, Sixty-card packs, containing 11 and 12-spots, are coming into general use for Fan Tan, as they divide equally among almost any number of players. With this pack eights are used for starters instead of sevens.

There is another form of Fan Tan in vogue, in which eldest hand leads any card he pleases and other players must play on it in ascending sequence until the entire suit is played. Each failure to play forfeits one chip. Player of last cards of a suit starts with any card he chooses for the next suit. After King has been reached, the sequence is continued by Ace, two, etc. The player who first plays out his entire hand wins the pool, and gets one chip from each other player for each card held at the time winner plays his last card.

HEARTS

The Pack.—Full pack, 52 cards.

Number of Players.—Two to six; best four-hand.

Rank of Cards.—Ace (high), K, Q, J, 10, etc., to 2 (low).

Cutting.—Cut for deal; high deals, Ace being high card.

Shuffling.—Any player may shuffle, dealer last, and player to dealer's right cuts, leaving at least five cards in each packet.

Dealing.—Deal out the entire deck, one at a time, in rotation to the left, beginning with eldest hand. Deal passes to the left.

Misdealing.—A misdeal loses the deal. The following are misdeals:

1. Failure to offer pack to be cut.

2. Dealing a card incorrectly and failing to correct the error before dealing another card.

3. Discovery, before the first trick is turned, that any player has incorrect number of cards.

4. Exposing a card in dealing.

If pack is found to be imperfect, a new deal is required by same dealer.

Objects of the Game.—To win, on tricks, as few hearts as possible.

The Play.—Eldest hand leads any card, and each succeeding player in turn to the left must follow suit, if possible. Holding no card of suit led, player must discard a card of another suit. Highest card played of suit led takes the trick. Winner of first trick leads for second, and so on, until the hands are played out. The Hearts taken by each player are then counted and settled for, and cards are bunched for a new deal.

190

Errors in Play.—A player is compelled to take last trick if he fails to play to one trick and plays to next; or if during the hand player is found to have too few cards, the other hands being correct.

All cards which are shown on the table face up or held in the hand so that partner can see any portion of the card face, except cards played regularly to tricks or those taken back after having been played to an erroneous lead, are *exposed cards*. Exposed cards must be laid face up on the table, liable to call of adversaries. If, when an adversary calls an exposed card, another card is led or played, such other card becomes an exposed card and is liable to call. A card cannot be called when to play it would constitute a revoke (see "Revoke"). If exposed card or cards can be used in the regular course of play, no penalty remains.

Players leading out of turn must take card back unless all have played to it, in which case lead stands. Card led out of turn is exposed and subject to call, and on his next turn to lead player may be compelled by next player to his right to lead or not to lead a Heart.

A card played out of turn must be taken back, and left hand adversary may compel player in error, when his proper turn comes, to play his highest or lowest of suit led or not to discard a Heart. If leader for the trick was left-hand adversary of offending player, either he or player whose proper turn it was to play may enforce the penalty.

Revoke.—If a player fails to follow suit when able, he "revokes." A revoke may be corrected if discovered before the trick is turned; otherwise, the hands are played out, and if revoke is discovered, revoking player must settle for all others, if a player other than himself wins. If he wins, he must put up the chips won for a *jack*. If two players revoke, each must pay the penalty as if he alone were in error. If revoking player wins with another, he must settle all losses, and put up his share of the winning for a *jack*.

Scoring.—A simple Method.—After hands are played out, each player puts up one counter for each Heart he has taken, and player taking fewest Hearts wins them all. If two or more players take a like number of fewest Hearts, they divide, odd counter remaining in pool for next deal.

Sweepstakes Method.—Each player puts up one counter for each Heart he has taken. If one player takes no Hearts, he wins the pool; if two players take no Hearts, they divide the pool, leaving odd counter up for next deal. If each player takes at least one Heart, or if one player takes them all, the pool is not won on that hand, but remains to be added to succeeding pools until it is won. The pool is then known as a *jack*.

Howell Method.—Each player puts up for each Heart he has taken as many counters as there are players besides himself in the game. He then takes out of the pool as many counters as the difference between the total number of Hearts in play (thirteen) and the number of Hearts he took on that hand. This does away with *jacks*.

Game.—Each deal is a game in itself, though by agreement this may be changed. Each player may begin with an equal number of counters, and the first player losing all his counters is considered the loser; or first player winning an agreed number of counters wins the game.

DOMINO HEARTS

Use 52-card pack, without joker.

Three to seven may play; best four or five-hand.

Deal six cards to each, one at a time, in rotation to the

left, beginning with eldest hand. Place remainder of pack (talon) face downward on table.

Eldest hand leads, and each player in turn must follow suit if possible. Having no card of suit led, player must draw one card at a time from top of talon in regular order until he draws a card of suit led, or until talon is exhausted. After talon is exhausted, player holding no card of suit led may discard a card of any suit. Highest card played of suit led wins trick. Winner of first trick leads for second, and so on, until the cards in talon and hands are exhausted, when the Hearts taken by each player are counted and cards are bunched for a new deal. Any player playing out all the cards in his hand retires from the play for the balance of that hand. Should a player win a trick with his last card, next active player to his left leads for next trick. If all but one player play out all their cards before talon is exhausted, the Hearts remaining in talon and such player's hand are counted against him. If all of the active players play out on the same trick, the remaining Hearts in the talon (if any) are counted against player who last plays on that trick.

Domino Hearts may be scored under any of the methods used in the regular game. Or, the Hearts taken by each player on each deal may be scored against him, and the first player taking a certain number (usually thirty-one) is loser of the game. Player having fewest number of Hearts scored against him at this time is winner.

AUCTION HEARTS

The same as the regular game of Hearts, except that players bid after the deal for the privilege of naming the suit to be avoided. In bidding player names the number

7 ·

of counters he will put up as a pool if allowed to name the suit. Bidding begins with eldest hand, and rotates to the left, each player being allowed one bid only. Each player must bid higher than all preceding bids or must pass.

Highest bidder puts up pool and names suit. He leads first, and thereafter play proceeds as in the regular game.

When the hands are played out, each player adds one counter to the pool for each card he has taken of the forbidden suit. Player taking no card of forbidden suit wins pool; if two players take no card of forbidden suit, they divide the pool, leaving odd counter, if any, for next pool, which is a *jack,* as at sweepstakes. If more than two players take no cards of the suit, or one player takes all thirteen, or each player takes at least one, no player wins. The deal passes, and successful bidder on original deal names suit to be avoided, without bidding. The play proceeds as before, and at the end of the play of the hand each player puts up a chip for each card of forbidden suit he has taken. If no player wins on this deal, a new deal ensues, and so on, until the pool is won.

HEARTSETTE

When three or four play, delete 2 of Spades; more than four, use full pack.

Deal three-hand, 16 cards; four-hand, 12 cards; five hand, 10 cards; six-hand, 8 cards to each player, one at a time in rotation to the left, beginning with eldest hand. The remaining cards are left face downward on the table, and are called the "widow."

The play is the same as in the regular game, except that winner of first trick must gather in the widow with the trick, and all Hearts contained therein count against him. He alone is allowed to examine the widow.

JOKER HEARTS

Played the same as the regular game, except that the joker is added and two of Hearts deleted from the pack. Joker ranks between the 10 and J of hearts, and wins any trick in which it is played unless a higher Heart is played, in which case the higher Heart wins, regardless of the suit led. Holder of joker must follow suit to Hearts, if they are led; but he need not follow suit to anything else if he can get rid of joker instead. If he plays the joker on a plain suit, he wins the trick, unless there is a Heart higher than the 10 on the same trick.

In scoring, joker counts as five Hearts. If player to whom it is dealt takes it, he adds five counters to the pool, but if another player takes it, he pays five counters to the player to whom it was dealt.

BLACK JACK

A variation of Hearts, in which the Jack of Spades (Black Jack) counts as 10 Hearts, but still retains its rank as a Spade. Holder of it must follow suit to Spades. If a suit is led of which player has no card, he must discard the Spade Jack before any other card.

BLACK LADY

The same as Black Jack, except that the Queen takes the place of the Jack of Spades. The Queen retains its original rank as a Spade.

SPOT HEARTS

A variation in which the various Hearts are settled for according to their denominations, Ace being worth 14 counters, K 13, Q 12, J 11, and the balance worth their spot value, *i.e.*, 10s 10, 9's 9, etc.

THE FASCINATING GAME OF HEARTS

Full pack, 52 cards. Game, 60 points. Queen of Spades counts 13 and with the 13 Hearts, makes 26 one player can get if all the tricks are taken. There are no partners. Each one plays independent of the others. The player who first gets 60 points loses.

Usually played by four persons. The cards are dealt from the top of the pack until all are distributed, 13 to each one. To make the game more interesting, if 4 are playing, 3 cards are passed to the right around the table, from the hand of each player, but no player is allowed to take up the discarded cards until his cards are passed to the next player; and so on until the circuit is completed. When all have received the discarded cards in the proper order, each one will have 13 cards, as when the play commenced. Of course, the main object of these exchange cards is to confuse, as far as possible, the opponents by giving them certain cards which may interfere seriously with a hand that has already been considered a winner.

The rule should be never to discard the Jack of Spades or any of the other smaller cards of the Spade suit, because with enough of these cards in the hand, the Ace of Spades, the King of Spades and the Queen of Spades will be guarded, but without this protection there is always danger of someone leading a Spade that will draw the higher cards from the hand, making it possible for someone to throw the Queen, which, if it takes the trick, counts 13 against the player taking it; while if another player holds King or Ace, and is compelled to take the trick (including the Queen), that player loses 13 points.

In discarding, the smaller cards of the other suits must also be held, but excepting the Ace, King and Queen of

Spades, always play the higher cards first, beginning with the Aces of the other suits, which leaves the smaller cards near the end of the hand to fight the battle to a successful finish. To a beginner the game of Hearts may not seem scientific at first, but the more it is played, the more interesting and intricate it becomes. The possibility many times of being put into a tight place proves exciting and enjoyable to any one of the adversaries who has succeeded in forcing the Queen on some one of the players.

Five persons also can play the game. Only 10 cards, however, are dealt, instead of 13, as with 4, discarding the 3 of Clubs and the 3 of Diamonds, leaving 50 cards to work with. To play the game scientifically, from start to finish, one should keep track of every card played on the table. To do this requires thought and strict attention, but it is not absolutely necessary in order to play an enjoyable game.

Deal to the left and discard to the right. The players, of course, must all follow suit as long as there are cards in the hand of the same suit, but if not any, they have the right to put on any other card. Here comes the opportunity to get rid of the Queen of Spades, but if not in the hand, then throw the highest Heart or any high suit card in the hand on trick, keeping in mind all the time that the Queen of Spades and the high Hearts are the cards to get rid of as quickly as possible or to avoid taking.

FIVE HUNDRED

The Pack.—Two-hand, 24-card pack. A (high) to 9 (low) ; three-hand, 32 cards, A (high) to 7 (low) ; four-hand, 42-card pack, A (high) to 4 (low) ; deleting two 4's; five-hand, regular 52-card pack; six-hand, 62-card pack, with 11, 12 and two 13 spots. The joker may or may not be added to any of these.

Number of Players.—Two to six. (A good three-hand game.)

Rank of Cards.—As in Euchre (the bowers being used), thus: Trump suit, J (right bower), high; J of same color (left bower) ; A, K, Q, 10, 9, etc. Suit same color as trumps: A, K, Q, 10, 9, etc. Two suits of opposite color: A, K, Q, J, 10, 9, etc. Joker, when used, is the highest trump, ranking above the right bower. In some localities a form of the game is played in which the bowers are not used.

Cutting.—Cut for deal. High deals, Ace being highest of a suit, joker highest of all. The player on the dealer's right cuts the cards, after they have been thoroughly shuffled, and he must leave at least five cards in each packet.

Dealing.—Each player must receive ten cards; balance of the pack is left face down on the table for a "widow," and must be laid out between the first and second rounds, thus: Deal three cards to each player, then lay out the widow, then four cards to each, then three, in rotation to the left, beginning with the eldest hand.

Misdealing.—There must be a new deal by the same dealer if too many or too few cards are given to any player, or if the same number of cards is not dealt to all the players in each round, or if a card be found faced in the pack; or if, during deal or play, the pack is found to be imperfect; but any prior score made by that pack shall stand.

If a card be exposed during the deal, opponents may decide whether to have a new deal or let the deal stand.

A deal by the wrong player may be stopped before the last round is dealt, but after that it stands.

If, after he has made a bid, a player is found to have either more or less than his correct number of cards, and adversaries have the right number, the widow must also be wrong. The player in error loses his bid on that deal, but his hand must be made good from the widow. If the hand is long, a card must be drawn from it face down, and added to the widow.

If two players have an incorrect number of cards, there must be a new deal.

Object of the Game.—To take tricks. Player or partners who name trump must take full number of tricks bid to score anything and to avoid being set back. (See "Set-Back.") Adversaries score for each trick they take. (See Scoring.)

Making the Trump.—Beginning at dealer's left, each player bids for privilege of naming trump, or "passes." Only one bid is allowed each player.

Bids are made to take a certain number of tricks, with a named suit as trumps; or, to take them without a trump. The form of bid is generally thus: six in Clubs, eight in Diamonds, etc. The value of these bids depends on the table of values used.

In bidding, suits rank as follows: Spades (lowest), Clubs, Diamonds, Hearts, "No Trump" (highest).

In some localities the rank of suits is: Clubs (lowest), Spades, Hearts, Diamonds, "No Trump" (highest).

No bid can be made for less than six tricks. If no one bids six or more tricks, the cards are bunched and the deal passes to the left.

In some localities, if no one bids, the hands are played "No Trump," and each trick taken scores ten. There is no set-back. (See "Set-Back" under Scoring.) In such case the widow is not used, being left face down. Or, if agreed, it may be turned face up to be looked at, but not drawn from.

A bid to raise a previous bid must be for a higher number of scoring points, or it must be to win a greater number of tricks to make the same number of points. Thus under the original schedule (see tables of scoring points) a bid of eight tricks in Spades, the value of which is 120 points, would raise a bid of seven in Clubs, which also has a value of 120. In the Avondale schedule there are no two bids of same value, hence there can be no complications or misunderstandings as to the relative value of bids. A player cannot raise his own bid if all other players pass.

Irregular Bidding.—If any player bids out of turn, such bid is void, and his partner or partners lose their right to make any bids that deal. Opponents may bid against each other for the privilege of naming the trump suit.

Discarding.—Highest bidder takes the widow into his hand and then discards to reduce his hand to ten cards. He may retain part or all or none of the cards taken up.

Leading.—After discarding, successful bidder leads any card he chooses. (In some localities player at dealer's left leads.) It is not obligatory to lead trumps.

The Play.—Each player in turn to the left must play to the trick, following suit if possible. If no suit be held, player can trump or throw off a card of any other suit. Winner of first trick leads for next one, and so on.

No-Trump Hand.—On "No Trump" bid, the hand is played without trumps.

The Joker.—This is the highest trump when there is a trump suit. In a No Trump bid the joker is a suit by itself, and is a trump, but the holder of the joker cannot trump with it while he is able to follow suit. If the holder of the joker leads it he has the privilege of naming the suit that shall be played to it, regardless of his previous play.

Exposed Cards.—The following are exposed cards, and may be called by an adversary:

Any card dropped face upward on the table, except cards played regularly to tricks.

Two cards played to the same trick.

Any card so held in the hand that player's partner may see any portion of its face.

Any card named by the player holding it.

All exposed cards must be left face upward on the table, and are liable to be called. When such demand is made, the player must lead or play them, if he can do so without revoking. The call may be repeated at each trick until the card is played, but if the exposed card can be disposed of in the course of play, no penalty remains.

A player having one or more exposed cards on the table must not play from his hand until the adversaries have had time to call the exposed card. If he plays another card without waiting for this demand, such other card must be withdrawn if adversaries demand, and becomes also an exposed card.

Irregularities in Play.—If, during the play, any person is found to have too many cards, his hand is foul, and neither he nor his partner can score that deal, but are subject to the set-back penalty if they have named the trump and failed to take as many tricks as bid. They must play the hand out, however, to permit adversaries to score. This applies, also, to a bidder who has failed to discard correctly.

If highest bidder discards too many cards, he scores if he makes good his bid, but is set back if he fails. Should he win a trick with his last card the lead goes to next player to the left.

Neither a player nor his partner can win a trick on which either of them has no card to play.

If a player leads out of turn, and all the others follow him, the trick stands good. If it be noticed before the trick is complete, the cards must be taken back, and the leader's card becomes an exposed card. If lead properly belongs to partner of the player in error his right-hand adversary may call upon the proper leader to lead or not to lead a trump, but he cannot demand that any particular one of the three plain suits be led.

If the third hand plays before the second, or the fourth before the third, the card cannot be recalled, but must remain on the trick, as if played in proper rotation.

If a player fails to follow suit, when able to do so, it is a revoke. Upon the revoke being claimed and proved, the hands shall be immediately abandoned. If it is an adversary of the bidder who has revoked, the bidder scores the full amount of his bid, while the side in error scores nothing. If it is the bidder who revokes, he is set back the full amount of his bid, and the adversaries score any tricks they may have taken in up to that time.

Partners.—The four, six and five-hand are partnership

games—the four-hand, two against two; six-hand, three pairs of partners. There are various forms of the five-hand game. In some localities, successful bidder designates any one player as his partner during that hand, and such player cannot refuse; in others, one partner on bid of six or seven, and two partners on bid of eight, nine or ten. In other localities he may call upon holder of a certain card to act as his partner; as, the player holding a named trump which is missing from bidder's hand, or a high card of a plain suit which he needs to strengthen his hand. Bidder does not know who his partner is until card called for falls in the natural course of play. In some locaities the holder of the card called for announces it at once.

Scoring.—After hands are played out, if bidder takes as many tricks as he bid, he scores as per the schedule used.

In no case can the bidder score more than amount he bid, unless the bid was for less than 250 and he takes all ten tricks, when he may score 250 instead of amount bid.

Each player or set of partners, opposed to bidder, scores ten for each trick taken.

Set Back.—If bidder fails to take as many tricks as he bid, he is "set back;" that is, the number of points bid are deducted from his previous score. If a player is set back before he has scored anything, or more points than he has scored, he is "in the hole" (indicated by drawing a ring around the amount). Partners are set back together the full amount bid.

Game.—Game is 500, but in partnership, if one side is in the hole the other side wins if it get 500 ahead.

If more than one player scores game on the same hand, and one of them is bidder, bidder wins if he makes good his bid. If neither is the bidder, player first winning enough tricks to make his score 500 wins.

If any player scores out during play of a hand, balance of hand is not played, unless the bidder can win out. Abandoned hands must be shown, to prove there has been no revoke.

A player may be 100 in the hole and score out on a ten-trick No Trump.

TWO-HAND FIVE HUNDRED

When two wish to play Five Hundred, the 32-card pack may be used and a dead hand dealt to the left of the dealer, besides the usual widow in the center of the table.

This dead hand must not be touched nor any card in it looked at, the idea of the game being that the bidder speculate on the Aces and Kings which are out against him being in the dead hand, and not among his adversary's cards. This makes bids of seven or eight at No Trump quite common.

The higher bidder takes the widow as usual, and in all other respects the game is the same as the regular Five Hundred for three players. The Avondale schedule is recommended for the scoring, as there are no ties.

TABLES OF SCORING POINTS
AVONDALE SCHEDULE
TABLE OF POINTS—GAME OF FIVE HUNDRED

If Bid is	6 tricks	7 tricks	8 tricks	9 tricks	10 tricks
Spades	40	140	240	340	440
Clubs	60	160	260	360	460
Diamonds	80	180	280	380	480
Hearts	100	200	300	400	500
No Trump	120	220	320	420	520

ORIGINAL SCHEDULE

If Bid is	6 tricks	7 tricks	8 tricks	9 tricks	10 tricks
Spades	40	80	120	160	200
Clubs	60	120	180	240	300
Diamonds	80	160	240	320	400
Hearts	100	200	300	400	500
No Trump	120	240	360	480	600

INVERTED SCHEDULE

If Bid is	6 tricks	7 tricks	8 tricks	9 tricks	10 tricks
Clubs	40	80	120	160	200
Spades	60	120	180	240	300
Hearts	80	160	240	320	400
Diamonds	100	200	300	400	500
No Trump	120	240	360	480	600

1,000 AND 1,500

The pack, rank of cards, deal, bid, lead and play are the same as in 500. In counting the hands, each player scores additional points, as follows: For each Ace taken in, 1 point; each K, Q, J and 10, 10 points; each 9, 9 points; each 8, 8 points, etc., each card taken in being counted at its numerical value. Joker does not count. These additional points are not reckoned toward making the bid good, and are thrown out if bidder is set back through failure to take the number of tricks bid.

In 24-card pack there are 50 of these additional points to each suit, or 200 in all; 32-card pack, 65 to a suit, or 260

·in all; 44-card pack, 80 to a suit, 320 in all; 52-card pack, 85 to a suit, 340 in all; 60-card pack, 108 to a suit, 432 in all.

In some localities the K's, Q's and J's are not counted.

Game.—1,000 or 1,500 points, as agreed upon.

PROGRESSIVE FIVE HUNDRED

Before play, each player is furnished with a score or tally card, designating table at which he is to begin play. For four and six-hand play it is also necessary to designate partners. Thus, 4-hand tally cards may be marked: Table A 1, A 2, A 3, A 4; one and three playing partners against two and four. Six-hand: Table A 1, A 2, A 3, A 4, A 5 and A 6, the odd numbers playing partners against the even.

The game then proceeds as in the regular game of Five Hundred.

Scoring.—A pad of score sheets is furnished each table. After hands are played out, count all points made or set back, and enter score of each player individually on score-sheet. (In partnership play each player is credited with entire amount made by the partners.) Entry on score-sheet is made by one player and O.K.'d by adversary. Score-sheet is then turned over to scorer. Scorer keeps a general score sheet, with plus and minus column for each player. At end of each game, amounts made or lost by the various players are entered in the proper columns (all points won being entered in the plus column and all "set-backs" in the minus column). At the end of the afternoon's or evening's play the points won by each are added up, and the points lost (through "set-backs") are deducted therefrom. The player having the highest number of points, after all "set-backs" are deducted, wins.

Progressions.—Play one deal for each player at table, and then progress. Three-hand, high player progresses; four-hand, winning partners; five-hand, two players with highest scores; six-hand, three winning partners. Any preferred style of progression may be used.

FIVE HUNDRED—"NULLO BID"

Some players favor a variation in which a player may bid "Nullo" and obligate himself not to take a trick. Bidder leads, and in partnership game plays alone against opponents. The value of the bid is 250 and in the Avondale schedule it ranks between eight Spades and eight Clubs; in Original schedule it goes over nine Clubs or eight Diamonds, or seven Hearts or seven No Trump; in Inverted schedule it goes over nine Spades or eight Hearts or seven Diamonds or seven No Trump.

In case bidder takes one or more tricks, he is set back 250 points and opponents score 10 for each trick he takes. In non-partnership games each opponent scores for tricks bidder takes.

As Nullos are No Trumps, there is no trump except the joker, which is always a trump and will always win any trick on which it is played. In the ordinary game the holder of the joker may lead it and name the suit which shall be played to it, but in Nullos the players may discard what they please. If the player of the Nullo happens to hold the joker, or gets it in the widow, it is obvious that he must lay it away in his discard, or it will be impossible for him to avoid taking a trick.

GRAND

The Pack.—52 cards, which rank from the A, K, Q down to the 2 in each suit. Two packs should be used, so as to mark the position of the deal, as the highest bidder always leads, but the deal goes to the left in order.

Players.—Four—two playing against two as partners.

Cutting.—The lowest two cuts are partners against the highest two and the highest of all has the choice of seats and cards, and deals the first hand. Ties cut again.

Dealing.—Each player receives thirteen cards, dealt one at a time, no trump turned. A misdeal does not lose the deal.

Objects of the Game.—The game is 100 points, and the object is to reach that number or to be nearer to it than your adversaries when the time agreed upon to stop playing arrives. These points are made by scoring so much apiece for tricks over the book when the game is Whist or Grand; for three tricks, or four tricks, or a march, when the game is Euchre; and for no Hearts taken in when the game is Hearts.

Quitting Time.—As this is a game in which the bidder is continually being set back, it is often impossible for either side to reach 100 points, so a quitting time should always be agreed upon in case of an unfinished game. The side that is farthest from 100 when this time arrives, owes the other side the number of points they are short, together with 10 points for each time they have been set back.

Set Backs.—The set backs must be marked on the score card with a cross, so that they may be counted up at the end of the play. Suppose A and B have 55 points and eleven set backs, while Y and Z have 70 points and eight set backs, A-B lose the 45 they are short of 100 and 30 for the three set backs in excess of those scored against Y and Z. If Y and Z were the ones with eleven set backs, to A-B's eight, then the net loss for A-B would be 15 points only, instead of 75.

Bidding.—The eldest hand always has the first bid and he must either call a certain number of points, five or more, or pass. Nothing is said about the game he purposes to play or the trump suit, only so many points, usually multiples of five. Only one bid is allowed to each player in turn, and the highest bidder then names the game. If all pass, the dealer must bid five and play something.

The highest bidder always leads for the first trick.

Game Values.—In Straight Whist, each trick over the book is worth 5 points. Grand slam, 30 extra. The highest possible score at Whist is, therefore, 65. Honors have no scoring value.

In Euchre, the odd trick, commonly called the Point, is worth 5. Four tricks are worth 10, and a march made by two players is worth 20, unless the bidder has declared to play alone and asked for his partner's best. If he has not bid more than 20 he need not ask for his partner's best.

If the bidder is willing to play alone to make 25, he must ask for his partner's best and give the adversaries the same privilege, so that if one of them has the King or Queen, he may get as many guards to it as he can. The bidder almost invariably holds both bowers and the Ace, unless the bid is forced.

When the game is Euchre, each player discards down to five cards, and nothing lower than the eight may be kept in the trump suit. Any player found with a smaller trump, or more than five cards, has a foul hand. The bidder must discard before seeing what card his partner is about to give him.

Hearts is a safety bid more than anything else. When the dealer's side is 70 or more, the eldest hand may declare to play Hearts without bidding at all. He leads a card at once and says, "This is Hearts." At any lower score, or when it is not the dealer that is 70 or better, this cannot be done, and the privilege is restricted to the eldest hand always.

If neither the eldest hand nor his partner takes in a Heart, they score 50 points, and the dealer is set back 13, one for each heart. If the eldest hand or his partner take in any Hearts, they score nothing, but are set back a point for each Heart, so that both sides go back more or less. Should the dealer's side get no Hearts, they would score 50 and set their opponents back 13.

If the dealer's score is not as good as 70, and the eldest hand passes without making a bid, it is usually a sign that he is willing to play Hearts but does not want to call them for fear his partner might have something better. When he does not want to play Hearts, he should make a bid of some kind, if only 5 points.

The highest bidder can always make the game Hearts, unless he has bid more than 50, and if neither he nor his partner take in a Heart, they score 50 and set the other side 13. But if the bidder or his partner take in any Hearts they are set back the amount of the bid and one extra for each Heart they take, so that both sides go back.

Grand is Whist without a trump. Each trick over the book is worth 9, and grand slam is worth 40, so that it is possible to make 103. A grand slam at Grand wins the game, even if the bidder is in the hole when it is played.

All bids are usually in multiples of five, not in nines,

because even if the bidder intends to play a Grand, he should not betray the fact, but he may overcall his partner's 15 with 18, or an adversary's 25 with 27.

In all games, the bidder can score as much more than his actual bid as he can make. He may make five by cards at Grand, worth 45, on a bid of 5.

Lost Games.—When the bidder fails to make good, he is set back the amount of his bid and has to pay his opponents for any tricks they win that score. Suppose that after bidding 15 he makes Clubs trumps for Whist and gets only two by cards, worth 10. He is set back the 15 that he bid, but his opponents do not score anything, because they did not make the odd trick. Had the bidder won only five tricks out of the 13, he would have been set back 15 just the same, but the other side would have scored 10 points for the two by cards they made.

In Grand, there is a double penalty. Suppose the bid is 20 and the player says "Grand." To cover his bid he must make three by cards, or 27. If his adversaries get the odd trick, they score 9 points for it and set the bidder back the 20 he bid and 9 for the trick he lost—29 altogether.

In Euchre, the bidder is always penalized what he might have made, which is supposed to be a march, worth 20. If he bids 10, and says "Euchre" with Clubs for trumps, he must win four tricks to make good. If he gets three only, he is set back the 10 he bid and the 20 he might have made —30 points.

If he bids 20, says it is "Euchre" and does not play alone, he and his partner must make a march. If they fail, they go back the 20 bid and 20 they might have made—40 points. If the bidder goes alone after bidding 20 and fails to make all the tricks, he goes back 40 just the same.

When the bid is 25 and the game is Euchre, the bidder

must play alone and must ask for his partner's best, discarding down to four cards before he looks at the card his partner passes to him. Either adversary can then ask for his partner's best. When the bid is a lone hand and fails, it loses 50, of which 25 is the bid and 25 is what he should have made.

RUSSIAN BANK
(Or Crapette)

This game, which is sometimes called Double Solitaire, has lately come into great favor as being probably the best game for two players ever invented.

The Pack.—Two full packs of 52 cards each, with backs of different colors.

Number of Players.—Two, either or both of whom may, by agreement with the adversary, have a consulting partner to give advice but who takes no part in the actual play of the cards, and is not allowed to point out or call stops on the opponent.

Ranks of the Cards.—From the Ace, deuce up to the King on the foundations. The suits have no rank.

Cutting.—One pack is spread face downward and each player draws a card. The highest has the choice of packs and seats and has the first play.

Shuffling.—The winning cut having made his choice of packs, each shuffles and cuts the pack to be used by his adversary. The packs are then exchanged.

Dealing.—Each player deals from the top of his own pack, 12 cards, one at a time, face down, in a pile to his right. These are his "stock." He then deals 4 cards face

up, one at a time, to his right, in a line toward his opponent. The 8 cards form the tableau. Space must be
left between the two lines of cards so dealt for 8 Aces,
as they come out which will form the 8 foundations. The
remaining 36 cards are then placed face down in a pile on
the player's left, and form his "hand."

The Play.—The person who has the winning cut plays
first, removing any Aces which are face up, and placing
them between the two lines of cards that form the tableau.
Any cards which can be built up in sequence and suit on
those Aces (Ace, deuce, trey of Spades, for instance) must
be played into the foundations before making any other
move, under penalty of having a "stop" called on the player.
A card once played on a foundation cannot again be moved
under any circumstances. Any card touched, even if not
moved, when another card should have been played on the
foundations, is a stop, if called by the adversary.

There being no further possibility of building on the
foundations, the player proceeds to make as many changes
as he pleases in the tableau itself, by building upon any card
in descending sequence, but alternating colors; such as a
red 7 on a black 8; or a black Jack on a red Queen.

In making changes from one part of the tableau to another, only the top card of any pile may be moved at a
time, so that if it were desirable to separate a 5 and 6, in
order to build them on a 7 elsewhere, a space must be
found for the five in order to free the 6.

The player is not obliged to make any changes in the
tableau, but when he ceases to do so, or has none to make,
he turns up the top card from his "stock" on his right. If
this is playable on any foundation, it must be put there at
once. Otherwise it may be played into a space, if one is

vacant, or in descending sequence and alternate color with any card in the tableau.

If there is no space, and he cannot play from his stock, he leaves the last card turned up on the top of his stock, and turns up the top card from his hand, the pile on his left. If this is playable, he may be able to make changes which will enable him to play the top card from his stock, in which case he resumes turning up from his stock, as it is always most desirable to get rid of all the stock cards as soon as possible. In this way he may turn from hand to stock alternately, until he comes to a stop, and can make no further plays. The last card turned from his hand must be laid face up between his hand and his stock and forms the first card of his discard or trash pile. It then becomes the turn of his adversary to play, and he proceeds to make whatever changes he may be able to, turning up the top cards from his stock as long as he can play them, and then from his hand, when he can no longer play from his stock. The last card turned, which will always be from his hand, starts his trash pile.

A player has the privilege of playing on the up-turned cards of his opponents stock, or trash pile, in either ascending or descending sequence in the same suit. Suppose the Spade 8 is on the opponent's trash pile, the Spade 7 or 9 may be played on it, and the 6 or 8 on the 7 again, or the 8 or 10 on the 9. The player is not allowed to play on his own stock or discard in this manner; only on his adversary's, but cards from any part of the tableau, or from his hand or stock, may be so played.

In his plays in the tableau, he may use his opponent's stock cards that are face up; but neither player is allowed to use any card that is face up on a trash pile, except to be placed on a foundation. Cards that fit on any of the foundations must be played there before another card is touched.

When the player's stock is exhausted he turns from his hand alone. As soon as his hand is exhausted, if it is his turn to play, he turns his discard pile face downward and it then becomes his hand, to be turned up one card at a time as before, forming a new trash pile.

Penalties and Stops.—There is no penalty for making a false move, such as playing a red 7 on a red 8, or a 7 on a 9, but the mistake must be corrected by the adversary, and the card taken back.

If there is anywhere a card face up that can be played on the foundations, and the person whose turn it is to play touches any other card before playing that card on the foundation, his opponent may call a stop, and take up the play himself. If the card has been turned from the hand or stock, it must be returned to its position when the stop is called. Toward the middle of the game, with 14 or more cards in sight, it requires a sharp eye to prevent overlooking stops.

Game.—The player who first gets rid of all of his cards, by placing them on the tableau, the foundations, or his opponent's stock, or trash piles, wins the game, for which he gets 30 points. In addition to this he gets 2 points for each card remaining in his opponent's stock, if any, and 1 for each card remaining in his opponent's hand or trash pile.

SINGLE PACK RUSSIAN BANK

Only one pack is used and the dealer gives 26 cards to each player, 2 the first time, then 3 at a time. Each picks up the cards face down, and the non-dealer lays out the top four, face up, in a row. If he can make any builds, he does so at once, filling the spaces until he has to stop. The dealer then lays out four, and makes any changes in the eight piles until he has to stop. Aces are placed in the center to be built up upon in suits. These are the foundations.

All changes are made by building in both sequence and suit, and the sequences may be started either way, according to the player's choice, but once started they must be kept going that way. Suppose the first four cards are H 7, C 6, D 8, H 8. The player may put the H 7 on the 8, or the 8 on the 7. He then fills the space with a card from his hand. If that makes no change, say S 10, the dealer lays out, let us say, the H 9, C 5, C 7, D K. He puts the H 9 on the 8, the Club 6 on the 7 and the 5 on that, and fills the three spaces from his hand.

Suppose he turns up the C 4, D 7 and H J. He builds and still has two spaces, turning H K and S 6. His four spaces being now filled, and no further play possible, the non-dealer turns a card. If this cannot be played, he puts it face up on his trash pile. As long as he can play he turns up. As soon as all the cards are in the trash pile, it is turned face down and run through again. The winner is the one that first gets rid of all his cards, the loser paying for each he has left in hand or trash pile.

As the cards are built in suit as well as in sequence, the player is allowed to move an entire file to another file, provided it continues the sequence, so as to get a space. For example: One file shows the 5, 6, 7 of Hearts, with the 5 on the top. Another file contains the 9, 10, J of Hearts, with the 9 on the top. If the player draws the 8, he can put it on the 9, and lift the 5, 6, 7, making one pile from the 5 to the J, and giving him a space.

There being a space, he can now reverse the sequence if he wishes to do so, starting with the 5, which will now be the bottom card, and bringing the J to the top. This may be desirable if the K of Hearts is in another pile, and he hopes to turn up the Q, or if he knows the Q is in his trash pile, which he will presently have to turn over and play through again. Any sequence may be reversed in this manner if there is a space in which to do it. Reversing may also shut off an opponent's cards. If a card is drawn that will fit at the bottom of a sequence, such as drawing the 9 of Spades when the 6, 7, 8 are on the table, with the 6 on the top, the 9 cannot be played unless there is a space. If there is a space, the 9 can be slipped under the 8, as that is the same thing as putting the 9 in the space and shifting the 6, 7, 8 to it.

Cards turned up, or from the tableau, may be placed on the opponent's trash pile, if they fit in sequence and suit, but cards cannot be taken from the foundations for this purpose.

STUNG

The Pack.—Full pack of 52 cards. Ace (low) to King (high).

Number of Players.—Any number from two to eight may play.

Cutting.—Pack is spread and one card drawn by each player, high dealing.

Shuffling.—Any player may shuffle, the dealer last. Player to dealer's right cuts the pack, leaving at least five cards in each packet.

Dealing.—Cards are dealt to the left, one at a time, until the pack is exhausted. On the last round, if cards do not divide evenly, remaining cards are faced in the center of the table. Cards dealt cannot be sorted or examined by players and are laid in packets, face down, in front of the players. Deal passes to the left.

Objects of the Game.—To get rid of all cards in the hand before the other players have done so, in the following manner:

By building up on Aces with cards of the same suit in sequence.

By building down on other cards with cards of opposite color in sequence.

By playing from pack upon exposed cards of other players.

By giving cards to other players who make misplays during the course of the game.

The Play.—Player to dealer's left turns top card from his pack. This card is placed in the center of the table. Next player to the left turns one card and places it in the center of the table. Play continues to the left until four cards have been placed in the center of the table. (If cards do not deal evenly and part of the pack is placed in center of table, cards are added in the above manner to make four.)

After first row is laid out players continue in the same manner. Aces are placed in another row as soon as exposed. If a card turned is in sequence to an Ace or any card which has been played on the Ace, in ascending sequence, it must be played on this sequence. If it is in descending sequence and of opposite color to any card exposed in the first row of "starters," it must be played in this row. If the card cannot be played, it is placed face up on the table to form part of another packet, which is kept face up. Player continues to turn cards until he exposes a card which will not apply to any combination on the table.

When original packet has been transferred to exposed packet, exposed packet is turned face down and is used as before.

After the first player has turned cards he will have one card exposed, as will all other players, after the first round. When cards are thus exposed, a player turning a card which will play to form either an ascending or descending sequence of different color with any exposed card, he must play on the exposed packet, provided the card will not play in the center of the table. Card is played on the first exposed packet to the left if more than one play is possible.

Play continues in this manner until one player disposes of all of his cards and those given him by other players. He then drops out and the others play until but one player has cards remaining in his hand, who loses the game. If desired, first player disposing of all of his cards may be declared the winner.

As the addition of cards to the "starters" will naturally permit top card of one row to be placed on bottom card of another row, the different rows must be combined when possible. Cards in this row will also, during the game, play in ascending sequence with the Aces, and must be so moved when possible. Therefore, in addition to disposing of cards from his own hand in the manner described above, player must make all possible plays from the board.

Plays must be made in the following order: (1) From the lower rows to the Ace sequences. (2) From one lower row to another lower row. (3) From one lower row into a space to permit a card being placed in the Ace sequence. (4) From the top of player's exposed packet onto Ace sequence. (5) From top of exposed pack to space if space exists. (6) From top of exposed pack to descending sequence. (7) From top of exposed pack to exposed pack of some other player, under above conditions. If top card of exposed pack will not play in any manner, then another card is turned. This card is played as would be the exposed card. When card from packet is played, card beneath it must be played if possible before another card is turned.

When a player makes a misplay, by failing to make a possible play, by exposing card when top card of exposed packet could be played, by examining cards in unexposed packet, by exposing card out of turn or by failing in any way to play the game correctly, player discovering such misplay calls out "Stung." Each player, beginning with the one to his left, then gives player making misplay one card from top of exposed packet or from top of original packet, if no cards are exposed. Cards thus given him are placed face up on his exposed packet in the order that they come. If such player has played cards in error, cards misplaced must be taken back, play passing to the left.

NORWEGIAN WHIST

The Pack.—Full pack of 52 cards.

Number of Players.—Four (two against two as partners). In cutting, the lowest two pair against the highest two and the highest of the four deals the first hand.

Rank of Cards.—In play, the Ace is high and the other cards rank from the K, Q, J, etc., down to the deuce.

Shuffling.—Any player may shuffle the cards, the dealer last. In cutting to the dealer, at least four cards must be left in each packet.

Dealing.—Deal thirteen cards to each player, one at a time, in rotation to the left. The deal passes to the left.

No trump is turned, as every hand is a No Trumper.

Misdealing.—A misdeal does not lose the deal, but the cards must be dealt again by the same dealer. It is a misdeal if any card is exposed during the deal or if any player has an incorrect number of cards.

Objects of the Game.—To win or to lose tricks, according to the declaration. In Grand, the play is to win tricks; in Nullo to lose them.

Bidding.—The eldest hand has the first bid. He can declare to play Grand or Nullo, or he can pass. If he passes, the next player to his left has a chance to name the game. If all pass without bidding, the hand is played as a Nullo.

The Play.—If the game is declared to be a Grand, the player to the RIGHT of the bidder leads any card he pleases. If the game is a Nullo, the player to the LEFT of the bidder leads. If no bid is made, the player to the left of the dealer leads for the first trick for a Nullo.

The Game.—The game is usually 50 points, each trick being worth 4. In some localities the tricks are worth only 2 in Nullo, but 4 in Grand. No matter what the values may be, they are so proportioned to the game that it takes thirteen tricks, or a grand slam, at Grand, to win the game in one hand.

The first six tricks do not count for either side, but all over the book won by the bidder count for him in Grand and against him in Nullo. If he bids a Grand and fails to get seven tricks, each trick over the book taken by his opponents counts double for them. In Nullo they remain at the same value either way.

If a player revokes, he gives three tricks to the other side in Grand or takes three from them in Nullo. If a wrong player leads, the player on the right of the one whose turn it is to lead, if that leader be the partner of the one in

error, can call a suit. If it is not the lead of either adversary, a lead can be called when next either of them gets
the lead. If a player corrects a revoke before the trick
is turned and quitted, he may be called on to play his highest or lowest of the suit led, and the card he takes back is
exposed and liable to call. If a player bids out of turn,
he forfeits 20 points and loses his bid on that deal.

SHEEPSHEAD (Schafkopf)
GAME No. 1

The Pack.—32-card pack, all below the sevens are deleted.
Number of Players.—Four.
Rank of Cards.—The four Jacks are permanent trumps
and rank Clubs (highest), Spades, Hearts, Diamonds
(lowest). In addition to the four Jacks, one suit is named
trump (see Making the Trump) for each deal, the cards
of which rank below the Jacks and with relation to each
other as follows: Ace (highest), 10, K, Q, 9, 8, 7 (lowest).
No Trump suits rank Ace (highest), 10, K, Q, 9, 8, 7,
(lowest).
Cutting.—Cut for partners and deal, the higher two
being partners against the lower two, and the highest
of all is dealer.
Shuffling.—Any player may shuffle the cards, dealer last,
and player to dealer's right cuts.
Dealing.—Deal eight cards to each player—four cards at
a time in rotation to the left, beginning with player to left
of dealer. Deal passes to the left.
Objects of the Game.—To win in tricks certain cards of
counting value as follows: Aces, 11; tens, 10; Kings, 4;
Queens, 3, and Jacks, 2.

Each side puts up an equal number of counters before the deal.

Making the Trump.—The side making the trump must win 60 points and as many more as they bid; thus, side bidding fifteen must win 75 points, etc.

Eldest hand has first bid, and the bidding passes in rotation to the left, each player being allowed but one bid. Highest bidder names trump suit. If all pass, player holding Jack of Clubs must make the trump.

The Play.—Eldest hand leads any card, and each player in turn to the left plays and must follow suit if possible. Holding no card of suit led, player may either trump or play a card of another suit.

Winner of first trick leads for second, and so on until the hands are played out. Points are then counted, and cards are bunched and a new deal ensues.

Scoring.—If the side which makes the trump wins as many points as they bid, they win the pool. If they win 91 points they win double the amount, provided they made good their bid. If they win 120 points, they win four times the amount. In case of no bid, the side which holds the Jack of Clubs and names the trump wins the pool if they win 60 points. If the side making the trump fails to make 60 points (or as much as they bid, if their bid was for more than that amount) their opponents win the pool. If opponents of side making trump win 91 points, they win double; if they win 120 points, they win four times the amount.

Game No. 2.—The same as Game No. 1, except that there are six permanent trumps, which rank as follows: Queen of Clubs (highest), Queen of Spades, Jack of Clubs, Jack of Spades, Jack of Hearts, Jack of Diamonds. The rules for Game No. 1 apply.

Game No. 3.—Played by four players as individuals. Diamonds always trumps. Each player forfeits one chip for each trick he takes less than two, and receives one chip for each trick he takes more than two. Tricks and not points are scored. In all other respects the rules for Game No. 1 apply.

Game No. 4.—Four players (two partners against the other two). There are six permanent trumps, as in Game No. 2. Player holding Queen of Clubs, with his partner, must make 61 points, or pay double the forfeit. Otherwise the rules for Game No. 1 apply.

Game No. 5.—For four players (two partners against the other two). There are fourteen trumps, which rank as follows: Queen of Clubs (highest), Queen of Spades, Queen of Hearts, Queen of Diamonds, Jack of Clubs, Jack of Spades, Jack of Hearts, Jack of Diamonds, Ace, ten, King, nine, 8, 7 of Diamonds. As a general rule, Diamonds are trumps, but trump may be announced as in Game No. 1. Score as in Game No. 1.

Game No. 6.—For six players (three partners against the other three), partner being seated alternately. There are fourteen trumps, as in Game No. 5. Other rules the same as Game No. 5.

Game No. 7.—Played with a double pack—48 cards (9's low). Diamonds are permanent trump suit, and trumps rank as in Game No. 5, making twenty-four trumps in all. If two cards of the same suit and denomination fall upon the same trick, the first played ranks above the second. Game is 121 points.

Game No. 8.—Played with double pack of 48 cards, by six players (three partners against the other three), partners being seated alternately, each player receiving eight cards. Other rules the same as Game No. 7.

Game No. 9.—Played with a double pack of 64 cards (7's low), by eight players (four partners against the other four), partners being seated alternately. Diamonds are always trumps. Other rules the same as in Game No. 7.

THREE-HAND SHEEPSHEAD

The 32-card pack is used and 10 cards are dealt to each player, the last two cards being left as a widow. The successful bidder takes the widow and discards two cards before announcing the trump. If all pass, the player holding the highest Jack must name the trump.

The rules of Game No. 1 regarding the number of trumps, bidding, scoring, etc., apply.

FIVE-HAND SHEEPSHEAD

This is played the same as the three-hand game except that a 40-card pack (made by deleting twos, threes and fours) is used.

RED DOG

Or High-Card Pool

The Pack.—52 cards, ranking from the A, K down to the 2.

Players.—Any number from 3 to 8. Positions at the table may be cut for. The highest takes his seat and the first deal; the next highest to his left, and so on.

The Pool.—Before the deal, each player contributes one counter to the pool. If any player wins the entire pool, all contribute one counter each to form a fresh pool.

Dealing.—Any player may shuffle, the dealer last. Player on the right cuts, leaving at least 5 cards in each packet.

8

Cards are dealt from left to right, one at a time, until each player has 5. The remainder of the pack is left on the table, face down, for the stock.

The Play.—Player on dealer's left has the first say. After examining his cards he can pass, paying one counter forfeit to the pool and abandoning his hand; or he can bet any amount, not exceeding the number of chips then in the pool, that he holds a card of the same suit as the one then on the top of the stock, and of higher rank. As soon as he puts up his bet the dealer turns up the top card of the stock.

Suppose it is the Spade 8. If the one who bet can show a higher Spade he wins as many chips from the pool as he bet. If he fails, his bet goes into the pool. He shows only one card. The card turned up from the stock goes into the deadwood, with the hand of the one who bet, and the next player to the left has a chance to bet or pass. It is obvious that two high cards in two different suits are required to make a safe bet. Four Aces would be a certainty.

When all have bet or passed, including the dealer, all the cards are gathered up and the deal passes to the left. Any chips remaining in the pool are added to by the usual contribution from each player of one counter for the new deal.

SKAT

The Pack.—32-card pack, Ace (high) to 7 (low).

Number of Players.—For three players. If more than three play, cards are dealt to the two players next to the dealer on the left and the one player next to him on the right. The players not receiving cards share the fortunes of the two who play against the successful bidder. (See Bidding.)

Rank of Cards.—The four Jacks (called Wentzels) are always the four best trumps, and rank: Clubs (highest), Spades, Hearts, Diamonds (lowest). After the four Jacks, the cards of the suit named as trump rank: A, 10, K, Q, 9, 8, 7. Non-trump suits rank: A (high) 10, K, Q, 9, 8, 7.

The four suits rank: Clubs (highest), Spades, Hearts, Diamonds, but this rank has nothing to do with trick-taking value, merely increasing or diminishing the value of the game played according to the suit named as trump.

Matadores.—When a player holds the Jack of Clubs, it and each trump in *unbroken* sequence with it is called a Matadore. Thus, with Spades as trump, player holding the four Jacks and Ace, 10 and King of Spades, would have 7 Matadores, but if the Jack of Hearts were missing, he would have only two Matadores, the Jack of Clubs and Jack of Spades.

There are always one or more Matadores in the hands of the three players. If in the hand of highest bidder, he is said to play *with* a certain number of Matadores, or if in the hands of his opponents, he is said to play *without* a certain number. The number of Matadores either *with* or *without* affects the value of the game played.

Cutting.—Cut for choice of seats; low has choice of seats and deals first, the cards and suits ranking in cutting as they do in play. Player to right of first dealer should keep the score, thus showing when each round of deals is completed.

Shuffling.—Any player may shuffle, dealer last, and player to dealer's right cuts, leaving at least five cards in each packet.

Dealing.—Beginning with player to left of dealer, deal three cards to each active player in rotation to the left. When more than three are in the game, only three players receive cards. (See Number of Players.) Then deal two cards to the table, face downward (called the "Skat"). Then deal two more rounds to the players, four cards, then three, making in all ten·cards to each player and two to the Skat.

Misdealing.—In case of a misdeal, same dealer deals again, and ten points are deducted from his score as a penalty for the misdeal. The following are misdeals:

(a) Failure to offer the pack to be cut.

(b) Exposing a card in dealing.

(c) Dealing too many or too few cards to any player on any round.

(d) Not dealing the Skat cards in their proper turn.

If the pack is found to be imperfect, such discovery renders the current deal void, but does not affect any previous scores.

A player dealing out of turn may be stopped if discovered before the last card is dealt; otherwise the deal stands. Next deal must be by player whose proper turn it was to deal, and then proceed as if no misdeal had been made, omitting, however, the player who dealt out of turn. Thus each player deals but once in each round.

Objects of the Game.—There are two general classes of games—those in which the player's object is to take no trick, and those in which the player's object is to win enough counting cards in tricks to make 61, counting each Ace 11, ten 10, King 4, Queen 3, and Jack 2. The former are called *Null* (or *Nullo*), and *Null Ouvert*. Player declaring Null Ouvert endeavors not to take a trick, as he does in Nullo, but in addition his cards are exposed face up on the table. There are no trumps in Nullo and Null Ouvert. The cards of each suit rank: Ace (high), K, Q, J, 10, 9, 8, 7 (low).

In games of the other class, player naming the form of game endeavors to win points in tricks; failure to make 61 points loses the game. These games are as follows:

Tournée.—The successful bidder turns up one card of the Skat, declaring the suit of such card trump. If the turned card be a Jack, however, he may declare the suit of the Jack to be trump or play a Grand Tournée, the four Jacks being the only trumps. After declaring, player takes the other Skat card into his hand and discards two cards. If the discarded cards are of any counting value, they are counted for the maker of the trump.

Solo.—The successful bidder declares a suit trump from his hand, without looking at the Skat. He must play with the cards which are dealt to him, and cannot use the Skat in play. The Skat belongs to him, however, and any points and Matadores found therein at the end of the play are counted for him.

Grand.—When a Grand is played, the four Jacks are the only trumps. There are four varieties of Grand: Guckser (or Grand Frage), Grand Tournée, Grand Solo, and Grand Ouvert.

In Guckser, player takes both Skat cards and announces the four Jacks to be the only trumps. He discards two cards from his hand as in Tournée.

If a player, intending to play a Tournée, turns a Jack for trump he may change his game from Tournée to Grand. This is called *Grand Tournée.*

Successful bidder may announce a Grand before looking at either of the Skat cards. This is called *Grand Solo.* The Skat cards are not seen by any player until the hand is played out, when, if of any counting value, the cards are counted for successful bidder.

Successful bidder may announce a Grand, and spread his

cards face up on the table, and play them in that manner, though his cards are not subject to call. This is called *Grand Ouvert*. The player declaring Grand Ouvert must win every trick to win his game.

Bidding.—The three active players are known by the following names: Player to left of dealer is called "Vorhand"; the second player is called "Mittelhand," and third, "Hinterhand."

Vorhand has the right to name the game, but the others may bid to take this privilege from him by naming a certain number of points, which must never be less than 10 and must represent the value of some game.

Mittelhand has first bid, and if Vorhand thinks he can make as many points as bid, he says "Yes," whereupon Mittelhand must bid higher or pass. If Vorhand is offered more than he thinks he can make, he passes. As soon as either Vorhand or Mittelhand passes, Hinterhand has the privilege of bidding with the survivor. These two bid in the same way, until one or the other passes. Highest bidder then declares the form of game to be played. Bidder may play any game he chooses, provided the value equals or exceeds the amount of his bid. He is known as the "player."

Nullo.—This is a bid not to win a trick. In Nullo there are no trumps, no Wentzels, and no Matadores. The cards rank A, K, Q, J, 10, 9, 8, 7. Nothing will increase the value of a Nullo, which is always 20, if played out of hand.

Null Ouvert is a Nullo which is laid open on the table before a card is led. It counts double—40 points.

Gucki Nullo is a bid to take the Skat cards and discard two in their place, afterward playing a Nullo. Before touching the Skat it must be distinctly stated that it is a Gucki Nullo and not a Gucki Grand. If successful, this is worth 15, but if lost, it counts double—30. A player may announce an open Gucki Nullo, which is to lay the cards face up after taking the Skat and discarding. This is worth 30, but counts double if lost—60 points.

Passt-Mir-Nicht Tournée.—When a player turns one of the Skat cards for a Tournée, and it does not suit him, he may so declare without showing it. He must then turn the other card, which shall be trump. Should this second card be a Jack, the player may either declare that suit trump, or declare a Grand Tournée. The player must show the second card, however, before he mixes it with his other cards; otherwise his opponents may determine what game shall be played; the opponent naming the highest having the privilege. If player playing Passt-Mir-Nicht Tournée wins, it counts as Tournée; if he fails, it counts double against him.

Ramsch.—When both players pass without making a bid, Vorhand may declare Ramsch. The cards rank as in Grand, the Jacks being the only trumps. If each player takes at least one trick, the player winning the greatest number of points loses the value of the game, 20 points; if one player has taken no trick (Jungfer), the loss is 30 points.

Values of Games.—Each of the above games has a unit value, and in the first six of the following games these values may be increased by certain conditions of the game. (See Multipliers.) These unit values are, as follows:

When trumps are	Clubs	Spades	Hearts	Diamonds
Tournée	8	7	6	5
Solo	12	11	10	9

When the four Jacks, only, are trumps:

Grand Tournée	12
Guckser (double if lost)	16

Grand Solo 20

Grand Ouvert 24

When there are no trumps:

Nullo 20

Null Ouvert 40

Gucki Nullo (double if lost)............................ 15

Gucki Null Ouvert (double of lost)................ 30

Multipliers.—In the games where a trump suit is named, the above values are increased, as follows: If a player declaring the form of game makes 61 points, he wins a "simple game." If he makes 91 points, he makes his opponents Schneider, and if he wins every trick, he makes his opponents Schwarz. Beginning with the simple game, which scores only the unit value, the value of the game is multiplied by making Schneider and Schwarz, as follows:

Game, 1; Schneider, 2; Schneider announced in advance, or Schwarz without having announced Schneider, 3; Schwarz, after having announced Schneider, 4; Schwarz, announced in advance, 5. Thus, a Tournée in Clubs is worth 8; if Schneider is made 2x8=16; if Schwarz is made, 3x8=24, etc. Schneider or Schwarz may not be announced in any game in which the Skat cards are used. Grand Ouvert is always Schwarz announced.

In addition to the above values, the value of each game is enhanced by the number of Matadores player is *with* or *without.* Bidder playing with Jack of Clubs, and not having Jack of Spades, plays *with one,* no matter what else he holds. With Jack of Clubs and Spades, the Jack of Hearts missing, he plays *with two.* *Without* Matadores, establishes the same values; that is—having Jack of Spades without Jack of Clubs is *without one;* with Jack of Hearts in hand, and two black Jacks missing, is *without two,* etc. Value is then established by counting the value of the game, to which is added the number of Matadores, *with* or *without*.

Example: With or without the first three Jacks in a Spade Tournée—3 (Matadores), plus 1 (game) equals 4, multiplied by 7 (unit value of Spade Tournée) equals 28.

Schneider and Schwarz.—If the player succeeds in getting 61 points, he wins his game, whatever it may be. If he gets 91, he wins a double game, which is called Schneider. If he takes every trick, he wins a treble game, called Schwarz.

If the single player fails to reach 61, he loses. If he fails to get 31, he is made Schneider; if he fails to win a single trick, he is made Schwarz.

These multipliers add to the value of the game he loses, just as they would add to the value of the game if he won.

In solos the player may announce Schneider or Schwarz in advance, but his adversaries cannot announce anything.

The game multipliers are as follows: 1 for the game; 2 for a Schneider; 3 for a Schwarz. Suppose a player is with two Matadores and makes Schneider, he is with 2, 2 for Schneider, 4 times the unit value of the game.

Announcing adds one multiplier. Schneider announced is worth 3. Making Schwarz after having announced to make Schneider is worth 4. Making Schwarz after having announced it is worth 5; because the announcement is a double one, to make Schneider and Schwarz both.

The Play.—After successful bidder has named the form of game he will play and disposed of the Skat cards, Vorhand leads any card, and the others must follow suit, if possible. Holding no card of suit led, player may trump or discard a card of another suit. Highest card played of suit led wins the trick, unless trumped when highest trump played wins. Winner of first trick leads for second, and so on until the hands are played out. In a Grand, if a Jack be led, holder of another Jack must play it, as the four Jacks are trumps.

Abandoned Hands.—In a Tournée, if, before he plays to the second trick, successful bidder announces that he cannot win his game, he may abandon his hand, losing the value of the game, but escaping a probable Schneider or Schwarz. This cannot be done in a Solo game, however.

Irregularities in the Hands and Play.—If, during the play, a player is discovered to have too few cards, as the result of having dropped a card, or unconsciously played two cards to one trick, he loses, but his opponent may demand that the hand be played out, to try for a Schneider or Schwarz. The last trick, with the missing card, is considered as won by opponent of player in error. If player in error is not the single player, his partner suffers with him. If player finds the missing card, he cannot take it into his hand if he has, in the meantime, played to a trick.

Playing Out of Turn.—If an adversary of the single player leads or plays out of turn, he loses the game. The single player may demand that the error be corrected and the hand played out, for the purpose of increasing the value of the game. If the single player leads out of turn, the cards must be taken back if either adversary demands it, provided both of them have not played to the trick.

The Revoke.—If a player, having a card of the suit led, neglects to follow suit, he revokes. A player who revokes loses the game, but opponent may demand that the error be corrected and the hand played out, in order to increase the value of the game.

Examining Tricks.—A player who examines the tricks taken (except the last made trick), or counts the points therein, loses the game announced, but any one of the participants may demand that the game be played out in order to increase the player's loss.

Scoring.—The player winning the game he has made or announced receives its value from each other player. If he loses, he must pay to each the value of the game lost. If more than three are playing, the players receiving no cards share the fortunes of the two who play against the single player. Payments may be made with chips, or the score of each player may be kept on a sheet of paper, the amount won being added to his score and the amount lost deducted.

At the end of the sitting, the scores of the players are balanced one against the other. Suppose that at the end of the sitting, it is found that A is minus 7, B plus 88 and C plus 19. The last line shows this, as each single player has his score added to or reduced the amount of the game he wins or loses as soon as he plays the hand. We figure thus:

A	B	C
— 7	+ 88	+ 19
— 95	+ 95	+ 26
— 26	+ 69	— 69
Total, —121	+164	— 43

A has lost 7 to B and B has won 88 from A, showing A's loss to B is 95 points. A's loss to C is 26, and so on.

AMERICAN SKAT

Although not yet officially recognized by the laws of the American Skat League, the following variety of the game is rapidly superseding all others throughout the United States, chiefly because it does away with the objectionable features of finding cards in the Skat which completely alter the value of a solo player's game. In the new game, every card in play is known to the highest bidder.

The preliminaries, including the bidding, are as in the

regular game, but the lowest bid is 18, and the highest is 504. There is no variation in the value of the suits, which are always Diamonds, 9; Hearts, 10; Spades, 11, and Clubs 12. There is only one Grand, worth 24, and Nullo is worth 23; or if played open, 46.

Skat Cards.—The highest bidder always takes the Skat cards and lays out two cards to reduce his hand to ten before announcing his game, so that every hand is practically a Gucki, the difference being that in the old game Guckis were always Grands, with Jacks only for trumps, whereas in American Skat they may be anything.

Scoring.—If the player wins the game he announces, and it makes his bid good, it is scored as in the ordinary game; but if he loses, he loses double, no matter what game he is playing.

Schneider and Schwarz.—The highest bidder is allowed to announce either Schneider or Schwarz, even after he has seen the Skat. If he succeeds in winning an announced Schneider the total value of his game is doubled instead of simply adding another multiplier to it, as in ordinary Skat. If he wins an announced Schwarz, the total value of his game is trebled.

Example: Suppose the highest bidder plays Spades without the best Jack, and announces Schneider. His game is 1 for game, 1 for Schneider, without 1, 3 times 11, or 33, doubled for announcing Schneider, 66. If he loses after announcing it, he loses 132. Should he make Schwarz after announcing Schneider he would get only the added multiplier. In the foregoing case, he would get 66 for his announced game, plus 11 for Schwarz, 77 in all.

If the highest bidder announces Schwarz and succeeds, he wins three times the value of the ordinary game. Suppose he plays a Grand with three Matadores, Schwarz announced. His game is worth 1 for game, 1 for Schneider, 1 for Schwarz, with 3, or 6 times 24, equal to 144, multiplied by 3 for announcing it, 432 points. If he lost it, it would cost him 864.

The smallest possible game to win is a Diamond with one, worth 18. The largest possible game to lose is a Grand, Schwarz announced, with four, worth 1,008.

CINCH

(High Five—Double Pedro)

Full pack, 52 cards. Four players (partners, two against two).

Rank of Cards.—Trumps rank: A (high), K, Q, J, 10, 9, 8, 7, 6, 5, 5 of suit same color as trump, 4, 3, 2 (low). Suit same color as trump: A (high), K, Q, J, 10, 9, 8, 7, 6, 4, 3, 2 (low). Other two suits: A (high), K, Q, J, 10, 9, 8, 7, 6, 5, 4, 3, 2 (low).

Cutting and Shuffling.—Cut for partners, choice of seats and deal. Highest cut wins, and Ace is high. Any player may shuffle cards, dealer last, and player to dealer's right cuts, leaving at least four cards in each packet.

Dealing.—Beginning with eldest hand, nine cards to each, three at a time, in rotation to the left. Deal passes to the left.

Dealer giving a player incorrect number of cards or failing to give each player three cards on each round, forfeits deal. Deal out of turn may be stopped before last three cards are dealt; otherwise deal must stand. If, after a bid has been made, a player discovers that he has incorrect number of cards, deal must stand if the other hands are correct.

Objects of the Game.—To hold in hand Ace and 2 of

trumps (high and low), and to take tricks in which J, 10 and 5 of trumps and 5 of suit of same color as trumps are played.

The Play.—Bidding.—Beginning with eldest hand, each player may bid for the privilege of naming the trump suit, naming the number of points he thinks he can make. Each player must bid higher than preceding bids or pass, and only one bid is allowed each player. Fourteen is highest possible bid. Highest bidder names trump suit.

Discarding and Drawing.—The trump having been named, each player discards, face upward, all cards in his hand, except trumps, and dealer gives each in turn, beginning with eldest hand, enough cards to fill his hand out to six. After helping the others, dealer may search through remainder of the pack and take what cards he wishes to fill his hand to six cards. This is called "robbing the deck."

A player having discarded a trump by mistake, may take it back, provided he has not taken into his hand the cards given him by the dealer to fill his hand; otherwise it must not be taken by any player.

If player who discarded it is highest bidder's adversary, and card is of any counting value, it is scored for highest bidder. If discarded by highest bidder or partner, it cannot be counted for either side.

Leading and Playing.—All having discarded and drawn, successful bidder leads any card. Each other player in turn plays to the lead, and if he has card of suit led, must follow suit or trump. If he has no card of suit led, he may either trump or discard a card of another suit. Highest card of suit led wins the trick, unless trumped, when highest trump played wins. Winner of first trick leads for second, etc., until the hands are played out. Cards are then bunched and new deal ensues. If, during the play, a player revokes (*i.e.*, having a card of suit led, neither follows suit nor trumps), or is found to have too many cards, the hands are played out, but neither the offending player nor his partner can score on that hand. If revoking player be bidder's opponent, bidder and partner score all they make, whether they make amount bid or not.

Cards played on a lead out of turn must be taken back, unless all have played to such lead, when trick must stand. If it was offending player's partner's turn to lead, right-hand adversary may compel him to lead trumps or not to lead trumps. If it was not the turn of that side to lead, card led out of turn must be laid face up on the table subject to call of adversaries.

Scoring.—Scoring points are as follows:

High.—Ace of trumps; counts one point for player to whom dealt.

Low.—Two of trumps; counts one point for player winning trick upon which it is played.

Low is frequently counted by player to whom it is dealt, which practice often leads to disputes as to who played it. To avoid such disputes when this method is used, the card should not be played on the trick but should be laid face up in front of its holder.

Jack.—J of trumps; counts one point for player winning trick upon which it is played.

Game.—10 of trumps; counts one point for player winning trick upon which it is played.

Right Pedro.—5 of trumps; counts five points for player winning trick upon which it is played.

Left Pedro.—5 of suit same color as trumps; counts five points for player winning trick upon which it is played.

If the bidder's side makes as many as bid, or any in excess of that figure, they score it all, and the adversaries then score any points they may have made.

If bidder and his partner fail to make the number of points bid, they not only lose any points they do make, but are *set back* amount of bid, *i.e.*, amount bid is deducted from their previous score. If they are set back before they have scored anything or more points than they have to their credit, they are said to be "in the hole," indicated by drawing a ring around the minus amount. Bidder's opponents score whatever they make.

Another method of scoring is to subtract points of side making fewer points from those of side making the more, providing bidder makes amount bid. If he fails his side scores nothing, and amount of bid is added to points made by opponents.

Under first method, if both sides go out on same deal, bidder's side wins. Under second method, as one side only scores on each hand, there can be no tie for winning the game.

Game.—Usually 51 points, but can be changed by agreement.

CINCH WITH WIDOW

Cinch is sometimes played with a widow. Deal one round of three cards to each player, beginning with eldest hand; then a widow of four cards to each, then two rounds more of three cards to each.

The four cards constituting the widow are left face down and the nine cards are taken into the hand.

Each player in turn to the left, beginning with eldest hand, bids from the nine cards in the hand for the privilege of naming trump, but before successful bidder names trump suit, each player takes up his widow. After trump is named players discard all but six cards, and play proceeds as in regular game.

PROGRESSIVE CINCH

Positions are allotted as in Progressive Euchre. Each table is provided with a bell, and the side scoring thirty-two points rings the bell at their table. Play immediately ceases at all tables, and the partners at each table having scored the greatest number of points, up to and including the last hand scored, progress.

Ties may cut to progress and score, or a half game may be scored for each player, cutting to progress only.

SIXTY-THREE

This game is a modification of Cinch. Nine cards are dealt, and after discarding the hands are filled out to nine again.

One hundred and fifty-two points constitute a game. The trump-suit cards count as follows: Ace (high), 1; King, 25; three-spot, 15; nine, 9; ten (game), 1; Jack, 1; five (right pedro), 5; five of same color suit (left pedro), 5; two (low), 1. All of these points (including low) count to the player taking them. Bidding for privilege of making the trump continues round and round until no one will bid higher. Sixty-three is the highest bid possible to make. In all other respects the rules of Cinch apply. In progressive play, four hands are played at each table, or individual scores may be counted as in Cinch.

SOLO

The Pack.—32 cards—A, K, Q, J, 10, 9, 8 and 7 of each suit.

Number of Players.—Four.

Rank of Cards.—Queen Clubs, (Spadilla) is always highest trump; 7 of trump suit (Manilla) next highest trump;

Queen Spades (Basta) next highest. Aside from these three cards, all suits rank A (highest), K, Q, J, 10, 9, 8, 7 (low).

One suit is selected (generally Clubs) as "color" for the entire sitting. When this suit is named as trump, it is called "in color," and it increases the value of the game played. (See Values of Games.)

Matadores.—Spadilla, Manilla and Basta are called Higher Matadores. When all of them are held by one player or side, each other trump held by the same player or side in uninterrupted sequence with the Higher Matadores, beginning with Ace, is called a Lower Matadore, and each adds one chip to the value of the game.

Cutting.—Instead of cutting, any player deals cards around to the left, one at a time; player first receiving a Club deals for the play.

Shuffling.—Any player may shuffle, dealer last, and player at dealer's right cuts, leaving at least five cards in each packet.

Stakes.—Each player begins with a certain number of counters, or chips. Each dealer, in turn, puts into the pool before his deal an agreed number of chips, usually 2 or 4. These chips constitute a pool, which is added to by forfeits (Bete) or subtracted from by winnings (Stamm). A Bete or a Stamm consists of as many chips as are in the pool at the time player becomes liable to the forfeit (Bete) or wins a Stamm. A Bete or a Stamm cannot exceed 16 chips, and if there are more than 16 in the pool, the player adds only 16 for a Bete, or takes 16 from the pool for a Stamm.

Dealing.—Deal eight cards to each in three rounds—three, then two, then three, in rotation to the left, beginning with eldest hand.

Object of the Game.—To win a certain number of tricks, with or without a partner.

Forms of Games.—*Simple Game.*—Bidder names trump suit, and calls for the Ace of another suit. Player holding this Ace becomes bidder's parter. Players do not know who this partner is until the called Ace is played. If player calls for an Ace of a suit of which he holds none, he must so declare before play begins, and place a card face downward before him, which is then considered as belonging to suit of called Ace, and must be played when such suit is led. Bidder and partner win the value of the game from opponents if they win five tricks; if they fail to win five tricks, they lose the value of the game to opponents.

Solo.—Bidder names trump suit, and plays alone against the three others. If he wins five tricks, he wins the value of the game from each opponent. If he fails to win five tricks, he loses the value of the game to each opponent.

Winner of Solo in color draws a Stamm from the pool, in addition to his winnings from each other player. If he loses he pays a Bete into the pool in addition to his losses to each other player.

In playing Solo or Simple Game, the player or side that wins the first five tricks may continue to play in order to take all eight tricks, but failure to win all eight forfeits the winnings of the five tricks. Success, in suit, wins double the amount of the original stake; in color, four times the original stake. Failure forfeits a like amount to opponents.

Tout.—Bidder names trump suit, and plays alone against the three others. If he wins eight tricks, he wins the value of the game from each opponent. If he fails to win eight tricks, he loses the value of the game to each opponent.

Bidding.—Players bid for the privilege of naming trump.

Bids rank: (1) Simple Game in suit (lowest); (2) Simple Game in color; (3) Solo in suit; (4) Solo in color; (5) Tout in suit; (6) Tout in color (highest).

Eldest hand has first bid. If he wishes to play a Simple Game, he says, "I ask." Player to left of eldest hand may then make the next higher bid, by asking, "Is it in color?" If eldest hand is willing to make color trump, he says, "Yes"; if not, he passes, when next player in turn takes up the bidding or passes. This order of bidding continues until no player will bid higher.

Example: A is eldest hand and says, "I ask." B, having a fair hand in Clubs, asks, "Is it in color?" A passes. C announces Solo, which bid outranks B's, as he cannot play Solo after having asked. D has a good Club Solo hand and asks C, "Is it in color?" whereupon C passes. D is highest bidder and plays alone against A, B and C with Clubs (color) as trump.

If no bid is made, holder of Spadilla must call on Ace and play simple.

Forcee.—If no higher bid than Simple Game (ask) has been made, and any player holds both Spadilla and Basta he must name the trump and play a Solo against the three others. If he wins five tricks he wins the value of the Solo from each opponent. If he fails to win five tricks he loses to each.

Or, he may call for an Ace, and holder of this Ace names the trump (any suit other than that of the called Ace), and is bidder's partner. Bidder and partner win the value of a simple game from opponents if they win five tricks. If they fail to win five tricks, they lose the value of a simple game to opponents.

If player holding Spadilla and Basta fails to play in accordance with above, he forfeits a Bete to the pool.

The Play.—After trump is named, eldest hand leads any card. Each player, in turn to the left plays a card, and must follow suit, if possible. Holding no card of suit led, player may trump or discard a card of another suit. Highest card played of suit led wins the trick, unless trumped, when highest trump played wins. Winner of first trick leads for second, and so on, until the hands are played out, or until bidder wins or loses his game. In playing Simple Game or Solo, if side or player making the trump win the first five tricks, they must abandon their hands; or, if they continue playing, they must win all eight tricks or forfeit.

A player who revokes loses the game, and must settle the losses for each other player.

Lead Out of Turn.—If the player of Solo leads or plays out of turn, or exposes a card, the error should be corrected, but does not score against him. Should one of his opponents commit any of the above errors, he loses the game and must settle the losses for each other player. If any of these errors are made in a Simple Game, the player in error must pay a Bete into the pool, and he and his partner lose the game.

Values of Games.—The values of the games are as follows:

Simple Game, in suit (any suit but color trumps)   2 chips
Simple Game, in color (color trumps) .... 4 chips
Solo, in suit .... 4 chips
Solo, in color .... 8 chips
Tout, in suit... 16 chips
Tout, in color .... 32 chips

(Among some players, these values are varied.)

THREE-HAND SOLO

Use a regular 32-card pack, reduced to 24 cards, by discarding 8 of Hearts, and all Diamonds except the 7. Diamonds are always color and there are only three trumps in this suit, Spadilla, Manilla and Basta. Solo is the only play. If no one bids, the hands are played in color, and the player taking the last trick loses the value of a Solo.

FROG OR SOLO SIXTY

The Pack.—36 cards, which rank A (high), 10, K, Q, J, 9, 8, 7, 6 (low). Each Ace is worth 11; each ten, 10; King, 4; Queen, 3; Jack, 2.

Number of Players.—Three, four or five can play, but only three are active in each deal. If four play, the dealer takes no cards. If five play, the dealer gives cards to two on his left and one on his right.

The Deal.—Anyone can deal the first hand, after which it passes to the left. Three cards to each player, then three for the widow, and then two rounds of four cards to each player.

Objects of the Game.—Each player bids to secure the privilege of naming a certain game to be played, which suits his own hand. No player can increase his own bid unless he is overbid by another.

The Games, or Bids.—There are three principal games, or bids, and the highest bidder becomes the player against the two others.

1. *Frog.*—When the bid is Frog, Hearts must be trumps. The bidder turns the widow face up to show what it contained, and then takes the cards into his hand, discarding to reduce to eleven again. Points laid out will count for him at the end of the play.

The player to the left of the dealer always leads for the

first trick any card he pleases. Others must follow suit if they can, and highest card played, if of suit led, wins the trick. Trumps win all other suits. A player is not obliged to head the trick unless he cannot follow suit, in which case he must trump, if he can. Should the third player not be able to follow suit either, he must play a trump, but he is not obliged to overtrump.

The eleven tricks played, each side turns over the cards taken in and counts the points won. If the single player gets more than 60 he must be paid, by each of his adversaries who held cards, one counter for every point he has over 60. If the bidder fails to reach 60, he must pay to each of the others at the table, including those who held no cards, one counter for every point his adversaries get more than 60.

2. *Chico.*—This outbids Frog. The bidder may name any suit but Hearts for trumps, but he must play without seeing the widow, the points in which will count for him at the end, just as in Frog. Each point under or over 60 is worth two counters in Chico.

3. *Grand.*—This is the highest bid and Hearts must be trumps, the bidder not touching the widow, although its points count toward his 60 at the end. Grand is worth four counters for every point under or over 60.

SIX BID SOLO

This is a variety of Solo Sixty, eliminating the Frog bid, as played in Salt Lake City and elsewhere.

The Pack.—36 cards, ranking from the A, 10, K, Q, down to the 6. In play, the Aces are worth 11 points each, each ten, 10; King, 4; Queen, 3; Jack, 2. This gives 120 for the pack.

Number of Players.—Three are active. If there are four at the table, the dealer takes no cards, but is paid if the bidder fails. If the bidder succeeds, the dealer (4th player) does not pay him.

Counters.—Each player should have the equivalent of at least 200 counters, the value being agreed upon.

The Deal.—Anyone can deal the first hand, after which it passes in turn to the left. The pack being properly shuffled and cut, 4 cards are dealt to each of the three active players, then 3 to each and 3 for the widow, then 4 to each player. This gives 11 cards as the playing hand on which bids are made.

Objects of the Game.—Each player in turn, beginning to the left of the dealer, bids to secure the privilege of playing a certain game, which he considers best suited to his hand. There are six of these games, which outrank one another in the order following. No player can change his bid, except to make a higher call when he is overcalled by another player. To win his game, the bidder must take in at least 60 of the 120 points on the cards.. The points in the widow count for him.

The Games, or Bids.—These are as follows:

1. Solo.—If this is not overcalled, the player names Spades, Clubs, or Diamonds, for the trump, and the player to the left of the dealer leads any card he pleases. The widow is not touched until the last trick is played. For every point the bidder takes in beyond 60, he receives 2 chips from each of the two active players. If he fails to reach 60, even with the aid of the points in the widow, he pays 2 chips to each, including the 4th player, if there is a 4th.

2. Heart Solo.—This overcalls Solo. Hearts must be trumps, and the bidder wins or loses 3 chips for each point above or below 60.

3. Misère.—There are no trumps, and the bidder under-

takes to avoid taking in a single counting card. The moment he takes a trick with a counting card in it, the hand is abandoned, and his game is lost. The cards in the widow are not counted. This bid wins or loses a flat rate of 30 chips to each of the other players, with the usual rule for the 4th player.

4. Guarantee Solo.—If the player names Hearts for trumps, he must make at least 74 points, in play and widow. If he names any other suit for the trump, he must make 80 points. This game wins or loses 40 chips flat to each player.

5. Spread Misère.—There are no trumps, and the player to the left of the bidder leads, no matter who dealt. The other plays to the lead, and the bidder's cards are then laid on the table face up, but his opponents cannot dictate the order in which he shall play them. The widow is disregarded. If the player does not take in a single counting card he wins 60 chips. If he loses, he pays 60 to each.

6. Call Solo.—The bidder asks for a named card. Any player holding that card must give it to the bidder, and take one in exchange. If the card asked for is in the widow, there is no exchange of cards. After the exchange, if any, the bidder names the trump, and undertakes to win the whole 120 points, counting those in the widow. The moment the opponents take in a counting card, the bidder's game is lost. If he has named Hearts, he wins or loses a flat rate of 150 chips to each player; if he has named any other suit, 100 chips.

Ties.—In the first two bids, Solo and Heart Solo, if each side takes in 60 points, it is a tie, and the bidder neither wins nor loses.

The Widow.—After the hand is played out, the widow is turned face up, and any points in it are counted to the bidder, except in misère, when the widow is not touched.

The Play.—Except in a spread misère, the player to the left of the dealer always leads for the first trick, any card he pleases. The next player must follow suit if he can and is obliged to trump if he cannot follow suit.

Revokes.—If the bidder revokes, he cannot win anything even if he makes the number of points required by his bid, but he does not lose anything. If he fails to make the required number of points, he must pay. If one of his adversaries revokes, neither of them can win anything, but they must pay losses, if any. In a misère, a revoke loses the game at once.

PROGRESSIVE SOLO

The Bids.—In this variation the Frog is added, and there are five standard bids, which outrank one another in order. These are: Frog, Spade Solo, Club Solo, Diamond Solo, Heart Solo. The player to the left of the dealer bids or passes, and each in turn to the left must overcall or pass. If a player's first bid is overcalled, he may bid again, if he can go higher. In the lowest bid, Frog, the three widow cards are not exposed and are taken into the hand of the bidder, who then discards any three cards face down. The cards that bidder discards face down always count for him at the end of the hand. The widow is not taken up in any of the solo bids but points in it are counted without bidder's cards.

Payments.—The bidder wins or loses according to the rank of his call, for every point over or under 60. For a Frog, 1 chip; for Spade Solo, 2 chips; for Club Solo, 3 chips; for Diamond Solo, 4 chips; and for Heart Solo, 5 chips. If both sides make 60, it is a tie.

The Double.—Any player in his turn may double a bid instead of overcalling it. If the doubled bid stands, the bidder wins or loses twice the usual amount. If the bidder redoubles, he wins or loses four times the usual amount. If the double or redouble is taken out with a higher bid, it is void.

The Pots.—It is usually agreed to make up two pots, each player contributing an agreed number of chips to the Frog pot, and twice as many to the Solo pot. These are kept separate. If the bidder succeeds, he takes the pot he plays for; but if he loses, he must double the number of chips in that pot. This is in addition to the usual payments for each point over or under 60.

RAMS—BIERSPIEL—ROUNCE

These are all American variations of the old German game Ramsch and are played by three to six players. In the first two games 32 cards are used (seven-spot low), in *Rounce* 52 cards (deuce low). In *Rams,* as generally played in the United States, the King is high, with the Ace ranking after the King. In *Bierspiel* the seven of Diamonds ranks as the second best trump. The rules given below apply to all three games, except where special rules are noted for *Rounce* and *Bierspiel.* The first deal is determined by any player dealing cards face up in rotation to the left, first player receiving a Jack being the first dealer.

Any player may shuffle cards, dealer last, and player to dealer's right cuts, leaving at least five cards in each packet. Five cards, by twos and threes, are dealt to each player, and an extra hand (or "widow") is dealt face down just before dealer helps himself in each round. The next card is turned for trump. In *Rounce* six cards are dealt to widow. In six-hand *Rounce* dealer takes no cards. In *Bierspiel,*

if seven of Diamonds is turned for trump, next card is
turned up, and this indicates trump suit. Dealer may take
both cards into his hand, discarding two others. If dealer
passes, eldest hand has privilege of taking up trump.

The Play.—Eldest hand may play either with original
hand or widow, or may pass. If he passes or takes widow,
he discards original hand and lays it, face down, on table.
(In *Rounce* player taking widow must discard one card.)
Each player after eldest hand may in turn pass or declare
to play, but hands of those who pass must not be discarded
until every player has had his say. The widow may be
taken up by any player unless another has already taken it.
Hands must not be examined after they are discarded. If
all others have passed pone must play with dealer. If all
but one pass, dealer must play with him. If two or more
declare to play, dealer may play or pass. Dealer may discard
one card and take up turned trump card. Each player who
plays must take at least one trick or forfeit five counters
to the next pool.

A "general rams" may be declared by any player, who
then has the lead and must win all five tricks. Each of the
other players must play in "general rams" even though he
has previously passed. (There is no "general rams" in
Rounce.)

Except a "general rams" is declared, eldest hand of those
who have not passed leads a card of any suit. Each player
in turn must follow suit, and must head the trick if he can.
If he cannot head the trick, he may play any card he has
of suit led. ·If unable to follow suit, player must trump (or
overtrump, if trumps have already been played). Even
though he cannot overtrump he must still play a trump; if
he can neither follow suit nor trump, he discards a card of
another suit. Highest card played of suit led wins trick,

unless trumped, when highest trump played wins. Winner of a trick leads to the next.

Rounce.—Player is not obliged to take trick, but must follow suit, if possible. Winner of first trick must play trump for second lead; thereafter any suit may be led.

Bierspiel.—Players may not look at their cards until dealer has turned trump and said "Auf," which is the signal for players to take up their hands. If four players declare to play, the first three leads must be trump; if three play, first two leads trump; if two, the first lead trump. If leader has no trump, he must play, face down, the lowest card in his hand, and the other players having trumps must play trump on it.

Scoring.—Players begin with an equal number of counters. Each dealer in turn puts up five counters for pool. If any player, who does not. pass, fails to take at least one trick, he is "ramsed," or "rounced," and must add five counters to next pool. At end of each hand player takes one-fifth of the amount of pool for each trick he has taken.

Pool containing only dealer's five counters is called "Simple," and all players must play. If it contains more than dealer's counters by reason of a player's having been ramsed, or having failed to succeed at "general rams," the pool is called "Double," and players may play or pass as they choose. If a player declaring "general rams" takes all five tricks, he takes pool, and each other player pays him five counters. If he fails, he must pay each other player five counters and must double the pool.

Bierspiel.—Scored by points, each trick taken counting 1 point. Each player starts with an equal number of points, from which his scores are deducted.

Game.—In *Rams* and *Rounce* first player losing all his counters loses game, or player first winning an agreed

number of counters wins game. In *Bierspiel* player cancel-
ing all his points wins game.

AMERICAN PINOCHLE
Two-Hand

Pinochle is played in America with 48 cards (two each
of A, K, Q, J, 10 and 9 of each suit), or 64 cards (adding
the 8's and 7's). The cards rank: A (high), 10, K, Q, J,
9, 8, 7. If two cards of same suit and denomination are
played on one trick the card that is played first wins.

In cutting for deal, high deals. Either player may shuffle
the cards, dealer last, and pone cuts, leaving at least five
cards in each pack. With the 48-card pack twelve cards are
dealt to each player, four at a time, and the next card
turned for trump. With the 64-card pack sixteen cards
are dealt to each player. If the card turned for trump
should be the lowest of the suit (the 9-spot or 7-spot, respectively) the dealer scores 10 points for it at once. This
trump is called *Dix* (pronounced "deece"). The rest of the
pack is laid beside it, face down. In case of a misdeal, a new
deal is required by the same player.

Objects of the Game.—To score certain combinations of
high cards (called melds), and to win play tricks containing
cards of counting value. The combinations of counting
value, or melds, are as follows:

Class A

Marriage (K and Q of any plain suit) .... 20 points
Royal Marriage (K and Q of trump suit) .... 40 points
Royal Sequence (A, K, Q, J and 10 of trumps) 150 points

Class B

Pinochle (Q of Spades and J of Diamonds)........ 40 points
Double Pinochle (2 Q's of Spades and 2 J's of
    Diamonds) .... 80 points
    In some localities Double Pinochle counts 500.

Class C

Four Jacks	(one each of the four suits)....	40 points
Four Queens	(one each of the four suits)....	60 points
Four Kings	(one each of the four suits)....	80 points
Four Aces	(one each of the four suits)....	100 points
8 Jacks		80 points
8 Queens		120 points
8 Kings		160 points
8 Aces		200 points

Cards taken in on tricks have the following values: Aces and tens, each count 10 points; Kings and Queens, each 5 points. The last trick counts 10 points for player taking it.

The Dix (lowest trump) counts 10 points to dealer turning it up or to holder under conditions elsewhere stated.

Melds are of no value unless the player making them wins at least one trick in play. Incorrect melds such as three Kings and a Jack in place of four Kings, stand unless corrected by the opponent.

The Play.—Eldest hand leads any card and dealer plays on it any card he chooses, it not being necessary to follow suit until the stock is exhaused. The high card of suit led wins unless trumped. Winner of trick may meld (or announce) any *one* combination which he holds, but he must do this before drawing his card from the stock by laying the cards composing the combination face up on the table. The meld is then scored immediately. A player who holds the lowest trump (9 or 7 as it may be) may, upon taking a trick, exchange it for the trump card originally turned up and score 10 points for the Dix, but if he makes any other meld on the same trick the 10 points are lost.

Cards used in one combination cannot be used in any other combination of less or equal value if both melds are in the same class. The lower must always be shown first and the higher added to it. At least one fresh card from the hand must be added to the cards already on the table for each additional meld.

After melding (if he has a meld) winner of trick draws top card from stock, his opponent taking the next, and leads for the next trick. In this way the play continues until the stock is exhausted. After all the cards have been drawn from the stock the second player on each trick must not only follow suit, but must take the trick if he can; if he has no card of suit led he must trump if he has a trump.

Only one combination can be melded for each trick taken. Cards used for melds may be afterwards led or played on tricks.

Irregular Plays.—If a player fails to take a trick when possible after the stock is exhausted, the opponent may demand that the cards be replayed from the trick in which the error was made.

If, after the first draw, a player has too many or too few cards, his opponent may allow him to play without drawing until his hand is reduced to the right number of cards or to fill his hand from the stock.

A card led out of turn may be taken back without penalty if the error is discovered before opponent has played; otherwise it must stand.

Irregularities in Drawing.—A player who draws two cards at once may put the second card back without penalty if he has not seen it; otherwise he must show it to opponent.

If loser of a trick looks at two cards in drawing, his opponent may look at two cards after the next trick and may take whichever one he chooses, without showing it.

If a player, at his proper turn, neglects to draw, his opponent may allow him to draw two cards after the next trick or may, at his option, declare the deal void.

Should there, through error, remain only two cards besides the trump card in the talon after the next to the last trick, the winner of the last preceding trick must take the top card, his opponent taking the trump, and the last card in the stock must remain unexposed.

Calling Out.—The first player who correctly declares that he has reached 1,000 points wins the game, no matter what the opponent's score may be. It therefore behooves each player to keep track of his points toward the end of the game. A player may call out at any time before the last trick is taken, whether he is in the lead or not, but not after he has picked up his cards to count his points. If he calls when he is not out, he loses the game. If both are 1,000 and neither has called out, the game is continued to 1,250 points.

If a meld is enough to put a player out, it is not necessary for him to win another trick to make the meld good. If the 10 points for the last trick complete a player's score he must call out before he takes the trick.

Scoring.—When the hands have been played out the points taken in tricks by each player are counted and added to the meld scores. The game is 1,000 points, unless extended to 1,250, as previously stated.

9

THREE- AND FOUR-HAND PINOCHLE

Three-hand Pinochle is played with 48 cards; four-hand, either 48 or 64. Deal is determined by cutting as in two-hand game; in four-hand, higher two are partners against lower two. In three-hand game (and in four-hand when 64 cards are used), 16 cards are dealt to each player, four at a time; in four-hand, with 48-card pack, 12 cards to each. Last card is turned for trump. Eldest hand, if he holds it, may exchange lowest trump (9 or 7) for turned trump, and score 10 for Dix. If not, next player has the privilege, and so on around the table until trump is exchanged. Holder of other 9 or 7 may then show it and also score 10 for Dix. Dix is a meld in three-hand even if dealer turns it up, and is scored with the other melds after winning a trick.

Each player, beginning with eldest hand, exposes whatever melding combinations he holds, and their values are noted. In four-hand Pinochle combinations cannot be formed by combining cards from two partners' hands. At least one fresh card must be taken from the hand for each additional meld. Thus four K's and Q's score 220 only, because the last card laid down cannot be used for two melds at one time. The trump sequence scores 190 if the marriage is laid down first and the A, J, 10 added.

After the melds are noted they are taken back into the hand and eldest hand leads any card. The other players, in turn to left, must follow suit and must head the trick if they can. A player holding no card of suit led must trump, and if the suit has already been trumped he must, if he has it, play a higher trump even if this wins his partner's trick. Also, if a trick has already been trumped and he has no card of the suit led, he must play a trump if he has one, even though it should not be higher than those already played. Player having neither suit nor trump may discard anything he pleases. Winner of first trick leads for next, etc.

After taking a trick, a player may score all of his melds. If he has no tricks he can score no melds. In partnership games both partners may score their melds if either takes a trick.

The game is 1,000 points. The rules as to calling out, etc., are the same as in the two-hand game. In partnership games a player calling out binds his partner.

AUCTION PINOCHLE WITH WIDOW

This is today the most popular form of Pinochle and has superseded nearly all of the other forms of the game. It is played with 48 cards (two each of the A, 10, K, Q, J, and 9 of each suit). It is played by three or four persons; if four play, the dealer takes no cards but shares the fortunes of the two opposed to the highest bidder.

Fifteen cards are dealt to each active player, three at a time, and three are laid aside, face down, after the first round, for the widow.

The player at the left of the dealer bids first and the bidding proceeds towards the left until two players in succession pass. Each bid must be at least 10 points higher than the previous one and a player who passes may enter the bidding upon the next round if he desires to do so.

When the bidding has been finished, the cards in the widow are turned face up for all to see and the successful bidder takes them into his hand and names the trump. He then lays out three cards in place of the widow, the points in which count for him at the end of the play. It is important that the bidder discard before melding, as no part of his melds may be laid away.

If a player takes up the widow before the bidding is finished, he cannot bid on that deal and must allow the highest bidder to draw three cards from his hand, face down, to take the place of the widow. Should a player expose the widow without taking it into his hand, he must shuffle it with his other cards, under the same penalty.

If successful bidder neglects to lay out for the widow before melding, he must be called upon to show his melds again after discarding. If he leads for the first trick without having discarded, his opponent must call upon him to discard before playing to the lead, or they condone the error. If the widow is found to contain more or less than three cards, opponents having their right number, the bidder's hand is foul and he is set back, provided there was no claim of irregularity in the pack when the deal was made.

Melds and scoring points are the same as stated under the head of Two-hand Pinochle.

The bidder then makes his melds and as he makes all of them at once, the trump sequence counts only 150, the royal marriage being lost. The opponents are not allowed to make any melds or to score anything for cards in the tricks which they take.

The play then begins by the successful bidder leading any card that he pleases for the first trick. The rules laid down under the head of Three- and Four-hand Pinochle as to following suit and trumping apply here.

If either of bidder's opponents leads or *plays out of turn*, the bidder cannot be set back, and he may either let the card led or played in error stand or may call upon the proper player to lead, the card played in error being left on the table subject to call. There is no penalty if the bidder leads out of turn.

A player *failing to follow suit* or to head a trick when possible is guilty of a revoke. If he is the bidder and his melds alone do not cover the amount bid, he is set back. If either of his adversaries revokes he cannot be set back, and he may play out the hand to score all he can in cards.

Any player found to have *too many cards* after playing to the first trick forfeits his entire score. If he has *too few* the card must be found, and he is then held responsible for any revokes just as if the card had been in his hand. If one opponent is short and the other has too many, the bidder cannot be set back, but may play out the hand. The superfluous card at the end belongs to the bidder, whether or not he wins the last trick. If the bidder has too many cards he is set back. If he has too few, the opponents having their proper number, the bidder's hand is foul and he is set back.

Any player turning up *and looking at any but the last* trick is not allowed to score anything for cards. This rule applies to all forms of Pinochle.

If bidder's melds equal his bid, the hand is not played, as only the amount bid can be scored. But if the melds are not sufficient to enable him to win, he may play the hand in an effort to win by cards enough when added to his melds, to equal his bid. If he does this he scores the amount of his bid. If after turning up the widow he decides that he cannot win enough by cards to increase his melds to the amount of his bid, he may acknowledge defeat, throw down the cards and accept a loss equal to his bid but if he plays the hand and still fails to make his bid, he loses double the amount of his bid.

In some localities one suit is considered better than the others and when it is trump the bidder scores double his bid. In the East, the Heart suit is so designated while in the Middle West Spades are the favorite suit. This is an optional provision and should be agreed upon by any set of players.

Some players vary the general rules by giving greatly increased values to *double* melds such as, 8 Aces, Kings, Queens or Jacks or the double Pinochle, double Royal Marriage or double trump sequence. Of course it is much harder to obtain such combinations which would seem to justify higher premiums for them, but the best authorities do not sanction such variations.

BEZIQUE

The Pack.—64 cards, two each (A, K, Q, J, 10, 9, 8 and 7 of each suit).

Number of Players.—Two.

Rank of Cards.—A (high), 10, K, Q, J, 9, 8, 7 (low). If two cards of the same suit and denomination fall on the same trick, the first played wins.

Cutting.—Cut for deal—high deals, cards ranking as above. Ties recut.

Shuffling.—Either player may shuffle and dealer's opponent (pone) cuts, leaving at least five cards in each packet.

Dealing.—Eight cards to each, beginning with pone, three to each, then two, then three. The 17th card is turned up for trump. The balance of the pack (called the talon) is placed face downward on the table, and the trump card is placed beside it, face upward. If this trump card is seven, dealer scores 10 points for it at once.

Misdealing.—Misdeal does not lose the deal. New deal by same dealer is required as follows:

If dealer exposes a card belonging to pone or to talon, pone may require a new deal.

If, before first trick is turned down, either player is discovered to have too many cards.

If a card, faced in pack, is discovered before first trick is turned down.

If pack is found to be incorrect.

If either player exposes one of his own cards, deal must stand.

A card faced in the talon after first trick is turned, must be turned face down in its proper position in the pack.

If, before first trick is turned, a hand is found to be short of correct number of cards, pone may require a new deal, or require dealer to supply deficiency from top of pack.

Objects of the Game.—To form, during play, certain combinations of cards of counting value, as shown in the following table; also to take in Aces and tens (called "Brisques") on tricks:

Class A

Marriage (K and Q of any suit) .... 20 points
Royal Marriage (K and Q of trumps) .... 40 points
Sequence (A, K, Q, J, 10 of trumps) .... 250 points

Class B

Bézique (Q Spades and J Diamonds) .... 40 points
Double Bézique (2 Q's Spades and 2 J's of
  Diamonds) .... 500 points

Class C

Four Aces	(any suits)	100 points
Four Kings	" "	80 points
Four Queens	" "	60 points
Four Jacks	" "	40 points

Each brisque counts 10 points for player winning it in tricks, and is scored as soon as taken in. Winner of last trick adds 10 points to his score.

The Play.—Pone leads any card, and dealer plays any card on it. Neither player is obliged to follow suit or trump, but may play any card he chooses. Higher card played of suit led wins the trick unless trumped, when trump wins. Winner of each trick takes the top card from the talon before leading for next trick, his opponent taking the next card. This continues until the talon is exhausted.

Either player, after winning a trick, and before drawing from the talon, may declare any one combination he holds, by laying the component cards of such combination face upward on the table. He scores for such combination at once. Only one combination may be declared after each trick, but a player holding more than one combination may announce them all, score for one of them, holding the others in abeyance, to be scored, one at a time, after each trick that he wins subsequently. If, before he has scored all of his declarations, he should draw cards which form another combination which he would prefer to declare, he may announce it and score it upon taking a trick, still holding in abeyance the combinations already on the table.

A card used in one combination cannot be used in another combination of less or equal value in the same class. For instance: King and Queen of trumps declared as Royal Marriage may be used again in sequence, but if used in the sequence first, they cannot thereafter be scored as a marriage, the latter being a combination of less value and of the same class as the sequence. Again, if King and Queen of any suit have been declared, another King or Queen cannot be added to either of the cards to reform the marriage; but three other Queens or Kings may be added to the Queen or King to make four Queens or four Kings.

Player holding the seven of trumps may, upon taking a trick, exchange it for the turned trump and score 10 points. Should he hold both sevens, he may score 10 points for each. Player holding the second seven may show it upon taking a trick, and score 10 points for it. Neither player can announce a combination and score the seven at the same time.

Player exposing and scoring a combination which is found to be erroneous must deduct the amount from his score, and his opponent may designate and compel him to lead any card of that combination. If he has in his hand the card or cards to correct the error, however, he may do so without penalty, provided he has not in the meantime drawn a card from the talon.

When only one card besides the trump card remains in the talon, winner of the last trick takes it, his opponent taking the trump. All declarations then cease, and each player takes into his hand whatever cards he has exposed on the table. Winner of the last trick then leads any card, and thereafter each player must not only follow suit, but must win the trick if he can. Holding no card of suit led he must trump, if possible.

Irregularities in Play.—A lead out of turn may be taken back without penalty, if discovered before opponent has played to it; otherwise it must stand.

If either player has too many or too few cards after the first draw, opponent may allow player in error to play without drawing until his hand is reduced to eight cards, if he has too many; or to fill his hand from the talon, if he has too few.

If, after the talon is exhausted, a player fails to win a trick when possible, his opponent may demand that the cards be taken up and replayed from the trick in which the error was made.

Irregularities in Drawing.—If a player neglects to draw at his proper turn, his opponent may declare the deal void, or may allow player to draw two cards after the next trick.

Player drawing two cards at once may put the second card back without penalty, if he has not seen it; otherwise he must show it to his opponent.

Player drawing out of turn must put back card drawn, and if such card belongs to opponent, player in error must show his own card to opponent. If both players draw erroneously the draws must stand.

If the loser of a trick in drawing looks at two cards, his opponent may look at two cards after the next trick, and may take into his hand whichever he chooses. If he takes the second card, he need not show it.

Should there, through error, remain only two cards in the talon besides the trump card after the next to the last trick, the winner of the last trick must take the top card, his opponent taking the trump, leaving the last card of the talon unexposed.

Scoring.—All scores are counted as soon as made, for combinations, brisques, sevens of trumps, and last trick.

There are many devices made for scoring Bézique, but it may be scored on a sheet of paper after the method used in Cribbage.

A convenient method of scoring is with Poker chips—nine blue chips representing 100 points each; four red chips, 20 points each; and two whites, 10 points each. These are arranged in a row on the table, and chips representing the proper number of points are moved forward on the table as the points are made.

Example.—Supposing A and B are playing. A wins first trick, and, announcing Royal Marriage, he pushes two red chips forward. `On next trick he announces four Queens, taking back two red chips and pushing forward one blue chip. In this way any number of points may be indicated with the chips as apportioned above.

Game.—Usually 1,000 points.

BEZIQUE WITHOUT A TRUMP

Played the same as the regular game, except that no trump is turned; the first marriage declared and scored determines trump suit. Seven of trumps does not count; all other combinations count as in the regular game.

THREE-HAND BEZIQUE

The three-hand game requires three packs of cards. A Triple Bézique (three Queens of Spades and three Jacks of Diamonds) counts 1,500 points. All other combinations count the same as in the regular game.

Game.—2,000 points.

FOUR-HAND BEZIQUE

Four-hand game requires four packs of cards. Play may be as partners or as individuals. Combinations are the same as in the regular game, and Triple Bézique counts 1,500 points.

Player, upon taking a trick, may announce all of the combinations which he holds, or may pass the privilege to his partner. Only one combination may be scored after each trick. Partners may combine the cards held by each other to form combinations, provided one part of such combinations is already on the table.

Game.—2,000 points.

RUBICON BEZIQUE

Rubicon Bézique differs from the regular two-hand game in the following particulars:

Four packs of 32 cards each are used; there are two players, and nine cards are dealt to each player, no trump being turned. The first marriage declared and scored determines the trump suit.

In addition to the regular combinations, the following are allowed: Sequence in plain suit counts 150 points; Triple Bézique counts 1,500 points; Quadruple Bézique counts 4,500 points. The last trick counts 50 points for the player winning it.

Player receiving neither a Jack, Queen nor King on the original deal may expose his hand and score 50 points for Carte Blanche. If on the first draw he gets neither Jack, Queen, nor King, he may show the card drawn and score another 50 points for Carte Blanche, and so on until he draws a Jack, Queen or King. The first Carte Blanche can be counted only from the hand as originally dealt.

Combinations which have been scored may be broken into, a new card or cards substituted, and the combination scored again. For instance: Four Aces have been declared and scored and one of the Aces has been played. A new Ace of any suit may be substituted, and four Aces scored again. The same principle applies to all other combinations. A player cannot use a card as part of a combination when such card has been used in a combination of equal or greater value of the same class. Thus, a King used in a sequence could not thereafter be combined with a Queen to form a marriage.

Scoring.—Each deal is a game in itself. After the deal is played out, the points for combinations, Carte Blanche and the last trick are counted up and the lower score is deducted from the higher. In counting, all fractions of 100 are disregarded, the score being counted by 100's only. Brisques are not counted until after all other scores are counted, and then only where the score is close enough for the brisque count to change the result; or where, by counting the brisques, a player may save himself from a rubicon. (See below.) In case the difference between the two scores is less than 100 on the final count, the higher adds 100 points to his score for bonus. To this is added 500 points for game, the sum being the value of the game.

A player scoring less than 1,000 points is *rubiconed,* and all points he has made are *added* to the higher score. Winner of a rubicon also adds 1,000 points to his score (a double game) for the rubicon, and 300 points for all the brisques, no matter by whom won. If rubiconed player has scored less than 100, his adversary adds 100 points for bonus, in addition to above.

If a player can bring his score up to 1,000 by adding the brisques he has won, he has not been rubiconed. In this case, the other is also allowed to count his brisques.

RUM

This game is best adapted to four, five or six players, but may be played also by two or three. The full pack of 52 cards is used, ranking sequence from King to Ace. Deal and choice of seats are determined by drawing from the spread deck, highest winning. With four or more playing, six cards are given to each; with three players, seven; with two players, ten. The cards are dealt one at a time, and the next card, face up, is placed beside the stock in the center of the table to start the discard pack.

The object of the game is to get rid of the cards by laying them out in sequence and suit of three or more or in triplets and fours.

The play begins by eldest hand drawing a card from the top of the stock without showing it or taking the card lying face up beside the stock. If he should hold in his hand any three or four of a kind, as three 7's, or any suit in sequence of three or more, as 9, 10, J of Hearts, he may lay them face up on the table. Whether he exposes some combination or not he discards one card which is placed face up upon the discard pack covering the card which was previously on top.

After the eldest hand each player in turn to the left proceeds in like manner, but, as the game is generally played, only one combination can be laid down at one time.

Another way to get rid of cards is to add them to combinations already on the table. Thus if three Kings have been laid down a player may add the fourth if he has it, or he may add the 7 or Jack of Hearts to the 8, 9 and 10 of Hearts already laid down. Sequences may thus be extended indefinitely, but the Ace must always end a sequence. As the game is generally played only one card at a time can be laid down in this way, but this rule as well as the one on combinations may be set aside by agreement.

No player may get rid of any card except in his proper turn. If a player cannot use the exposed card he must draw from the stock. In case of doubt it is well to draw for the smaller combinations.

If all the cards are drawn from the stock before any player gets rid of all his cards the game may be ended by all players showing their hands, the lowest pip value winning, or the game may be continued by gathering up the discards and, after shuffling and cutting, turning up the top card and leaving the rest face down, then proceeding as if it were the original stock.

The player who first gets rid of all the cards dealt him or drawn wins the game, the others settling with him according to the number of pips on the cards remaining in their hands, the Ace counting one and so on up, Jack 11, Queen 12 and King 13.

The game is sometimes varied so that a player holding combinations which include every card in his hand may lay them all down at once, in which case he scores double the pip value of his opponents' hands.

QUINZE

This is a French game. It is usually played by only two persons, and is much admired for its simplicity and fairness; as it depends entirely upon chance, is soon decided, and does not require that attention which most other card games do; it is, therefore, particularly calculated for those who love to sport upon an equal chance.

It is called Quinze from fifteen being the game, and is played as follows:

1. The cards must be shuffled by the two players, and when they have cut for deal, which falls to him who cuts the

highest, the dealer has the liberty to shuffle them again.

2. When this is done, the adversary cuts them; after which the dealer gives one card to his opponent and one to himself.

3. Should the adversary's card be a small one, he is entitled to have as many cards given to him, one after the other, as will make fifteen, or come nearest to that number, which are given face up from the top of the pack. For example, if his first card is a deuce, and he draws a five, which amount to seven, he must continue, in expectation of coming nearer to fifteen. If he then draws an eight, which will make him just fifteen, he, as being the eldest hand, is sure of winning the game. But if he overdraw, and make more than fifteen, he loses, unless the dealer should happen to do the same; which circumstance constitutes a drawn game, and the stakes are consequently doubled. In this manner they continue, until one of them has won the game by being nearest to fifteen.

4. At the end of each game, the cards are shuffled, and the players again cut for deal.

SOLITAIRE CARD GAMES
NAPOLEON AT ST. HELENA
("Big Forty" or "Forty Thieves.")

Shuffle two entire packs of cards together and deal off upon the table, face up, four rows of ten cards each, from left to right—forty cards in all—called the *tableau*.

The object is to relase the cards from the tableau and *talon* (see below), according to the following rules, so that

·they can build up in eight suits, beginning with Ace, then deuce, etc., up to King.

In building, only the top card of the talon or a bottom card in the tableau can be used; the rule regarding the tableau being that no card can be used that has another card lying beneath it. Thus, at the beginning of the play, the cards in the bottom row of the tableau only are available, but as soon as one has been used the card which lies just above it can be used.

To play: If there are any Aces in the bottom row of the tableau, release them, and lay them in a row beneath the tableau, the Aces forming the *foundations* for building.

Then examine the tableau and endeavor to release cards so as to build upon the *foundations* (following suit, or to build down in sequence within the tableau itself, following suit). Thus, if you have a King of Hearts near the top of the tableau, and a Queen of Hearts which is available for use (no card beneath it), the Queen may be played on the King, and so on, playing the available cards in descending sequence on to any card in the tableau. This should be done as long as such a play can be made, as it releases other cards desired for use. It is called marriage, and should be proceeded with cautiously, as a sequence formed in a lower row may block a desired card above it, which might soon have been released.

As fast as Aces are released place them in the foundation row.

In plays in the tableau, create, if possible, a vacancy (in a straight line) in the top row. This space will be of great advantage in releasing other cards in the tableau or talon. Vacancies in the top row may be filled with any available card, either from the tableau or talon. The player will use his judgment about filling the vacancies as created, or wait for a more opportune time. Only one card may be moved at a time so that if the bottom card in any row of the tableau has another on it, it cannot be moved until it can be placed on a foundation.

When all the available cards are played, deal out the remainder of the pack one card at a time, playing all suitble ones in descending sequence on the tableau or in ascending sequence on the foundations.

The cards that canot be played, either on the foundations or tableau, are laid aside, one on top of the other, face up, forming the talon.

If the foundations cannot all be completed in the ascending sequence to the Kings, thus consuming all the cards in the tableau and talon in one deal of the cards, the game is lost. There is no redeal.

TWENTY-FOUR CARD TABLEAU

This game is played according to the rules governing Napoleon, with the following exceptions:

Deal the tableau, four rows of six cards each. The foundations can only be built upon in suits ascending in sequence to the King. The tableau can only be built upon in descending sequence in alternate colors. The player is entitled to redeal the talon.

TWENTY-EIGHT CARD TABLEAU

This game is played under the same rules as Napoleon, except in the following points:

Deal four rows of seven cards each. The foundations must be built upon in ascending sequence, in alternate colors, regardless of suit, and the tableau in descending sequence in the same manner.

THIRTY-TWO CARD TABLEAU

Deal four rows of eight cards each, to form the tableau. Any Aces or suitable cards for the foundations may be played direct on the foundations, while dealing the cards to form the tableau. Build upon the foundations in ascending sequence, in suits only. Build down on the available cards in the tableau, in descending sequence, in alternate colors. Deal once only. In all other respects the rules for Napoleon will apply.

THIRTY-SIX CARD TABLEAU·

Deal four rows of nine cards each. Build upon the foundation, in ascending sequence, in suits only. Build down on the available cards in the tableau, in descending sequence, in alternate colors. In all other respects the rules for Napoleon will apply.

AULD LANG SYNE

Take four Aces from a pack of cards and lay them out in a horizontal row (*foundations*). Then deal out the pack, one card at a time, into four piles, watching the cards closely and building on the foundations from any of the four piles whenever possible (it is not necessary to follow suit). No redeal is permitted.

A more difficult way is to leave the Aces in the pack and place them in position as they come out in the deal.

Still another way. is to follow suit in building. Two redeals are permitted when played this way.

STREETS AND ALLEYS

Shuffle a full pack of 52 cards, and then lay down a vertical row of four cards. To the right of these, lay down another row of four cards, both face up, with a good space between the two rows. To the left of the first row lay four more, letting them overlap the first row a little. Do the same with the row to the right, putting the second row still further to the right. Continue this until you have laid out the whole pack, when you will find that you have four rows of cards, seven in each row, on your left, and four rows, six in each row, on your right, with an alley between.

Let us suppose this is the layout:

D9	C9	H6	HJ	DA	HK	C3		H8	S7	CK	C6	DK	H2
H5	HA	D3	CA	S4	C7	H3		C5	S9	CQ	H4	SQ	D6
C4	D10	S6	C10	H7	C8	S5		D4	DJ	D5	DQ	C2	H10
S8	HQ	S10	S3	D2	SA	SK		CJ	SJ	H9	D8	S2	D7

The only cards that are in play are the eight that are on the extreme ends of the four rows. In the example given above these are the D9, H5, C4, S8, H2, D6, H10, and D7. Any of these eight may be used upon any other of the eight to build down in sequence, regardless of suit or color. As soon as a card is so used, it will expose the card next to it and bring it into play.

Assume that we play the H5 on the D6, we expose and bring into play the HA, and all Aces must be immediately placed in the alley, between the two sets of cards, to be built upon, in sequence and suit, until the King is reached.

Having placed the HA in the alley, you have uncovered the D3. Put the H2 on the HA, and you uncover the DK, and so on. As soon as any row of cards on either side of the alley is cleared up by this shifting and covering, any of the end cards on any row may be taken and placed in the space. But for this provision it would be impossible to get rid of a blocking card like the DK, for instance.

Although the player is obliged to place the Aces in the alley as soon as they are free, he is not obliged to build upon them unless he wishes to, and it will usually be found better not to be in too great a hurry about it.

A variation of this game is to place the Aces in the alley as the cards are dealt, instead of leaving them to be uncovered by transfers, but this makes both rows contain only six cards and renders the solution somewhat easier.

GOOD MEASURE

One entire pack of cards. Lay out two Aces as the beginning of the foundations (the other two to be found and placed alongside as the deal progresses).

Deal out ten packets of five cards each, face down, but as each packet is completed turn the top card of each packet face up.

As the other two Aces appear, use them in the foundations. Should a King appear, place just above the ten packets.

Play can now commence by building in suit and ascending sequence on the Aces (foundations); or in descending sequence, without regard to suit, on the ten packets and on the Kings as they are placed in position. The uppermost card only of each of the ten packets is available. Vacated places cannot again be occupied.

A more difficult way is to make the play on the Kings a black on a red, and *vice versa*.

THE RAINBOW

One entire pack of cards. Shuffle cards thoroughly.

Deal thirteen cards into a packet, face up. To the right of this packet lay four single cards, face up; use the first of these four cards to form the nucleus of the foundations, place it just above its present position, and fill the space vacated by using the uppermost card from the thirteen packet.

The nucleus of the foundations now being known, the

three other cards of the same denomination are to be placed at its right, as they come out in dealing. These foundations must be built up in suit and ascending sequence. The play then continues by a descending sequence on the four cards to the right of the thirteen packet, putting a red on a black, and *vice versa*, using, whenever possible, the top card from the thirteen packet; this card must always be used for filling vacant places.

Hold balance of pack, face down, and deal off one card at a time. Cards not suitable can be placed to one side in a talon.

Two redeals of this talon are permissible.

MULTIPLE SOLITAIRE

Although called solitaire, this is a game for two, three or four players, and the object is to see which one can get rid of his thirteen pack first and play the most cards on the Ace foundations, which are being common property.

Each player shuffles and cuts a pack of cards, which he passes to his right-hand neighbor, receiving a pack from the player on his left.

Thirteen cards are first dealt off the top of the pack, and placed face up at the player's left. Then four cards are laid out in a row, face up, in front of the player.

Any Ace that shows at any time must be at once placed in the center of the table for any of the four persons to build on. These foundation Aces are built on in sequence and suit only, and if two players can use the same Ace, the first one to get to it has it, so that quickness is a great point.

The stock is held in the left hand, face down, and the cards are run off three at a time and turned face up, the card showing being available for building. If the top card of three can be used, the next one is available, but if not the three are laid on the table, face up, and another three taken, and so on, three at a time, until the whole pack has been gone through. The stock is then lifted, without disturbing its order, turned face down and gone through again, three cards at a time.

The four cards laid out in a row may be built upon in descending sequence and alternate colors, a black six on a red seven, and so on. A player is not obliged to build upon the Aces unless he wishes to do so, nor is he obliged to build on his own four cards if he prefers to pass a possible play.

As soon as a space is left in the four rows, the top card from the thirteen pack must be used to fill it. As soon as the first thirteen pack is exhausted all play must stop. The cards played upon the foundations are sorted to their proper owners and counted. The one whose thirteen pack is exhausted adds 10 to the number of cards he had on the foundations. The number of cards left in the thirteen pack of each other player is subtracted from the number he had on the foundations. Score is kept and 100 is the game.

The secret of success in this game is quickness of perception, because the faster player will run through his cards and get on the foundation Aces ahead of the others. An expert will go through his stock three times to an ordinary player's twice.

KLONDIKE

The Pack.—52 cards, which have no rank except that they are in sequence from the A, 2, 3 up to the J, Q, K.

The Layout.—The player pays 52 counters for the pack and he is paid five counters for every card he gets down in the foundations. The cards being shuffled and cut, the

first is turned face up and laid on the table. To the right
of this card, but face down, are placed six more cards in
a row. Immediately below the left-hand card of this row
that is face down, another card is placed face up, and five
to the right of it face down. Another card face up below
and four to the right face down, and so on until there are
seven cards face up and twenty-eight in the layout.

Any Aces showing are picked out and placed by themselves above the layout for foundations. These Aces are
built on in sequence and suit up to Kings. The moment
any card in the layout is uncovered by playing away the
bottom of the row it is turned face up. Cards in the layout
are built upon in descending sequence, K, Q, J down to
4, 3, 2, and must alternate in color; red on black, black on
red. If there be more than one card at the bottom of a
row, all may be removed together. Spaces are filled with
Kings only.

The stock is run through one card at a time and any
card showing can be used, either on the layout or foundations. The pack may be run through once only.

WHITEHEAD

This is a variation of 7-card Klondike, played with 52
cards. Instead of dealing one card face up and then six
more to the right of this, face down, all are dealt face up.
Then a row of six, under the first, also all face up, and so on
until 28 cards are laid out. The 29th is turned up for the
starter, and placed above the layout.

All cards moved in the layout from one column to another must be built in descending sequence (from the 8 to
the 7), and must be of the same color, but not necessarily
of the same suit. Any number of cards in sequence may
be moved from one pile to another if they are all in the

same suit as well as sequence. For example, if a pile reads, 7, 8, 9, 10 of Hearts, J of Diamonds, Q of Hearts. The four Hearts could be moved into a space, or onto the J of Hearts in another pile, but to release the Q of Hearts, the J of Diamonds would have to be played on the Q of Diamonds or a space. When there is no play in the layout, the top card of the stock is turned up, and the top of the passed stock is always available. Starters are placed above the layout as fast as they appear, and are built up, 7 to 8, etc.

CANFIELD

This differs from Klondike in the layout and in the play, although the two games are often thought to be the same under different names.

In Canfield, after shuffling and cutting, thirteen cards are counted off, and laid to the left, face up. The next card turned up is the one to build on. Suppose it is a Jack. Place it above as a foundation and then lay out four cards, face up, in a line with the thirteen pile, which is your stock.

Holding the remainder of the pack, face down, in your left hand, take three at a time from the top and turn them up. If you can use the card that shows, do so by building up in sequence and suit on the Jacks in the foundations, or by building down in sequence, red on black and black on red, on the four line. Use the top of your stock if you can.

If you can clear off one of your four line, fill up the place with the top card from your stock. The stock must never be built on.

After running off the pack in threes, it may be taken up again and without any shuffling run off in threes again. If there are only two cards in one of your four lines at any time and the top card can be used on another pile, it may be taken for that purpose.

THE IDIOT'S DELIGHT

This is considered the most interesting and difficult of all solitaires. The person who can get it out more than once in four attempts, on the average, is unusually fortunate or skillful.

The full pack of 52 cards is used, well shuffled, and cut. Nine cards are laid out in a row from the left to right, all face up. Upon these a row of eight cards, also face up. Then rows of seven, six, five, four, three, two and one. This leaves seven cards, which are spread on the table face up, separate from the tableau. There will now be nine rows of cards from left to right, and nine files, up and down, the card at the bottom of a file being the only one that can be moved.

Aces are taken out when they are at the bottom of any file, to start the foundations, for building up to Kings in sequence and suit. Only one card may be moved at a time from one file to another, and all cards moved must be placed on another card of a different color, red on black, or black on red, and in descending sequence, as the H 5 on the S 6. Spaces may be filled by anything. The player is not obliged to play on the foundations unless he wishes to, but cards once placed there cannot be taken back. Any of the seven cards that lie free can be used at any time to continue a build or to go on the foundation, but once used they cannot be put back.

The object is to get the entire 52 cards built onto the four Ace foundations.

TABLE GAMES
ROUGE ET NOIR

Rouge et Noir (Red and Black), or Trente-un (Thirty-one), is a table game, so styled, not from the cards, but from the colors marked on the tapis or green cloth with which the table is covered. To form the game, it is necessary that there should be a banker, or dealer and players, or punters, the number of whom is unlimited.

The table usually employed is of an oblong form, thirty feet long and four feet wide, covered with a green cloth, in the middle of which the bank is placed; in other words, the money that belongs to the banker. The company are at liberty to place their money on the right and left of this table, upon the chances that seem to them most likely to win.

Six packs of 52 cards each are shuffled together and used as one, the dealer taking in hand a convenient number, deals first for black, turning up the cards one at a time and announcing the total pip value of the black ones. Face cards and tens are worth 10, Aces and others their face value. The dealer continues to turn up cards, one by one, until he reaches or passes 31. The number never exceeds 40.

He then deals for red in the same way, and whichever color comes nearer to 31 wins.

If the same number is dealt for each, all bets are a stand-off. If exactly 31 is dealt for each, the bank takes half the money on the table.

FARO

Faro (also known as Pharo, Pharaoh and Pharaon) is a

table game played with 52 cards by any number of players against a banker. The cards have no rank, the denominations being all that count. Bets are made and paid in counters, the red being usually worth five whites, the blue five reds and the yellow five blues. There is always a limit on the bets, which is doubled when only one card of the denomination bet on remains in the dealing-box. This is called a case card.

Upon the table is a complete suit of Spades, usually enameled on cloth. The Ace is nearer the banker on his left, and that row ends with the six. The seven turns the corner, and then the cards run up to the King, which is opposite the Ace, a space being left between each card and its neighbor.

The cards are shuffled and placed in a dealing-box, from which they can be drawn only one at a time. The top of this box is open and the face of the top card can be seen. This is called Soda. The dealer pulls out two cards, one at a time, the first card being laid aside, the one under it being placed close to the box, and the next one left showing. The card left in the box wins; the one beside the box loses. Players bet upon what the next card of any denomination will do, win or lose. "Stuss" is faro out of hand.

A bet placed flat upon a card says it will win when next it shows. A bet with a copper on it means that the card will lose. Bets may be placed in twenty-one different ways, between two cards, behind three, on the corners, and so forth, each taking in a different combination. If any card embraced in the combination shows, the bet is either won or lost. A player having two bets on different cards, one to win, the other to lose, and losing both bets on one turn, is whipsawed. If two cards of the same denomination win and lose on the same turn it is a split and the banker takes half the bets.

The banker pays even money on all bets except the last turn. When only three cards remain, all different, they must come in one of six ways and the bank pays four for one if the player can call the turn. When there are two cards of the same denomination left in for the last turn, it is a cathop, and the bank pays two for one. In "Stuss," he takes all.

BILLIARDS

The Standard American Billiard Table is ten feet by five, but one nine by four and a half is also used and of late many much smaller tables for home use have made their appearance. With the diminutive tables, the balls and cues are proportionately smaller than for the standard game.

Three balls are used which are known as the *red*, the *white* and the *spot-white*. The white ball belongs to one player and the spot-white to the other, and each player in turn strikes his ball (called the cue ball) with the tip of the cue in an effort to make it hit both of the other balls. Of these, the first one struck by the cue ball is called the object ball and the second one the carom ball, because the cue ball caroms off from the object ball to hit the second one.

To start a game the red ball is placed at the foot of the table on a spot at the middle of a line drawn across the table from the second diamond on one long side of the table to the second diamond on the other long side. One white ball is placed on a corresponding spot at the head of the table. The line across the table upon which this white ball is placed is called the "string." The player who opens the game must place his cue ball inside the string and within six inches to the right or left of the other white ball (which is his opponent's ball) and must make his cue ball strike the red ball first. After the first shot, either the red ball or the other white ball may be hit first.

When a player makes a successful carom, that is, when his cue ball strikes both of the other balls, he scores one point and shoots again with the three balls where the last shot has left them. When he fails to hit both balls, his inning or turn is ended and his opponent plays. A game consists of any number of points agreed upon.

If a player's cue ball is in contact with either of the other balls, they are said to be "frozen" and when this is the case the player is not allowed to make his cue ball hit the one with which it is frozen *first* but may, if possible, play in such a manner that his cue ball hits the other ball first and the one which touched his cue ball afterwards; or he may shoot to a cushion and strike both balls upon the rebound either one first; or his third privilege is to have the three balls respotted as at the start of the game and then continue his inning.

Billiards is essentially a game in which one acquires skill by practice, but it involves a few principles of physics, familiarity with which will greatly assist a beginner.

If a ball is struck upon its exact center, it will be rolled forward in a straight line and if it strikes a cushion perpendicularly, it will rebound perpendicularly, that is, it will return upon its former course, but if it strikes a cushion at any angle with the perpendicular to the cushion at that point, it will rebound at an equal angle the other side of this perpendicular. The angle of "incidence" equals the angle of "reflection." If the cue ball, struck squarely as just stated, hits another ball squarely upon its center, the object

ball will be driven forward in a straight line and the cue
ball will come to rest, but if the object ball is struck off
center, upon its right side for instance, the cue ball will be
deflected to the right and the object ball will be propelled
upon a line deflected a corresponding amount to the left.
One very important point to be remembered is that no
matter whether the cue ball is struck by the cue upon its
center or to the right or left, or above or below the center,
it will always travel in a direct line of the cue.

Now let us consider the effect of striking the cue ball upon
any point other than its exact center, that is, above or
below or to one side. By striking it directly above the
center, the effect is simply to increase the rapidity of its
forward rolling motion and upon hitting the object ball
squarely, only a portion of its motion would be imparted to
the object ball so that the cue ball would tend to continue
in the same straight line or to follow the object ball. This
is called, therefore, a "follow" shot.

If the cue ball is struck below the center, two motions are
imparted to it, one a sliding motion forward and the other
a tendency to roll backward. The latter effect strives to
overcome the former. If the cue ball strikes the object ball
squarely, the impact destroys the forward motion and the
retrograde tendance causes it to return upon its course.
This is called the "draw."

A stroke upon the right or left of center rolls the ball
forward, but also gives it a twist towards the right or left
so that after hitting the object ball its deflection is more
to that side upon which it was struck. This is called
"English."

The following diagram illustrates these points and it,
together with the instructions as to "How to obtain desired
results when striking the cue ball," has been furnished by

courtesy of Mr. C. A. Storer, President of The National
Billiard Association of America, formerly a nationally
known billiard instructor and the author of "Better Billiards."

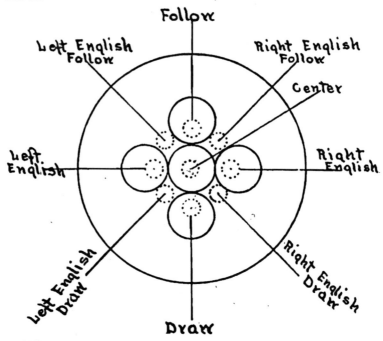

HOW TO OBTAIN DESIRED RESULTS WHEN STRIKING
THE CUE BALL

The billiard ball being round, naturally is difficult to hit
correctly and in such a manner as to avoid what is termed
a "miscue." There are, of course, certain portions of the
ball to hit where you should not miscue, and it is easy to
explain clearly just how and where to strike the cue ball
so as to get the desired results.

It is very seldom that a professional player miscues. The reason is not that he has some uncanny ability, but rather the fact that he knows where and how to hit the ball. A very important thing to practice is to deliver the stroke with the cue as near on a level as possible. This will aid greatly in striking the ball properly.

A youth, a novice at the game, was playing with a very good billiard player who was a stranger. The stranger was winning handily, while the youth was using every alibi possible to excuse his poor showing. Finally, the older man said, "Buddy, remember one thing sure; it is you, not the balls and cue, who are supposed to be educated." That helped the beginner with his game as much as any one thing could. It taught him to *think* while playing billiards. One should be careful to decide just what should be done before attempting it. As an example, never get into position to shoot until you are sure how you are going to play the shot. Then you will avoid shooting when in doubt, which is very harmful to your game. Try at all times to be certain that you will strike the ball just where you want to and you will avoid many mishaps.

It is not necessary to strike the ball on the extreme side to produce running or reverse English. That, coupled with the fact that you deliver your stroke with too tight a grip on the butt of the cue, at the same time not having a solid bridge hand on the table, is the usual cause of miscues.

Let us now discuss the details connected with properly striking the cue ball. The accompanying diagram shows the exact size of the ball used for straight rail, balkline and three-cushion billiards. The balls used for pocket billiards are a trifle smaller. The five large circles shown on this ball represent the width of the usual cue tip. The four large circles around the center one indicate the extreme distance you should ever cue the ball away from the center. This, it will be noticed, is exactly the width of the tip from the outer edge of the tip when the exact center is struck. The small dotted line circles inside the large ones show the approximate space covered on the ball by the cue tip when it comes in contact with the ball. The small dotted line circles among the four outside large circles indicate where to hit when executing the extreme follow or draw shot with the addition of left or right English.

From this diagram it is easy to understand why it is dangerous to try to cue the ball farther away from the center than shown by the outside circles. In fact, it is seldom that a shot requires such extreme off center cueing. It is surprising to see the follow, draw and English action which may be attained by striking the ball just a little off center. And remember, when you cue further away than this diagram shows, you will then commence to miscue. This is especially true when cueing to either side or above center. However, when striking below the center line, it is safe (when extreme action is desired) to cue lower than the width of the tip from the edge of the center circle. This may sound odd, but the explanation will no doubt convince you. When cueing the ball on the lower half (below center line) there is much more resistance felt when the ball is struck with the cue. This is because more of the weight of the ball is above when you are hitting. This extra weight, or resistance makes it less dangerous to cue a little further away from the outer edge of the center circle. For this same reason, the cue ball may be shot with greater accuracy. Professional players cue most of their shots below and near the center. They do this for the reasons just explained.

You will find that you can get about as much English,

follow or draw action as you will need, by striking the ball about the width of the tip from the outer edge of the center circle, which represents the edge of the tip when cueing direct center. Of course, most shots will not require this much action, so you will then move your tip a trifle, or about one-half to the side you desire. In connection with this, it is well to remember to deliver the stroke with the cue as near level as possible, and to follow through.

THE VARIOUS FORMS OF THE GAME

The simplest form of Billiards called the Three-ball Carom or Straight Rail Game has been described. In this game an expert player is often able to keep the three balls close together along the rail in such a manner that he can, by light strokes, make a large number of caroms without losing his turn of play. This is termed "nursing the rail" and in order to limit such a series of strokes, the "eighteen-inch balk line game" has been devised.

THE EIGHTEEN-INCH BALK LINE GAME: TWO SHOTS IN

Four lines are drawn across the table parallel to the sides and eighteen inches from the rails. This divides the table into eight spaces around the rail and a rectangular inner space. These eight spaces are called the balk spaces and when the two object balls are both in one of these spaces only one stroke may be made without driving at least one of the balls out of that space. In such a game, "anchor" spaces are also created, seven inches square, around each point where a balk line meets the rail so as to prevent nursing over the boundary between two balk spaces. When both object balls are within an anchor space, only one shot may be made without driving at least one ball out of that anchor space. Should one ball be driven out of an anchor or balk space and return, another carom may be scored, but again on the second stroke one ball must be driven out.

CUSHION CAROM GAME

Here one or more cushions must be struck either before either of the object balls is hit or after one object ball has been hit and before hitting the second one. If it is a three-cushion game, three cushions means three impacts, not necessarily three different cushions.

POOL OR POCKET BILLIARDS

Games of this class, of which there are many differing slightly from each other, are played upon a billiard table which has six pockets, one at each corner and one at the middle of each long rail and the object of the games is to drive the object balls into these pockets.

AMERICAN PYRAMID FIFTEEN BALL POCKET BILLIARDS

This, which is the simplest game, is played with fifteen numbered balls which are usually colored and one white one. The numbered balls are the object balls and the white one is the cue ball, which is used alternately by the players. The fifteen object balls are formed into a triangle with the apex ball upon the red spot and the others extending towards the foot of the table. The first player shoots from within the string and his first shot must either pocket one or more balls or cause two balls to hit a cushion. If he pockets one or more balls he continues to play with the cue ball as it lies. When he fails to pocket a ball, he removes the balls which he has pocketed, each of which counts one, and his opponent plays. The game is won by the player who pockets eight balls.

If the cue ball enters a pocket or jumps from the table, the player loses his turn and must restore one of his pocketed balls to the table.

Another form of the game is to have the object balls which are numbered from one to fifteen count, not one each, but according to their numbers so that the game is won, not necessarily by the one pocketing the most balls but by the one, the numbers of whose pocketed balls reaches 61 (since the sum of all the numbers is 120).

ROTATION POCKET BILLIARDS

In this game the numbered object balls must be pocketed in the order of their numbers. The placement of the fifteen object balls here differs from that already given in that ball number one is at the apex of the triangle and the largest numbered balls are at the base of the triangle. If a player strikes the lowest numbered ball with his cue ball and thereby pockets one or more balls they are all counted to his score no matter what their numbers may be, but if he fails to hit the lowest numbered ball, any balls which may be pocketed must be returned to the table, the player loses his turn and three points are deducted from his score.

BOTTLE POOL

The game of Bottle Pool is played with one white ball, the "one" ball, the "two" ball and a pool bottle.

The one and the two balls are spotted at the foot of the table at the left and right diamonds nearest each pocket and the bottle is placed standing upon its neck in the center of the table. When it falls it must be set up where it rests.

A carom on the two object balls counts one; pocketing the one ball counts one; pocketing the two ball counts two and a carom from an object ball which upsets the bottle counts five. The game consists of exactly thirty-one points.

The first player plays with the white ball from any point within the string at either the one or the two ball. If a player after a carom from either object ball strikes the bottle so as to turn it completely over and set it upon its base, he wins the game at once.

A player who makes more than thirty-one points is burst and must start over at nothing but all that he made on his first string in excess of thirty-one counts on his new string.

PIN POOL

This game is played with two white balls, one red one and five small wooden pins which are set up in the middle of the table in the following form:

4
x

3   **5**   **2**
x   x   x

1
x

The numbers by the pins represent the number of points each one counts. Each player is given a small ball bearing a number which his opponents should not see. The object of the game is for a player to knock down pins until the sum of their numbers added to the number upon his secret ball shall be exactly thirty-one.

At the beginning of the game one white ball is spotted

upon the center line of the table five inches from the foot rail. The red ball is spotted on its own spot near the foot of the table and the first player places his ball in the string and must hit one of the other balls before knocking down a pin. after the first shot a player may play with or at any ball, red or white, provided his cue-ball hits an object ball before knocking down a pin.

If a player knocks down a pin without hitting an object ball first, the pin is restored without counting anything for him and he loses his turn.

If a player with one stroke knocks down the four outside pins leaving the center one standing, it is called a "Natural" and wins the game at once.

If a player gets more than thirty-one he is said to be "burst." He may continue to play with his original number starting over at nothing or he may be given a new number ball and start over but in this case he must await his next turn to play.

BOWLING OR TEN PINS

This is one of the oldest and most popular of all games because in addition to the amusement it affords, it constitutes a most beneficial physical exercise.

The standard American game requires an alley 41 or 42 inches wide and 60 feet long from the head pin to the scratch line from behind which the player must deliver the ball. There should be at least 15 feet run back of the scratch line, in which a player runs to start his ball. The pins are spotted in a triangle with the apex towards the player and their centers should be 12 inches apart. The standard pins are 15 inches high with the base diameter $2\frac{1}{4}$ inches.

The balls must not exceed 27 inches in circumference but smaller balls may be used.

A game consists of 10 frames or innings and a player rolls one, two or three balls in each frame.

A *Strike* is made when all ten pins are knocked down with the first ball of a frame. The player does not roll another ball in that frame but a strike allows him to count his next two balls in addition to the ten pins knocked down by his one ball, all for the first frame. He therefore records a strike by a cross on the blackboard and adds the score for the first frame after he rolls his next two balls. If a player does not make a strike he rolls a second ball.

A *Spare* is made when all ten pins are knocked down with the two balls of a frame and this entitles the player to add to these ten pins the number that he knocks down with his next one ball. A spare is recorded on the board by a diagonal mark and the score is filled in after he rolls his next ball.

If a player fails to make either a strike or a spare, it is called a *Break*. This is recorded by a horizontal line on the board and the actual number of pins knocked down by the two balls is marked up at once.

The only case where a player rolls three balls in one frame is when he makes a strike or a spare on the tenth and last frame. Inasmuch as a strike gives him two more balls, or a spare one more, he rolls them at once to finish the game.

Counting. The scoring often gives difficulty to beginners therefore a diagram with careful explanation is here given.

Frames	1	2	3	4	5	6	7	8	9	10
Pins ..	7-3	10	10	8-0	10	8-2	4-5	10	9-0	10-8-2
Record	/	✕	✕	—	✕	/	—	✕	—	✕
Score..	20	48	66	74	94	108	117	136	145	165

The first ball knocks down 7 pins and the second one 3. This is a spare and the diagonal mark is all that is put in frame 1 at this time because the number of pins knocked down by the next ball (the first ball of frame 2) is to be added to the 7 and the 3 for the score of frame 1.

In frame 2 a strike is made. It is recorded by a cross and now the total for frame 1 can be put up—it is 20. In frame 3 another strike is made and recorded by a cross. Still the total score for frame 2 cannot be entered because a strike allows counting the following *two* balls. In frame 4 the first ball knocks down 8, therefore a second ball is rolled and misses. The score for frame 2 can now be counted, 10 and 10 and 8, or 28. This is added to the 20 of frame 1 and put up 48 as the total for the first two frames. Frame 3 can now be filled in, the count here is 10 for the strike and 8 for the next two balls or 18 which added to 48 makes 66. Frame 4 counts only 8 and so can be recorded at once giving 74 for the four frames.

In frame 5 a strike is made and in frame 6 a spare with 8 and 2 for the two balls. Frame 5 is therefore scored as 20 (10 plus 8 plus 2) giving 94. In frame 7 a break is made of 4 and 5 balls. The 4 is counted with the spare of frame 6 (8 plus 2 plus 4) giving 108 (94 plus 14) and for frame 7 the 9 are added making 117.

In frame 8 a strike is made and in frame 9 a break of 9 and 0. Frame 8 therefore counts 19 making 136 and frame 9 adds 9 giving 145. In frame 10 a strike is made and as this is the last frame two more balls are rolled at once adding 20 making the final score 165.

On the tenth frame no more than 3 balls can be rolled even if all three are strikes. The highest score possible is 300 made by rolling twelve strikes.

BRIDGE KENO

For playing this game, cardboards are provided each of which has pictures of twenty-five playing cards upon it, arranged in five rows of five cards each. Each player must have one of these boards and the sets contain four, eight or twelve boards providing for a corresponding number of persons to play at one time.

One person places a shuffled pack of playing cards face down on the table before him and turns up the cards, one at a time. Each player is provided with small discs and if the card turned up appears upon his board, he at once covers it with a disc. The first person to cover five in a row, vertically, horizontally or diagonally, calls "Keno" and wins the game. If two players each cover a row with the turning of the same card, the one calling Keno first wins.

CHESS

The game is played on a board the same as that used for Checkers, and the position of the board must give each player a white corner square at the right hand.

Each player has 16 men to start with, 8 pieces and 8 pawns. The pieces are called the King, Queen, Bishop,

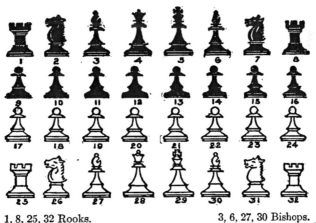

1, 8, 25, 32 Rooks.
2, 7, 26, 31 Knights.
3, 6, 27, 30 Bishops.
4, 28 Queens.
5, 29 Kings.

Knight and Rook. Those on the Queen's side of the board are called the Queen's pieces, as the Queen's Bishop, Rook, etc., and those on the King's side, the King's pieces. The pawns likewise assume the name of the King or Queen together with the name of the pieces they stand in front of, as the King's pawn, the King's Bishop's pawn, etc.

The Queen must stand on a square of her own color before game commences, but the King stands on a square colored opposite to that of his own color.

299

Kings and Queens must be exactly opposite each other across the board.

The King is the most important piece. If he cannot avoid capture he is checkmated and the game is lost. The King can only move one square at a time, in any direction, and can capture any adjacent squares not defended by opponent's pieces or pawns. The King is exempt from capture. Hostile Kings must always be separated by a square.

The Queen is the most powerful and moves in any direction, on any of the 4 center squares. She commands 27 out of the total 64 squares.

Following the Queen, the Rook is the next most powerful, moving backward, forward or laterally, but not diagonally, on unobstructed rows or files.

The Bishop moves and captures diagonally only backward or forward on squares of its own color. A White King's Bishop cannot capture or be captured by a Black King's Bishop. The Bishop commands 13 squares on a clear board. The Knight moves one square diagonally, then one forward, backward or sideways, or *vice versa*. He can move or capture in any direction, or can leap over his own men or any hostile man, and is the only piece that can play before any of the pawns have moved.

A Rook on same square on a similar clear board commands 14 squares; a Bishop on the same square, 13 squares diagonally; a Knight on the same square, 8 squares. The pawn only moves one square forward at a time, except on the first move, when it may move two squares. A hostile man may be captured right or left diagonally on immediately adjacent squares.

If a hostile pawn is on one of your fourth squares, your pawn having been played forward on either adjacent files to that occupied by the hostile pawn two squares on his first move in the game, the hostile pawn may take your pawn "in passing," leaping and placing himself on your captured pawn's third square. If he fails to capture on the move, he cannot do so afterwards. The pawn alone has privilege of promotion and capture in a direction other than his line of march.

RULES

A wrong position of the board or men may be corrected, provided four moves on each side have not been played.

If the first move is made by the wrong player, game is annulled, if discovered before fourth move. If a player moves out of his turn, his opponent decides whether it shall be retracted or whether both moves shall remain.

If a false move is made, the opponent may allow the move to remain, or he may compel the player to move it legally to another square or replace the man and move his King. If an adverse man be captured by an illegal move, the opponent may compel him to take it with a man that can legally take it, or to move his own man which has been touched.

The men must not be touched except by the right player, in playing, or for the purpose of adjustment, in which case the words "I adjust" must be said. Unless this is said when a player touches one of his own men (except accidentally) if it can be legally moved, he must move it, or if it is one of his adversary's men, he must capture it if he can legally do so. If a legal move cannot be made in either case, the offender must move his King, but if the King has no legal move, there is no penalty. If a player moves one of his opponent's men, his antagonist may compel him to replace the man and move his King or take the man moved, or allow the man to remain where moved.

As long as a player holds the pawn or piece touched, it may be played to any other than the square he took it from, but he cannot recall the move having quitted it. If a player takes one of his men with another, the opponent may compel him to move either.

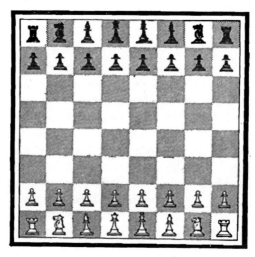

In castling (moving two squares in conjunction with either Rook) the King and Rook must be moved simultaneously, or touch the King first. If Rook is touched first he cannot quit it before having touched the King, or the opponent may claim the Rook's move as a complete move.

When the odds of either or both Rooks are given, the player giving the odds may move his King as in castling, and as though the Rooks were on the board. If moved as a penalty, the King cannot castle on that move.

When a hostile King has been checked, the player must say "check." If not announced when made, the move of the opponent which may obviate the check must stand.

If check be given and announced, if the opponent does not obviate it, he forfeits the option of capturing the check piece or of covering, but he must first move his King out of check; but there shall be no penalty if the King has no legal move. If the King has been in check for several moves and it cannot be accounted for, the player whose King is in check must free his King from the check by retracting his last move. If the moves made subsequent to the check are known, they must be retracted. If an opponent moves his King or touches a piece or pawn to interpose because a player has said check without giving it, he may retract the move, provided the other player has not played his last move.

When a pawn has reached the eighth square, the player may select a piece, whether it has been previously lost or not, whose name and powers it shall assume, or he may decide to have it remain a pawn.

An opponent may be called upon to draw the game or to mate the player within fifty moves on each side, whenever the opponent persists in repeating a particular check, or series of checks, or the same line of play, or whenever he has a King alone on the board; or King and Queen, King and Rook, King and Bishop, King and Knight against an equal or superior force; or King and two Bishops, King and two Knights, or King, Bishop and Knight against King and Queen; and whenever a player considers that his opponent can force the game or that neither side can win, he may submit the case to an umpire, who may decide whether it is one for the fifty-move counting. If not mated within the fifty moves, he may claim that the game shall proceed.

A stalemate is a drawn game.

The opponent may claim a draw if the same move or

series of moves has been made three times and in succession.

If a player can only move so as to take a pawn *en passant* he is bound to play that move.

CHECKERS

This game is played by two persons with red and black counters or men, 12 for each player; the board is divided into 64 squares alternately colored black and white. It should be placed between the players with white squares in upper left-hand corner and double white squares in lower left-hand corner. The counters of each player are placed on first three rows of colored spaces, on opposite sides of

the board, leaving two rows of colored spaces unoccupied between the counters of the two players.

The men are moved alternately on the dark squares only, in a diagonal forward direction, one square at each move. The last row of dark spaces on each side of the board is called the "King row" and the first object is to move the men across the board as quickly as possible in order to reach the "King row." As fast as accomplished each "man" is "crowned," or "kinged," by having another one of his men placed upon top of the piece that has reached this position.

A King may move either forward or backward, but on dark spaces only. The principle of the game is to capture or block all of the opponent's men. When all the pieces are properly placed, one of the opponents makes the first move, followed by the second player. If the player can leap over the piece or pieces of an opponent, one at a time, and find a resting-place on a dark square, the opponent loses the pieces or men jumped in this way.

If a player does not capture an opponent's man whenever possible, the other player, if he sees the omission, may remove the opponent's counter or man or he may compel his opponent to make the play. Players should endeavor to capture as many men with one move as possible.

If an opponent's "men" are blocked so no move can be made, he has lost the game. When a man reaches the "King row" the piece cannot move from that position until it has been "crowned" and the other player has moved.

It is better to keep the men as near the center of the board as possible. No advantage is gained by playing first. Giving away or allowing certain men to be captured often aids by exposing a greater number of the opponent's men. Do not touch the men until ready to make a move, as after a move has been made it cannot be changed.

Checkers when played by professionals or experts is a

scientific game that requires much study to master, but the few simple rules given above will answer the need of the great majority who have never played the game.

DOMINOES

Dominoes are pieces of ivory or bone, generally with ebony backs. On the face of each there are two compartments, in each of which there is found either a blank, or black pits, from one to six. These are called, according to the numbers shown, double blank, blank-ace, blank-deuce, etc., double ace, ace-deuce, ace-trey, etc., double deuce, deuce-trey, double trey, trey-four, double four, four-five, double five, five-six, and double-six—being twenty-eight in all. They are shuffled on the table face down, and each player draws at random the number that the game requires. There are various games, but those principally played are the Block, Draw, Muggins, Rounce, Euchre, Poker, Bingo, Matador and Bergen, the descriptions of which follow:

BLOCK GAME

Each player draws seven dominoes from the pool. The highest double plays first and after that each player plays alternately until the end of the game. The pieces are played one at a time, and each piece to be played must match the end of a piece that does not join any other. If a player cannot play, the next plays. If none can play, the set is blocked, and they count the number of spots on the pieces each still holds. Whoever has the lowest number of spots adds to his count the number held by his opponents. If there are two with the same number of spots, and they are lower than their opponents, there is no count. If any one is able to play his last piece while his opponents hold theirs, he cries "Domino," and wins the hand, and scores the number of spots the rest hold. The number required to win the game is one hundred, but it may be made less by agreement.

DRAW GAME

Each player draws seven dominoes and the game is subject to the same rules as Block, except that when a player cannot play he is obliged to draw from the pool until he can play or has exhausted the stock of pieces.

MUGGINS

Each player draws five dominoes. The highest double starts; after that they play alternately. The count is made by fives. If the one who leads can put down any domino containing spots that amount to five or ten, as the double five, six-four, five-blank, trey-deuce, etc., he counts that number to his score in the game. In matching, if a piece can be put down so as to make five, ten, fifteen or twenty, by adding the spots contained on both ends of the row, it counts to the score of the one setting it. Thus a trey being at one end, and a five being at the other, the next player in order putting down a deuce-five would score five; or, if double trey was at one end, and a player was successful in playing so as to get double deuce at the other end, it would score ten for him. A double six being at one end and four at the other, if the next player sets down a double four, he counts twenty—double six, *i.e.*, 12+double four, *i. e.*, 8=20. The player who makes a count must instantly announce it when he plays his piece, and if he fails to do so, or if he announces the count wrongly and any of his opponents call "Muggins," he is debarred from scoring the count. If a player cannot match he draws from the pool, the same as in the Draw game, until he gets the piece required to match either end or exhausts the pool. As in Draw or Block game, the first one who plays his last piece adds to his count the spots his opponents have; and when the game is blocked the one having the lowest number of spots wins and adds to his score the number of spots that the others have in excess of his. But the sum thus added to the score, must be some multiple of five nearest the actual amount. Thus, if his opponents have twenty spots, more than he has, he adds twenty to his score. If they have twenty-two, he adds twenty, because that is the nearest multiple of five; but if they have twenty-three he would add twenty-five, twenty-three being nearer that than to twenty. The game is two hundred if two play, but one hundred and fifty if there be three or more players.

BERGEN GAME

Each player draws six dominoes from the pool. The lowest double starts, and is called a double-header. After that the players play alternately from right to left. If no one has a double to start with, the lowest piece starts it. When a player sets down a piece which makes the extremities of the line the same, it is called a double-header. If one of the extremities be a double, and the next player can lay a piece that will make the other extremity of the same value, or if a double can be added to one end of a double-header, it makes a triple-header. If a player is not able to match from his hand, he draws one piece from the pool. If he is still not able to play, the next plays, or draws, and so on alternately. If domino is made, the one who makes it wins the hand. If it is blocked, they count and the lowest wins; but if the lowest holds a double in his hand, and his opponent none, the opponent wins. Or if there be two with doubles, and one with none, the last wins. If there be a double in each hand, the lowest double wins. If there be more than one double in any one's hand, and all have doubles, the one with the least number of doubles wins, without reference to the size of the doubles he holds. Thus: if a player hold two doubles, though they be the double blank and double Ace, and his adversary holds but one double, though it be the double six, the latter wins. The game is ten when three or four play, and fifteen when there are two. A hand won by either "domino" (getting rid of all dominoes) or counting, scores one. A double-header, either led or made, counts two. A triple-header counts three. But when either party is within two of being out, a double-header or a triple-header will count him but one; and if he be within three of being out, a triple-header will count him but two. A prudent player will retain the doubles in his hand as long as possible, in order to make triple-headers.

DOMINO ROUNCE

This is a pleasant game, and from two to four may participate in it. The pieces of rank are six to blank, and the doubles are the best of each suit, trump being superior to any other suit. The game begins by "turning for trump," and he who turns the highest domino is trump-holder for that hand. The dominoes are then shuffled, and each player takes five pieces, when the player at the right of the trump-holder turns the trump, and the end of the piece having the greatest number of spots upon it becomes trump for that round. The players to the left of the trump-holder then announce in regular succession whether they will stand, discard their hand and take a dummy, or pass. When four play there is only one dummy of seven pieces, and the eldest hand has the privilege of taking it. When all the players pass up to the trump-holder, the last player may elect to give the trump-holder a score of five points instead of standing or taking a dummy and playing. The trump-holder may, if he chooses, discard a weak piece and take in the trump turned, or he may discard his hand and take a dummy, provided there is one left, in which case he must abandon the trump turned. The player who takes a dummy must discard so as to leave only five pieces in his hand. After the first hand the trump passes to the players at the left in succession. The game begins at fifteen, and is counted down until the score is "wiped out," each trick counting one. The player who fails to take a trick with his hand is "rounced," *i. e.*, sent up five points. It is imperative that suit should be followed, and if holding one in hand, a trump must be led after a trick is taken, but a player is not compelled to "head," *i. e.*, take a trick when he cannot follow suit.

DOMINO EUCHRE

This game is usually played by four persons. The pieces rank as follows: The double of the trump suit is the right bower, and the next lower double is the left bower. There is, however, an exception to this rule, for when blank is the trump, it being impossible to have a lower double than the double blank, the double six is adopted instead, and becomes the left bower. In this instance the lowest double is right bower, and the highest double is left bower. After the right and left bower the value of the dominoes is governed by the number of spots following the trump. For instance, if six is trump, the double six is right bower, and the double five is left bower, followed by six-five, six-four, six-trey, and so on down to six-blank. If ace be the trump, the double ace is right bower, and the double blank is left bower, the ace-six is next in value, the ace-five is next, and so on down to the ace blank. But when the blank is trump, the double blank is right bower and the double six becomes left bower, the next trump in importance being blank-six, the next blank-five, and so on down to blank-ace, which is the lowest trump. When a suit is not trump, the pieces take rank from the double of the suit in regular order, downward.

At the beginning of the game, the players usually draw to decide who shall turn up trumps; he who draws the highest piece is entitled to the privilege, and is termed the dealer. When the dominoes have again been shuffled, each player draws five pieces, beginning with the eldest hand; the dealer then turns up one of the remaining pieces for trump. That portion of the domino which has the highest number of spots upon it determines the suit of the trump. Thus, if six-ace be the piece turned, then six is trump suit. After the first hand the privilege of turning trump passes to each player in succession. The eldest hand does not have the lead unless he exercises the privilege of ordering up or making the trump. Only the player who takes the responsibility of the trump, that is, the player who takes up, orders up, or makes the trump, has the right to lead. With this exception, Domino Euchre is like the card game of the same name.

DOMINO POKER

In this game only twenty pieces are employed, the double ace and all the blanks being discarded. The hands rank in regular order, from one pair up to the royal hand, which is the highest hand that can be held, as follows:

One Pair.—Any two doubles; double six and double deuce will beat double five and double four.

Flush.—Any five of a suit not in consecutive order; as six-ace, six-trey, six-four, six-five and double six.

Triplets, or Threes.—Any three doubles. The double ace and double blank being discarded, it follows that only one hand of triplets can be out in the same deal.

Straight Four.—A sequence of fours; as four-six, four-five, double four, four-trey, and four deuce.

Full Hand.—Three doubles and two of any suit; as double-six, double trey and double deuce, together with deuce-four and deuce-ace.

Straight Five.—A sequence of fives.

Fours.—Any four doubles.

Straight Six.—A sequence of· sixes.

Royal Hand, or Invincible.—Five doubles.

When none of the above hands are out, the best is determined by the rank of the highest leading pieces; thus, a hand headed by double six is superior to a hand headed by double five, but a hand headed by double deuce will beat six-five, and six-five will outrank five-four.

Domino Poker is governed by the same laws as the card game called Straight Poker, and is played in precisely the same manner.

BINGO

This game is played as similarly to the card game of Sixty-Six as the difference between dominoes and cards will permit. The rank of pieces is the same as in other Domino games, except that blanks count as seven-spots. The double blank, which is called Bingo, and counts for fourteen spots, is the highest domino, and will take the double of trumps.

The game is played by two persons and is commenced by

each drawing for the lead, and he who draws the highest piece has the lead. Each player then draws seven pieces, after which the eldest hand turns up another piece, the highest spot on which is trump. The eldest hand then leads, and the play is conducted in the same manner as Sixty-Six at cards.

The game consists of seven points, which are made in the following manner: The player who first counts seventy scores one point toward game; if he makes seventy before his opponent has counted thirty, he scores two points; if before his adversary has won a trick, three points. If Bingo captures the double of trumps, it adds at once one point to the winner of the trick.

The pieces count as follows to the winner of the trick containing them: The double of trumps always twenty-eight, the other doubles and all the other trumps according to their spots; the six-four and three-blank are always good for ten each, whether trumps or not; the other pieces have no value.

If a player has, at any time, two doubles in his hand, he can, when it is his turn to lead, play one, show the other, and announce twenty points, which are added to his count as soon as he has won a trick. If he holds three doubles, he counts forty, for four doubles, fifty, for five doubles, sixty, for six doubles, seventy points. If Bingo be among the doubles held, it adds ten more to the count.

MATADOR

This differs from all other games of Dominoes in this point, that each player, instead of matching the pieces, must make up the complement of seven. For instance, a five requires a two to be played to it, because two added to five makes *seven*. On a six an ace must be played; on a four, a three, and so on.

It will be seen that there is no piece capable of making a seven of a blank; to obviate this difficulty there are four matadors, the double blank, and three natural seven spots, namely—six-ace, five-two and four-three. These four matadors can be played anywhere, at any time, and are, of course, the only ones which can be played on a blank.

Each player at the commencement, draws three pieces; the one who has the highest double commences; or, if neither has a double, then the highest piece starts.

We will suppose double four to have been led. The player whose turn is next must play a three to it, or, failing to have a three in his hand, must draw till he gets one. Supposing it to be a three-five, the end spots will be a four and a five—the next player must then either play a three on the four or a two on the five, and so on.

This game may be played by two, three or four persons. When two play, there must be three pieces left undrawn, to prevent each from knowing exactly his opponent's hand. When more than two engage in the game, all the dominoes may be drawn. The player who makes domino first counts the spots on the other hand, or hands, and scores them toward game, which is one hundred or more, as agreed on before commencing the game.

If domino be not made before the drawing is ended, and a player cannot play in his turn, he must pass and await his next turn to play, but he must play if he can; the failure to do so deprives him of any count he may make with that hand.

In playing, a double counts only as a single piece; for instance, double six is a six, and can only be played on an ace-spot or on double ace; but if left in hand after domino is called it counts twelve points to the winner.

If the game be blocked, and neither player can make domino, then the one whose hand contains the least number of spots wins, and he scores the difference between his hand and the total of the other players.

The blanks are very valuable at this game—the double blank being the most valuable of all the matadors—as it is impossible to make a seven against a blank, so that if you hold blanks you may easily block the game and count.

When you have the worst of the game, and indeed at other times as well, guard against your adversary's blanks and prevent him from making them; which you may do by playing only those dominoes which fit with the blanks already down.

Never lay a blank at the lead unless you have a matador or a corresponding blank.

Keep back your double blank till your opponent makes it blanks all; you can then force him to play a matador or compel him to draw till he obtains one. It is better to have a mixed hand.

TIDDLE-A-WINK

This is a very amusing game, and suitable for a round party.

If six or more play, each takes three dominoes. The double six is then called for, and the person holding it plays it. If it is not out the next highest double is called forth, and so on downward until a start is made.

In this game he who plays a double, either at the lead or at any other part of the game, is entitled to play again if he can, thus obtaining two turns instead of one. The game then proceeds in the ordinary way, and he who plays

out first cries "Tiddle-a-Wink," having won. In the event
of the game being blocked, he who holds the lowest number
of spots wins.

BUNCO

AS PLAYED WITH NUMBERED CARDS

1. The pack consists of 10 "Bunco" cards, 5 "Stop" cards
and 10 series of cards, each numbered from 1 to 10—115
cards in all.

2. *Players.*—Two to 7 with 1 pack, up to 14 with 2 packs.

3. *Dealing.*—Shuffle and deal 10 cards, 1 at a time, to
each player for a Bunco pile, which the player places face
up in front of him with only the top card exposed. Next
deal 5 cards to each player for a hand. Then stack deck
in criss-cross piles of five cards face down.

4. *Game.*—The object of the game is to get rid of your
Bunco pile, and the player who first succeeds wins the game.

5. *Playing.*—All cards are played face up. The player
at the left of the dealer commences and *must* play all of his
No. 1 cards from hand *first* to the center of the table;
then, if possible, the top card from his Bunco pile. The
cards played from the hand and Bunco pile to the table
constitute the table piles, which are from 1 to 10 in sequence and are to be played on, and when filled are removed
from the table. The player then follows his No. 1 card with
a No. 2 card, and so on in sequence from his Bunco pile,
his hand or his surplus (hereafter described) until he can
play no longer; then he lays down a card to his surplus
and the next player plays in like manner. When a player

plays the _last card_ from his hand to some _table pile_, he takes another hand and continues; when he _lays_ his _last_ card to the _surplus_ he draws another hand, but cannot continue playing unless he draws a stop card, in which case should he wish to keep on playing he must play his stop card as provided in Rule No. 8. A player _must_ always play all of his No. 1 cards from his hand to the center of the table _first_ of all other plays. If he does not hold any No. 1 cards in his hand he must play from his Bunco pile if possible; all other cards played to the center of the table, whether from his hand or his surplus pile, the player may play at his option. When the deck is used up and no player has exhausted his Bunco pile, all removed piles are shuffled together and used for a new deck.

6. _Surplus._—Each time a player finishes playing, or is unable to play, he lays in front of him a card to form a surplus pile until he has four such piles; then he _must_ keep four surplus piles maintained before he can lay a card on any established surplus pile. When a player is stopped he does not lay a card to his surplus. A player may play from his surplus pile at his option. When playing from surplus piles the player must play from top of piles.

7. _Bunco Cards._—Bunco cards in the hand or surplus have the power of any number whatever in building a sequence on a table pile. When a Bunco card is played for a number card, the player must be able to follow the Bunco card with the next number in sequence, as: Bunco card on a No. 6, then a No. 8 on Bunco card. A player may also play one Bunco card on top of another and so on, if he has a number card to play on the last Bunco card, as: No. 4 —Bunco card—Bunco card—No. 7. If a Bunco card appears on a Bunco pile it _must_ be played to the table to stand for a No. 1 card. A Bunco card cannot be played for a No. 10

card. A Bunco card in hand or surplus may be played for a No. 1 card provided the player follows with a No. 2 card.

8. *Stop Card.*—A player holding a stop card in hand or surplus may at any time, and regardless of his position at the table, call "Stop" and take the turn to play. The player calling "Stop" *must* immediately play his stop card to any one of the table piles and that pile is removed, except when the stopped player has just played a Bunco card in building up his sequence; then the stop card must be played on *that* pile and the pile removed. The player calling "Stop" then goes on and plays from his Bunco pile, his hand or surplus, as long as possible or until he too is stopped by some player holding a stop card. When the player, who has just stopped another, finishes playing he lays a card to his surplus pile and the player to his left goes on. When a stop card appears on the Bunco pile it *must* be laid on the surplus and the next player takes his turn to play. The player who is stopped in this manner may immediately resume his play by playing his stop card as provided above. A stop card on the Bunco pile has no power until it is laid to the surplus. When two or more players call "Stop" at about the same time, the one calling first does the stopping. If it cannot be determined who called "Stop" first, the nearest player (calling "Stop") at the left of the stopped player makes the stop and takes the turn to play. A player is stopped when another player calls "Stop." If a stopped player holds a stop card he may resume his play immediately after being stopped by playing his stop card as provided above. Should the last card in the Bunco pile be a stop card, it must be laid to the surplus as provided elsewhere in Rule No. 8, and that ends the game.

9. Penalties.—Any player may call "Bunco" and place a

card from the deck under the buncoed player's Bunco pile for any of the following errors:

Failure to play all No. 1 cards from hand *first* of *all* other plays.

Failure to play from his Bunco pile when possible.

Any error in play.

For lifting cards from one surplus pile to another.

For looking at cards underneath his Bunco or surplus pile.

For giving information as to the best way to play.

For calling "Bunco" in error.

For calling "Stop" when he does not hold a stop card.

When a player is buncoed he loses his turn and the next player goes on.

10. *The Science of the Game* lies in so managing the surplus, your Bunco and stop cards as to aid yourself in getting rid of your Bunco pile and in hindering your opponents in getting rid of theirs. Keep track of the cards buried in your surplus without referring to them, however, arranging them as nearly as possible in sequence running down, and thus make it easier to remember the cards beneath, and do not play them except to benefit yourself or hinder your opponent, but rather keep them until you may be benefited by playing them. Never miss a chance to head off an opponent from playing from his Bunco pile.

11. *In Playing Partners* the same rules apply, except that you are at liberty to play from your partner's Bunco pile and surplus. If you have an opportunity to play from both your own and your partner's Bunco pile at the same time, you must play from your own first, and then from your partner's; otherwise you must play from your partner's Bunco pile whenever opportunity offers, the same as

from your own, and you may be buncoed for not doing so. When a stop card appears on your partner's Bunco pile you lay it to your partner's surplus, and the player to your left goes on. The game is finished when both partners' Bunco piles are exhausted.

12. To make the game more easy for children to play, omit the stop cards.

13. *Suggestions.*—Do not play a Bunco card except to aid yourself in reaching your Bunco pile, but hold it in your hand or surplus. Do not stop any player until he gets ready to play off his Bunco pile or until he builds some table pile high enough so that if you stopped him, you could play from your Bunco pile. Do not build up a table pile unless it will benefit you.

The Arbitrary Rules in the Game.

1. No. 1 cards in the hand *must* be played to the table first of all other plays.

2. A player *must* play from his Bunco pile whenever it is possible without conflicting with Rule No. 1.

3. A stopped player does not lay a card to his surplus.

4. When a Bunco card appears on the Bunco pile it *must* be played to the table to stand for a No. 1 card.

5. A Bunco card cannot be played for a No. 10 card.

6. When a stop card appears on the Bunco pile it *must* be laid to the surplus, and the next player takes his turn to play.

7. A stop card on the Bunco pile has no power until laid to the surplus.

8. When a player is "Buncoed" he loses his turn and the next player goes on.

PROGRESSIVE BUNCO

In parties, to play Bunco progressive, any number may be seated at a table, but each table should have the same number of players, if possible. Four at a table makes an interesting game. At the toll of a bell, play begins and continues until some player succeeds in getting rid of his Bunco pile, when all must cease playing, and the player at each table having the least number of cards in his Bunco pile gets a punch and moves to the next table, when the play resumes as usual, the player having the most punches in ten games being the winner. In case of a tie the players tied should cut the cards, the highest number winning. Stop cards and Bunco cards count for zero. In playing partners progressively apply partner rules. In case a shorter game is desired, 5 cards to a Bunco pile instead of 10 may be used.

BUNCO AS PLAYED WITH DICE

RULES FOR TABLE NO. 1.

Trump is made at Table No. 1.

Highest point on dice on first toss decides trump for all tables.

Three trumps made on one toss scores 23 points (Bunco).

First couple scoring 23 points (Bunco) shall announce Bunco, thereby stopping all play at all tables.

Points to be scored as follows:

One trump scores one point.

Two trumps scores two points.

Three trumps scores twenty-three points.

Three of any other number scores 5 points.

Continue to throw the dice until you have stopped scoring; then dice go to person sitting to your left.

11

RULES FOR ALL OTHER TABLES.

All play begins when table No. 1 announces trump and continues till table No. 1 calls Bunco, which stops all play at all tables.

No score allowed if dice have not touched table when Bunco is called, except that where no score has been made one hand around will decide winner at table.

If three trumps or 23 points are scored, continue the play. Score will sometimes reach 200 before Bunco is called.

Keep an account of points on scratch pad provided.

Winner's card will be punched for games won.

Winners advance toward head table and change partners; losers remain and change partners; losers at head table move to foot table.

In case of a tie score when Bunco is called, one hand around will decide winner. A tie on final games won will be decided by five tosses of the dice, highest being winner.

No card will be punched after you have left the table.

TECHNICAL TERMS

Definitions of technical terms used in the preceding pages are here given in alphabetical order.

Age.—Eldest hand; player to the dealer's left.

Ante.—A bet made before drawing cards in Poker.

Assist.—In Euchre, ordering the partner to take up the trump. In Bridge, increasing the partner's bid.

Blind.—A compulsory bet at Poker, before cards are dealt.

Bobtail.—A four-card flush or straight in Poker.

Book.—The first six tricks won by the declarer in Bridge.

Breathe.—In Poker, to pass the first opportunity to bet, with the privilege of coming in if any one else bets.

Burnt Cards.—Those turned face up on the bottom of the pack in banking games.

By Cards.—The number of tricks taken over the book by the declarer, at Bridge or Whist. Eight tricks would be two by cards.

Capot.—Winning all the tricks in Piquet.

Carte Blanche.—A hand without a face card.

Club Stakes.—The amount agreed upon as stakes if nothing is said before play begins.

Command.—The best card of a suit.

Coup.—A master stroke or brilliant play. A deal at Rouge-et-noir.

Deadwood.—The discard pile in Poker.

Deckhead.—Colloquial for the turned trump.

Declarer.—Player who makes the winning bid at Bridge and plays the dummy's cards in connection with his own.

Discarding.—When unable to follow suit or unwilling to trump, throwing away from another suit.

Doubleton.—Two cards of a suit at Bridge.

Doubling.—At Bridge, betting the declarer cannot make his contract; or, asking the partner to bid.

Dummy.—The exposed hand in Bridge.

Duplicate.—When the same hands are replayed by players at other tables in Whist or Bridge.

Dutch It.—To cross the suit, when trump is turned down by the dealer in Euchre, that is to make a suit of the opposite color trump.

Edge.—The same as "age"; eldest hand in Poker.

Elder or *Eldest Hand.*—The first player to receive cards in dealing, generally the player at dealer's left and leader in the play.

Exposed Cards.—Cards played in error, dropped on the table, or so held that the partner can see them.

Face Cards.—The K, Q and J.

Finesse.—Any attempt to win a trick with a card which is not the best you hold in the suit; such as Q, holding A and Q.

Flush.—All the cards of the same suit.

Force.—To compel a player to trump if he wants the trick.

Fourchette.—The cards above and below the one led, such as K and J over a Q.

Frozen Out.—A player who has lost his original stake and cannot come back into the game.

Guarded Cards.—Cards which cannot be caught by higher cards unless led through, such as K with a small one.

Heading a Trick.—Playing a card better than any so far on the trick.

Helping Partner.—Raising his bid at Bridge.

His Heels.—Turning up a Jack for a starter at Cribbage.

His Nobs.—The Jack of the same suit as the starter, at Cribbage.

Honors.—The highest cards in the suit when they have any counting value; such as A, K, Q, J, 10, or four Aces, at Bridge.

Horse and Horse.—Each player has a game in.

Inside Straight.—Sequences that are broken in the middle; such as 9, 8, 6, 5 at Poker.

Intricate Shuffle.—Butting the two parts of the pack together at the ends and forcing them into each other.

Jacks or Better.—Any hand that will beat a pair of tens; the opening qualification for jackpots at Poker.

Jeux de Regle.—Hands which should be played in a certain way on account of the mathematical expectation, in Ecarté.

Kitty.—A percentage taken out of the stakes to pay for expenses of any kind.

Knave.—Jack.

Lead.—The first card played in any trick.

Limit.—In Poker, the amount by which any player may increase the previous bet.

Losing Trump.—Any trump which is not the best, when only a few remain.

Love.—Nothing.

Love-All.—Nothing scored on either side.

Lurched.—Not half way toward game, especially at Cribbage.

Marriage.—The combination of a King and Queen of the same suit; if of the trump suit, it is called a royal marriage.

Master Card.—The best remaining card of a suit.

Matador (or matadore).—One of the highest trumps.

Meld.—In Pinochle, to declare; a declaration.

Milking.—Instead of shuffling, taking the top and bottom cards from the pack at the same time, with forefinger and thumb, and showering them on the table.

Misdeal.—Any failure to distribute the cards properly.

Mistigris.—A joker; also Poker with the joker in the pack.

Muggins.—Taking a score overlooked by an opponent, at Cribbage.

Negative Doubles.—Those made to obtain a bid from partner, at Bridge.

Next.—The suit of the same color as that turned down, at Euchre.

No-Trumps.—A hand played without a trump suit.

Nullo.—A bid to lose tricks instead of winning them.

Openers.—Cards that entitle a player to open a jackpot.

Overcalling.—Bidding higher than the last bid at Bridge.

Pair-Royal.—Any three cards of the same denomination, at Cribbage.

Pass.—To decline any undertaking in any game. To pass a card means to lead it and take a trick with it.

Pat Hand.—One played without discarding or drawing, in Poker.

Penultimate.—The lowest but one of a long suit.

Plain Suits.—Those which are not trumps.

Pone.—The player who cuts the cards; in a two-hand game, the dealer's opponent.

Positive Doubles.—Those made to defeat the contract, at Bridge.

Post-Mortems.—Discussions as to what might have been, sometimes called "if you hads."

Pot.—The amount to be played for in any round game.

Proil.—An abbreviation of pairs royal, at Cribbage.

Punters.—Those who play against the banker.

Puppy-Foot.—The Ace of Clubs.

Quart.—Any sequence of four cards.

Quart-Major.—The four highest cards of a suit.

Quick Tricks.—Cards that will win the first round or two.

Quitted.—A trick is quitted when it is turned down and the fingers removed from it. A score is quitted when the fingers are removed from the counters, the pegs or the pencil.

Redouble.—To double the player who doubles.

Re-entry Cards.—Cards with which the lead may be thrown to a hand.

Renege.—Failure to follow suit when able to do so.

Renounce.—Failure to follow suit.

Revoke.—Failure to follow suit or conform to a performable penalty when able to do so.

Robbing.—Exchanging a card in hand for the turned trump.

Round Trip.—The four Kings and Queen in Pinochle.

Rubber.—Best two out of three games. If the same player or partners win the first two games, the third is not played.

Ruff.—To trump a suit.

See-Saw.—A cross ruff, trumping alternate suits.

Sequence.—Three or more cards next to each other in numerical order.

Short Suits.—Those containing less than four cards.

Shuffling.—Mixing the cards so that no trace remains of their order during the previous play.

Singleton.—Only one card of any suit. If led, a sneak.

Skunked.—Losing without having scored a point.

Slam.—Winning every trick. All but one is little slam.

Sneak.—A singleton, led to ruff second round.

Squeezers.—Cards with corner indexes.

Starter.—The cut card at Cribbage.

Still Pack.—The one not in play when two are used.

Stock.—Cards left in the pack after completing the deal, but which are to be used in the play that follows.

Talon.—The same as "stock."

Tenace.—The best and third-best cards of any suit, such as A, Q (the major tenace), King, Jack (the minor tenace)'.

"Ten" Card.—One counting as ten.

Tierce.—A sequence of three. When headed by the highest card of suit it is called a tierce-major.

Two-Suiters.—Hands that contain two suits of at least five cards each.

Underplay.—Leading a card which is not the best you

hold when the best would be the natural lead, or holding up the best card, refusing to win an adverse trick.

Vole.—Winning all the tricks; a slam.

Whitewashed.—Defeated without having scored a point.

Wide Cards.—Those which are too far apart to be likely to form sequences in Cribbage or Rum.

Widow.—An extra hand dealt in any game, but available in the play.

Younger Hand.—The one who is at dealer's right in three-hand games. The opposite to elder hand.

LAWS OF AUCTION AND CONTRACT BRIDGE

(*Not given in the text, pages 21-47*)

In the present (1936) revision of the Laws of Bridge, they have been divided into five periods which makes reference to them much simpler than formerly. These periods are:

First Period—Preliminaries to the Rubber.
Second Period—The Shuffle, the Cut and the Deal.
Third Period—The Auction.
Fourth Period—The Play.
Fifth Period—The Score.

FIRST PERIOD

Cards.—The pack consists of fifty-two cards, divided into four suits, Spades, Hearts, Diamonds and Clubs, ranking downwards in this order. In each suit the Ace is highest followed by the King, Queen, Jack, 10, 9, etc., with the 2 as lowest. Two distinguishable packs should be used alternately.

Drawing Cards.—A shuffled pack is spread face down and each person draws a card. If more than four persons wish to play, those four drawing the highest cards form the table for the first rubber while the others sit out. The two with the highest ranking cards play as partners against the other two; the one with the highest card deals first and has the right to choose his seat and the pack with which he will deal.

SECOND PERIOD

The Shuffle, the Cut and the Deal.—For the first deal the player on the dealer's left shuffles the pack. During each deal the dealer's partner should shuffle the other cards and place them face down at his right.

Cutting.—The dealer presents the pack to the player on his right who lifts off a portion from the top and places it towards the dealer beside the bottom portion. The dealer then completes the cut by placing the bottom portion uppermost.

New Shuffle and Cut.—Upon the request of a player, made before the beginning of the deal, there must be a new shuffle and cut if:

(*a*) the cut is not made by the proper player.

(*b*) the cut leaves fewer than four cards in either portion.

(*c*) the face of a card is shown in cutting.

(*d*) a player other than the dealer completes the cut.

(*e*) there is doubt as to which was the top portion.

(*f*) a player shuffles the cards after the cut.

Dealing.—Players deal in rotation towards the left. The dealer must deal the fifty-two cards face down one at a time in rotation towards the left into four hands of thirteen cards each, the first card to the player on his left.

New Deal During the Deal.—There must be a new deal by the same dealer with the same or a correct pack if it is ascertained during the deal that:

- (a) the cards have not been dealt as provided in the preceding law.
- (b) a player has seen or can name a card dealt to another person.
- (c) a player has looked at a card dealt to him.

Dealing out of Rotation or with Wrong or Uncut Pack. Such procedure may be stopped before the last card is dealt; otherwise the deal stands as correct and the packs if changed, remain changed.

THIRD PERIOD—THE AUCTION

The Auction.—After the deal is completed, each player in turn, commencing with the dealer, must bid or pass. After the first bid each successive bid must either name a greater number of odd tricks than the preceding bid or an equal number of a higher value. The bids rank upwards as follows:—Clubs, Diamonds, Hearts, Spades, No Trump. If all four players pass in the first round of the auction, that deal is abandoned and the deal passes in rotation. After an opening bid the auction closes when three players pass successively.

Doubling and Redoubling.—Any player may in rotation double the last bid, if made by an opponent, or may redouble it, if it has been doubled by an opponent. Doubling and redoubling do not affect the number of tricks in the bid or its value for the purpose of the auction.

The Final Bid and the Declarer.—The final bid in the auction becomes the contract and the player who, for the side which made the final bid, *first* bid the denomination named in the contract, becomes the declarer.

Improper Calls.—A player may correct a misnomer without penalty.

If an improper call is overcalled in rotation before the non-offending side draws attention to the irregularity, the auction proceeds as if the improper call had been proper.

Insufficient Bid.—Unless overcalled (as provided above) an insufficient bid made in rotation must be made sufficient and if the offender selects: .

(*a*) the lowest sufficient bid of the same denomination, his partner must pass when next it is his turn to call;

(*b*) another bid, his partner must pass whenever it is his turn to call.

Call out of Rotation.—Unless overcalled, a proper call made out of rotation is cancelled, the auction reverts to the player whose turn it was to call, and, if it was:

(*a*) a pass made before the first bid, the offender must pass when next it is his turn to call;

(*b*) another call, the offender's partner must pass whenever it is his turn to call.

Card Faced, Seen or Disclosed.—If during the auction period, a player faces a card on the table, sees the face of a card of partner's or makes a remark which discloses to his partner a card in his hand, such card or cards must be placed face up on the table during the auction, and:

(a) if the owner becomes a defender, declarer may either prohibit the opening lead from being made in the suit of such card or cards or treat such card or cards as *penalty cards* (defined later) and

(b) if such card is of honor rank or if there are two or more such cards, the owner's partner must also pass whenever it is his turn to call.

FOURTH PERIOD—THE PLAY

Leads and Plays.—When the auction is closed, the defender on declarer's .left makes the opening lead. Declarer's partner then spreads his cards face up in front of him and declarer plays both his own hand and that of his partner.

Subsequent Play and Leads.—After a lead, a card is played from each hand in rotation and the four cards thus played constitute a completed trick.

The leader may lead any card. The other three hands must follow suit if they can, but if unable to follow suit may play any card.

A trick containing a trump or trumps is won by the hand playing the highest trump. A trick containing no trump is won by the hand playing the highest card of the suit led. The hand winning a trick leads to the next trick.

Played Cards.—A card is played:

(a) by declarer; from his own hand when it touches the table, after being detached from his remaining cards with apparent intent to play; from the faced hand when he touches it, unless for a purpose other than play, either manifest or mentioned by him;

(*b*) by a defender, when his partner sees its face, after being detached from his hand with apparent intent to play; and

(*c*) by declarer or a defender when named by him as the one he proposes to play.

Taking Back Card Played.—A player may not, on his own initiative, withdraw his played card except to correct a revoke.

If, when calling a penalty, a played card is duly withdrawn by specific or implied direction, it may be picked up unless it becomes a penalty card.

Player Unable to Play as Required.—If a player is unable to play as required to comply with a penalty, he may play any card subject to his obligation to follow suit, and the penalty lapses except that, in the case of a penalty card, the penalty lapses as to the current trick only.

Lead out of Turn.—A lead out of turn may be treated as a correct lead, and must be treated as such if, before the card wrongly led is withdrawn, a card is played to it by the other side. In all other cases, if a lead out of turn is made:

(*a*) by declarer from either hand; either defender may require him to take the lead back, and, if he has led from the wrong hand, he must lead a card of the same suit from the correct hand;

(*b*) by a defender, declarer may either treat the card led out of turn as a penalty card, or require the lead of a specified suit, from the other defender if he won the previous trick, otherwise from the defender who next wins a trick.

Simultaneous Lead by Defenders.—If the defenders lead

simultaneously the correct lead stands and the card wrongly played becomes a penalty card.

Premature Play by a Defender.—If a defender plays to a trick when it is his partner's turn to play; declarer, unless he has played from both hands, may require the other defender to play his highest or lowest card in the suit led and, should he be unable to follow suit, to play a specified suit.

Premature Lead by a Defender.—If a defender leads to the next trick before his partner has played to the current trick, declarer may require the other defender to play to the current trick his highest or lowest card in the suit led and, should he be unable to follow suit, to play a specified suit. The offender, should he not win the current trick, has led out of turn to the next trick.

The Revoke.—If a player revokes and corrects his error by withdrawing the revoke card before the revoke becomes established, he must substitute a correct card, and if the revoke card belongs to:

(a) a defender; declarer may treat it as a penalty card, or require him to play his highest or lowest correct card;

(b) declarer; it may be taken up, and, if the defender on declarer's left has played to the trick after declarer, he may require declarer to play his highest or lowest correct card;

(c) declarer's partner; it is put back without penalty. A card played by a player of the non-offending side after a revoke and before its correction may be taken back.

Acts which Establish a Revoke.—A revoke, other than one

made in leading becomes established when the offending side leads or plays to the next trick, except that such a revoke made in the twelfth trick never becomes established. A revoke made in leading becomes established when the offender's partner plays to the revoke trick.

Inquiries Regarding a Possible Revoke.—A player may ask whether a play constitutes a revoke and may demand that an opponent correct his revoke but nothing can alter or postpone the provisions of the previous section.

Declarer's partner may question only declarer, and, if he does so after intentionally looking at a card in a player's hand, declarer may not withdraw his card.

Established Revoke.—When a revoke has been established the trick stands as played; and, if the revoke is claimed, tricks won in play by the revoking side after its first revoke (including the revoke trick), are transferred to the non-offending side at the end of play—two such tricks for a side's first revoke and one such trick for each subsequent revoke by the same side; except that no tricks are transferred—

(*a*) if the revoke was made from a hand legally faced at the time;

(*b*) if the revoke is claimed or attention drawn to it after the cut for the next deal is completed or, if the revoke occurs in the last hand of a rubber, after the rubber score is agreed.

Scoring Transferred Tricks.—A transferred trick ranks for all scoring purposes as a trick won in play by the side receiving it.

Settling a Revoke Claim.—The tricks and unplayed cards may be inspected at the end of play to settle a revoke claim, and, if, after such claim, an opponent so mixes the cards that the claim cannot be established, it must be allowed.

Tricks.—Until a trick has been quitted, a player may require the players to specify which cards have been played from their respective hands.

Gathered Tricks.—Each completed trick must be gathered and turned face down on the table by a player of the side winning it. The cards of each quitted trick should be kept together so that its identity can be readily established, and the tricks taken by a side should be arranged together in such a manner that their number and sequence is apparent.

Inspecting Quitted Tricks.—If a quitted trick is looked at before the end of the hand, the opponents score 50 points in their premium score unless:

(*a*) there is difference of opinion as to which hand won it;

(*b*) it is found to contain an incorrect number of cards; or

(*c*) it is necessary to turn it in order to substitute a correct card.

Directing Partner's Attention to a Trick.—If a player's attention, before he has played and without a request by him, is directed to the current trick in any way by his partner, as by saying that it is his, by naming his card, or drawing the cards towards him; declarer or the defender on the left of declarer's partner, as the case may be, may require the offender's partner to play the highest or lowest card which he holds in the suit led and, should he be unable to follow suit, to play a specified suit.

Claim or Concession of Tricks by Declarer.—If declarer claims or concedes one or more of the remaining tricks or so implies by showing his hand or otherwise, he must leave his hand face up on the table, and forthwith make a comprehensive statement of how he intends to play the remaining tricks, specifying the order in which he intends to play his cards and the disposition of each card from each of his two hands. Either defender may demand such a statement or may require declarer to play on. Declarer may neither take any finesse unannounced at the time of such claim or concession nor depart from any statement he may have made.

Declarer may not treat cards shown in consequence of his claim or concession as penalty cards.

If both defenders have abandoned their hands, declarer's claim or concession must be allowed. An exposure of cards does not constitute an abandonment.

Claim or Concession of Tricks by a Defender.—A defender may show any of his cards to declarer for the purpose of claiming or conceding one or more of the remaining tricks. A concession of tricks by a defender is not valid unless the other defender accedes.

Tricks Conceded in Error.—If a side concedes a trick which it could not lose by any play of the cards, such concession is void.

Declarer's Partner.—Declarer's partner forfeits all his rights by intentionally looking at the face of a card in a player's hand. Thereafter he must remain silent in regard to any incident connected with the hand, and, if, after a defender has committed an irregularity, he fails to do so, declarer may not enforce any penalty for the offense.

If declarer's partner has not intentionally looked at the face of a card in a player's hand, he may:

(*a*) reply to a player's proper question;

(*b*) when requested, discuss questions of fact or law;

(c) question declarer regarding his possible revoke; and

(d) draw attention to a defender's irregularity and ask declarer whether he knows his rights.

Declarer's partner has no rights other than the above conditional ones. He does not rank as a player. If declarer's partner, by touching a card or otherwise, suggests the play of a card, the defender on his left may require declarer to play or not to play that card, unless such play would constitute a revoke.

If declarer's partner, on his own initiative, informs declarer which hand has the lead or warns him not to lead from the wrong hand; the defender on the left of declarer's partner may choose the hand from which declarer shall lead.

Claiming a Penalty During the Play.—When an irregularity is committed any player may draw attention to it, ask his partner whether he knows his rights, and give or obtain information as to the law covering it.

All questions as to what penalty applies to a given offense must be settled prior to the actual payment of a penalty or the taking of other action. A penalty once paid or action once taken stands, even though it is subsequently discovered to have been incorrect.

Unless a penalty is automatic, the right to any penalty lapses, if the partners consult as to which of alternative penalties to claim or as to the advantage to be gained by claiming any penalty, or if an unauthorized partner claims a penalty.

Penalty Card of a Defender.—If during the play a defender drops a card face up on the table, sees the face of any of his partner's cards, makes a remark which discloses any of his cards to his partner, or names any card in his partner's hand; such card becomes a penalty card.

A penalty card must be left face up on the table until played, and whenever it is the turn of the defender who owns it to play (subject to his duty to follow suit) ; if he has but one penalty card, he must play it; if he has two or more penalty cards, declarer may require him to play any one of them.

New Deal During the Play Period.—There must be a new deal by the same dealer with the same or a correct pack if it is found that the number of cards in the pack is incorrect or that a duplication exists.

Surplus Card.—There must be a new deal by the same dealer if one hand has a surplus card and either another has less than the proper number of cards or the surplusage is not due to omission to play to a trick. When the surplusage is due to omission to play to a trick, the offender must forthwith remove a card from the redundant hand; and, if possible, the card must be one which he could properly have played to the defective trick, and, if he has played to a later trick, his side transfers one trick won in play to the non-offending side.

Incomplete Hand.—There must be a new deal by the same dealer if one hand has less and no other more than the proper number of cards, and if, after due search which must be made, either the missing card cannot be found, or is found in such position as to show that it was not duly dealt to the deficient hand. In any other event, including the case where the missing card is found in the other pack, it shall be restored to its owner. The owner is subject to the revoke law but may not be penalized more than two tricks for established revokes made with a missing card. If a quitted trick contains more than four cards and there is doubt as to which card was included therein by error, declarer or the defender on the offender's left, as the case may be, may direct which card is to be restored to the deficient hand of the other side.

FIFTH PERIOD—THE SCORE

The method of scoring has been given in connection with the rules of the game at pages 39 and 40. One or two laws may here be added.

The Result of the Rubber.—At the end of the rubber the trick and premium score of each side is added up; the side with the larger total score wins the rubber, irrespective of the number of games, if any, which it has won, and the difference between the two totals represents the number of points won.

Correction of Score.—Proven errors are subject to correction as follows:

(a) In trick points, including errors in counting the number of tricks taken, before a call is made in the next hand, or if the error occurs in the final hand of a rubber, before the rubber score is agreed;

(b) In premium points or in addition or subtraction, before the rubber score has been made up and agreed upon.

MICHIGAN

This game is sometimes called Newmarket, Boodle or Stop. It is played with two regular decks of cards. Four cards, namely, the Ace of Hearts, the King of Clubs, the

Queen of Diamonds and the Jack of Spades are removed from one of the decks and placed face up in the center of the table. This is called the "Layout."

Any number may play the game from two to ten, but it is best with from four to eight players. The 100 cards are shuffled and dealt out one at a time, giving each player a hand and dealing one extra hand in front of the dealer which is called the "Widow."

Each player is provided with an equal number of chips or counters and before play begins each one puts one counter upon each card of the layout while the dealer must put two counters upon each one.

The object of the game is to be the first player to get rid of your cards and also to be able to play the duplicate of one or more of the layout cards.

The player at the left of the dealer starts by placing in front of him his lowest card of any suit. If he has others in sequence with it, he may play them one after the other calling each card as he puts it down. When he can play no more, the player who holds the next card in sequence plays it and others as long as he can continue the sequence after which the play is taken up by another player. This is continued until an Ace is played or until no player has the card next in sequence. This is called a "Stop" and the same player is allowed to start another suit. In starting one must always begin with his lowest card of that suit and it must be a different suit from the one last played.

Inasmuch as two decks of cards are being used, two players will often have the card which is to be played next and the one who calls it first has the right to play it and continue the game. This makes it a very exciting game.

When any player plays the duplicate of any of the lay-out cards he may take the pile of counters from that card.

Before the play, the dealer after looking at his hand may if he so desires exchange it for the Widow, but if he does not care to exchange he may sell the Widow to the player who bids the most for it.

The Widow if not used or sold or the hand for which it may have been exchanged is left face down and its cards not being in play produce breaks in sequences and thereby cause stops.

The player who first plays his last card wins and receives from each player as many counters as the number of cards which remain in that player's hand.

If the duplicate of any of the layout cards is not played or if a player in playing one forgets to take the counters from it, those counters remain there until the next round of play.

Each time a card is played it must be called out or another player may play and call the same card and continue to play.

A good hand is one containing one or more of the layout cards and if a player has none of them he may buy the Widow hoping that it will contain some.

PINOCHLE RUMMY

A number of variations of the common game of Rum or Rummy (See page 269) have been devised and have been called Pinochle or Five Hundred Rummy. The former name is much more appropriate as the game has no resemblance whatever to Five Hundred, but has a feature which is much like melding in Pinochle.

Instead of being allowed to pick up but one card from the discard pile, a player may take as many of them as he desires, provided he takes all of those which are above the lowest one which he desires. The other chief difference from ordinary Rummy is that the cards which a player places on the table in front of him count various amounts for him at the close of the hand. Each face card counts ten and all other cards their pip value, except the aces, which count fifteen each. The aces cannot be used for sequences either with the twos and threes or the kings and queens. When it is any player's turn to play he may lay down any number of combinations which he may hold— three or four of a kind or a sequence of three or more, or he may add a fourth to any three of a kind which any player has put down or continue any sequence which is upon the board. In case he wishes to add to a combination previously placed on the table by another player, he shows his card or cards and designates where they may properly be played, and then places them in front of his own place, as they count for him at the end of the hand.

When one player disposes of all of his cards he wins that round and scores first the amount due from the cards he has placed on the table and then the count of all cards remaining in the hands of his opponents. Each opponent counts the cards which he has placed on the table and subtracts from this amount the sum of those remaining in his hand. If he has a greater count in his hand than on the table he has a minus score.

CAMELOT*

Camelot is a game which will fascinate not only all true lovers of games but also all who are fond of romance. It is a medieval combat between two forces, each consisting of footmen and knights, and takes us back to the "days of old when knights were bold."

It is a two-hand game and therefore will fill a great need for a real test of skill when only two persons are available. It is played upon a checkered board with men or pieces somewhat similar to chessmen. The board is divided into 156 squares with 2 extra starred ones at each end which mark the castles, or goals. The protection and storming of these castles make the objectives of the game. The pieces are of two kinds: men and knights. There are 10 men and 4 knights for each player. The knights are easily distinguished from the men because they have black tops while the opposing pieces are of different colors.

The following plate shows the board with the pieces set ready to start the game.

The opposing forces are arranged facing each other in

Camelot is the invention of George S. Parker of Salem, Mass.

the middle of the field, like two armies—or in more modern parlance, like two football teams. The object of the game is to capture the enemy's castle. This is accomplished by getting 2 pieces, either 2 men or 2 knights or 1 of each, into the starred squares at the far end of the board. With the entire enemy army between your men and the goal, every step forward is a fight, and the goal is rarely attained until a large proportion of the enemy have been captured and removed from the field.

There are four kinds of moves: the plain move, the jump, the canter, and the knight's charge.

The Plain Move.—This consists of moving either a man or a knight one square in any direction—forward, backward, sidewise, or diagonally.

The Jump.—This move is similar to the jump in checkers. Either a man or a knight may jump an enemy man or knight which is upon an adjacent square if the square immediately beyond is vacant upon which the jumping piece may land. Unlike checkers, however, this move may be made in any one of the eight directions mentioned above. The enemy piece jumped is captured and removed from the field. This jumping may be continued so as to capture several pieces at one move, and the direction of each successive jump may be varied in any way.

The Canter.—This move is similar to a jump except that a friendly man or knight is leaped over for the purpose of obtaining a better position. Either a man or a knight may canter over one or more friendly pieces, one at a time, landing upon a vacant square immediately beyond the piece cantered. The canter may go as far and change directions as often as opportunity offers. The pieces cantered are, of course, not removed from the board.

Knight's Charge.—This move is the only special privilege

which belongs to a knight and is not enjoyed by a man. It is a combination into one move of the canter and the jump and is a most deadly attack when an opponent is careless enough to leave an opening. A knight may canter over one or more friendly pieces and then jump any number of enemy pieces which are in favorable positions. After jumping one or more enemy pieces, however, the knight cannot canter in the same move. In other words, a charge consists of cantering and then jumping, but it is not permissible to jump and then canter. The difference thus between knights and men is that a man may canter *or* jump but cannot do both in the same move, while a knight may combine the two moves into one play.

If a player can jump an enemy piece, he is compelled to do so if his opponent demands it; but if the opponent fails to see the opportunity and the player prefers not to jump, he may play elsewhere. If the opponent calls attention to a possible jump, demanding that it be made, and the player can make any other jump, either with a man or by a knight's charge, he may choose the jump to be made. Thus in place of making a simple jump of a piece which is on a square adjacent to one of his men, he may make a knight's charge, cantering over one or more of his own pieces and then jumping one or more enemy pieces.

After one or both of the armies have become somewhat depleted, the common practice is for each player to attempt to rush 2 of his pieces into the enemy's castle, at the same time defending his own castle. A player is not allowed to enter his own goal unless he is compelled to do so in jumping an enemy. If this happens, he is not allowed to jump out of the goal at the same play even though an enemy piece is upon an adjacent square. The play must be ended in the goal, the player must move or jump out at his next turn to play. After a piece has entered the opponent's goal, the player is not allowed to take it out, even to jump an enemy who may be upon an adjacent square. He may, however, move it back and forth from one starred square to the other as often as desired.

The first few moves are usually plain moves or canters to obtain better positions, and great skill and strategy may be used in arranging the pieces so as to prepare the way for a destructive knight's charge. It is frequently advisable to move a man where the enemy will have to jump and capture him if by so doing an opening will be made for a knight's charge which can capture several enemy pieces. Care should be taken, however, when this is done to see that the man exposed is the only one that can be jumped. The beginner will probably find his greatest difficulty in looking ahead and visualizing the positions of the pieces after he has made a knight's charge. While it is a great satisfaction to plan such a move and to be able to outwit the opponent by executing it, a player's pride has a great and sudden fall if the opponent steps into the openings which have been left and sweeps off half a dozen pieces.

After each move of the opponent, a player should carefully examine the whole line of battle, giving particular attention to each enemy knight to see if, by some round about charge, any one of them is in a position to make any captures. One's own knights should be so placed that charges may be possible in various directions whenever the opponent leaves any openings.

The following plates, used through the courtesy of Parker Bros., Inc., illustrate an unusually rapid game and show all four of the different moves. The beginner should play this out upon the board, setting up all of the pieces and making each move as indicated by the arrows.

19	20	21	22	23	24	25	26	27	28	29	30
31	32	33	34	35	36	37	38	39	40	41	42
43	44	45	46	47	48	49	50	51	52	53	54
55	56	57	58	59	60	61	62	63	64	65	66
67	68	69	70	71	72	73	74	75	76	77	78
79	80	81	82	83	84	85	86	87	88	89	90
91	92	93	94	95	96	97	98	99	100	101	102
103	104	105	106	107	108	109	110	111	112	113	114
115	116	117	118	119	120	121	122	123	124	125	126
127	128	129	130	131	132	133	134	135	136	137	138

First Moves.—Yellow opens by cantering a man from 107 to 83. Red makes plain move of knight from 52 to 64.

19	20	21	22	23	24	25	26	27	28	29	30
31	32	33	34	35	36	37	38	39	40	41	42
43	44	45	46	47	48	49	50	51	52	53	54
55	56	57	58	59	60	61	62	63	64	65	66
67	68	69	70	71	72	73	74	75	76	77	78
79	80	81	82	83	84	85	86	87	88	89	90
91	92	93	94	95	96	97	98	99	100	101	102
103	104	105	106	107	108	109	110	111	112	113	114
115	116	117	118	119	120	121	122	123	124	125	126
127	128	129	130	131	132	133	134	135	136	137	138

Second Moves.—Yellow now canters a knight from 105 to 107 to 85. Red makes a plain move of man from 62 to 75.

Third Moves.—Yellow canters a man from 108 to 84.
Red canters a man from 60 to 62 to 88 (to compel yellow
to jump into danger).

Fourth Moves.—Yellow now *must* jump with his knight

from 99 to 77, capturing enemy man on 88 and removing him. (This jump is compulsory because the opponent de- mands it and there is no other possible jump.)

Red knight on 64 must now jump because yellow knight is on adjacent square 77, but red player prefers to jump elsewhere by a knight's charge, cantering 64 to 86 and then jumping 86 to 108 and from 108 to 82 (thereby cap- turing and removing yellow man from 97 and 95).

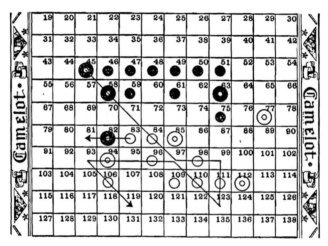

Fifth Moves.—Yellow is now obliged to jump and capture red knight on 82. He can do this by jumping a knight from 94 to 70 or a man from 83 to 81. He decides to use the lat- ter and jumps 83 to 81, capturing red knight.

Red now makes a decisive knight's charge, cantering a knight from 45 to 71 and jumping 71 to 97 to 99 to 123 to 97 to 95 to 93 to 119, capturing and removing 6 men and one knight, all in one move. Red is now very sure to win the game because yellow's forces are so depleted.

The following plate illustrates the position of two opposing forces towards the end of an actual game. Yellow's force, reduced to 2 knights and 2 men, is opposed by red with 2 knights and 3 men. Beginners will, by playing this out on a board with the men, see practical examples of all moves, as well as a fine example of a knight's charge.

From this position the game continues as follows: Yellow canters 73 to 47. Red threatens yellow knight with a plain move of man from 23 to 36. Yellow makes a plain move with knight from 71 to 59. (This move will win the game for yellow.) Red jumps a man over a knight, 36 to 58, removing yellow knight from 47. Red was compelled to jump, but he had a choice and might have captured yellow man on 60 by a knight's charge, cantering 27 to 49 and jumping 49 to 71. Either move is equally disastrous as in either case yellow can capture by a knight's charge 4 of red's pieces and win the game. Yellow now makes a knight's charge, consisting of canter 59 to 61 and 61 to 35, jump 35 to 14 to 37 to 39 to 16, capturing and removing 4 of red's pieces. This wins the game as red is left with only 1 piece.

CPSIA information can be obtained at www.ICGtesting.com
Printed in the USA
BVOW041049170413

318393BV00010B/719/P